AARON KIRSCHENBAUM

SONS, SLAVES AND FREEDMEN
IN ROMAN COMMERCE

SONS, SLAVES AND FREEDMEN
IN ROMAN COMMERCE

by

AARON KIRSCHENBAUM

Professor of Law, University of Tel Aviv

Preface by

ALAN WATSON

The Magnes Press, The Hebrew University
Jerusalem
The Catholic University of America Press
Washington, D.C.

Library of Congress Cataloging-in-Publication Data

Kirschenbaum, Aaron.
   Sons, slaves and freedmen in Roman commerce.

   Bibliography: p. 211
   Includes index.
   1. Agency (Roman law) 2. Contracts (Roman law)
   3. Master and servant (Roman law) I. Title.
KJA2534.K57   1987   346.37'029   87–1506
ISBN 0–8132–0644–8   343.70629

IN MEMORIAM

ANYU

Os suum aperuit sapientiae
et lex clementiae in lingua eius

CONTENTS

PREFACE

Ever since the famous insight of W.W. Buckland, it has been a commonplace that there is scarcely an institution of Roman law that will not be affected by the fact that one of the persons involved in a transaction is a slave. But another issue has been largely overlooked. What impact did the considerable presence of slaves in the society have on the development of legal institutions even when in a particular factual situation a slave need not be involved? For instance, the fact that many medical practitioners were slaves — though others were freedmen or free born — must have had an impact on the law relating to medical practice.

It is to one fundamental aspect of this issue that Aaron Kirschenbaum devotes this stimulating book. It is well-known that — surprisingly to modern jurists — Roman law failed to develop a theory of direct agency. Professor Kirschenbaum seeks a sociological answer and finds it in the abundance of slaves and other dependent persons who could be used as, or almost as, an extension of the head of the family. This leads him to a detailed examination of the diverse ways in which slaves and other dependent persons could be and were used to enter contracts, run businesses, acquire ownership and possession, and so forth, for the *paterfamilias*. A law of direct agency with free men as agents was, he concludes, just not needed by the Romans.

A slave economy downgrades the respect given to the paid labour of free persons. This affects social arrangements between the free born, and these arrangements in turn have an impact on the law. Paid employment may be eschewed, but this creates a special role for relationships which in appearance involve one person acting without reward to help another but which in reality cloak a system of mutual interdependence. The *duties* of friendship and the very nature of friendship are greatly affected by the prevalence of slave labour. This in turn, argues the author, has implications both for the law and for situations where the "law keeps out."

By skilfully relegating much controversial detail to the footnotes the author has produced a fascinating scholarly book that can readily be approached by those who are not specialists in Roman law. The subject is also one of wider interest and the book should be studied by anyone interested in law and society and in the development of the law. Moreover, although Professor Kirschenbaum sticks firmly to Roman conditions, the book has implications of great consequence to students of American slavery. The core of the book deals with institutions which are posited on the belief that, as human beings, slaves are the equal of free born citizens in business acumen, and that they can behave in similar ways. The impact on both society and law of regarding slaves as necessarily inferior is indirectly set in high relief.

ALAN WATSON

Professor of Law
University of Pennsylvania

ACKNOWLEDGEMENTS

The initial research out of which the present volume developed served as my Ph.D. dissertation at Columbia University. My doctoral studies were conducted under the guidance of Professor A. Arthur Schiller of blessed memory of the Columbia School of Law. It is with gratitude that I recall his tutelage.

Thanks are also due to Professors Reuven Yaron and Alfredo Mordechai Rabello of the Hebrew University Law School and to Professor Daniel Friedmann of the Tel Aviv University Law School for having encouraged me to have this study published. I should like to express my special appreciation to Professor Yaron for having read the complete work, for allowing me to benefit from his erudition and for suggesting a number of corrections and improvements. Professor Alan Watson of the University of Pennsylvania School of Law not only encouraged me but also graciously agreed to write the Preface.

I wish to express my appreciation to Tel Aviv University and to the Dean of the Faculty of Law, Professor Amos Shapira, for their financial assistance.

I am grateful to Mrs. Rachel Sandler, Mrs. Joan Hooper and Ms. Adele Zarmati for the preparation of the manuscript for publication during the various stages of its production; to Mr. Benzion D. Yehoshua, the director of The Magnes Press, and his assistant Mr. Dan Benovici, for their help in the production of this book.

I thank my wife, Judith, for the patience she showed and sacrifices she made during the many years of my study. I have dedicated the book to her mother, who was mine as well.

And, finally, I wish to offer my thanksgiving to the Almighty whose mercies and compassions have sustained me.

Ramat Gan, Israel　　　　　　　　　　**AARON KIRSCHENBAUM**
Sivan 5748
June 1986

ABBREVIATIONS

Ad Att.	Epistulae ad Atticum***
Ad fam.	Epistulae ad familiares***
C.	Justinian, Codex**
C.I.L.	Corpus Inscriptionum Latinarum
C. Th.	Theodosian, Codex
D.	Justinian, Digesta**
De ben.	De beneficiis
Ep.	Epistulae
G.	Gaius, Institutiones*
Gaius Epit.	Gaius, Institutionum Epitome*
I.L.S.	Dessau, ed., Inscriptiones Latinae Selectae
Inst.	Justinian, Institutiones**
N.N.D.I.	Novissimo Digesto Italiano, ed. Azara and Eula
P.S.	Paul, Sententiae*
R.E.	Realenzyklopädie der klassischen Altertumswissenschaft, ed. Paully, Wissowa, Kroll, Mittehaus, and Ziegler
Ulp.	Ulpian, Regulae*
V.F.	Vatican Fragments*
Z.S.S.	Zeitschrift der Savigny-Stiftung für Rechtsgeschichte (Romanistische Abteilung)

*   Contained in *Fontes Iuris Romani Anteiustiniani*; see Bibliography.
**   Contained in *Corpus Iuris Civilis*; see Bibliography.
***   See under Cicero in Bibliography.

1, 6

I¹
DE IUSTITIA ET IURE.

1 ULPIANUS *libro primo institutionum* Iuri operam daturum prius nosse oportet, unde nomen iuris descendat. est autem a iustitia appellatum: nam, ut ele-
10 ganter Celsus definit, ius est ars boni et aequi. Cuius merito quis nos sacerdotes appellet: iustitiam namque colimus et boni et aequi notitiam profitemur, aequum ab iniquo separantes, licitum ab illicito discernentes, bonos non solum metu poenarum, verum etiam praemiorum quoque exhortatione efficere cupientes, veram nisi fallor philosophiam, non simulatam affectantes.
2 ²Huius studii duae sunt positiones, publicum et
15 privatum. publicum ius est quod ad statum rei Romanae spectat, privatum quod ad singulorum utilitatem: sunt enim quaedam publice utilia, quaedam privatim. publicum ius in sacris, in sacerdotibus, in magistratibus consistit³. privatum ius tripertitum est: collectum etenim est ex naturalibus praeceptis aut
3 gentium aut civilibus. ⁴Ius naturale est, quod natura omnia animalia docuit: nam ius istud non humani generis proprium, sed omnium animalium, quae
20 in terra, quae in mari nascuntur, avium quoque commune est. hinc descendit maris atque feminae coniunctio, quam nos matrimonium appellamus, hinc liberorum procreatio, hinc educatio: videmus etenim cetera quoque animalia, feras etiam istius iuris peritia censeri. Ius gentium est, quo gentes humanae utuntur. quod a naturali recedere facile intellegere licet, quia illud omnibus animalibus, hoc solis hominibus inter se commune sit.
25 2 POMPONIUS *libro singulari enchiridii* Veluti erga deum religio: ut parentibus ita patriae pareamus:
3 FLORENTINUS *libro primo institutionum* ut vim atque iniuriam propulsemus: nam iure hoc evenit, ut
2, 1 quod quisque ob tutelam corporis sui fecerit, iure fecisse existimetur, et cum inter nos cognationem quandam natura constituit, consequens est hominem homini insidiari nefas esse.
4 ⁵ULPIANUS *libro primo institutionum* Manumissiones quoque iuris gentium sunt. est autem manumissio de manu missio, id est datio libertatis: nam
5 quamdiu quis in servitute est, manui et potestati suppositus est, manumissus liberatur potestate. quae res a iure gentium originem sumpsit, utpote cum iure naturali omnes liberi nascerentur nec esset nota manumissio, cum servitus esset incognita: sed posteaquam iure gentium servitus invasit, secutum est beneficium manumissionis. et cum uno naturali nomine homines appellaremur, iure gentium tria genera esse coe-

perunt: liberi et his contrarium servi et tertium genus liberti, id est hi qui desierant esse servi. 2, 9/10
5 HERMOGENIANUS *libro primo iuris epitomarum* Ex hoc iure gentium introducta bella, discretae gentes, regna condita, dominia distincta, agris termini positi, aedificia collocata, commercium, emptiones venditiones, locationes conductiones, obligationes institutae: exceptis quibusdam quae iure⁶ civili introductae⁷ sunt.
6 ULPIANUS *libro primo institutionum* Ius civile est, quod neque in totum a naturali vel gentium 15 recedit nec per omnia ei⁸ servit: itaque cum aliquid addimus vel detrahimus iuri communi, ius proprium,
1 id est civile efficimus. ⁹Hoc igitur ius nostrum constat aut ex scripto aut sine scripto, ut apud Graecos: τῶν νόμων οἱ μὲν ἔγγραφοι, οἱ δὲ ἄγραφοι¹⁰.
7 PAPINIANUS *libro secundo definitionum* Ius autem civile est, quod ex legibus, plebis scitis, senatus 20 consultis, decretis principum, auctoritate prudentium
1 venit. Ius praetorium est, quod praetores introduxerunt adiuvandi vel supplendi vel corrigendi iuris civilis gratia propter utilitatem publicam. quod et honorarium dicitur ad honorem¹¹ praetorum sic nominatum.
8 MARCIANUS *libro primo institutionum* Nam et ipsum ius honorarium viva vox est iuris civilis. 25
9 ¹²GAIUS *libro primo institutionum* Omnes populi, qui legibus et moribus reguntur, partim suo proprio, partim communi omnium hominum iure utuntur. nam quod quisque populus ipse sibi ius constituit, id ipsius proprium civitatis¹³ est vocaturque ius civile, quasi ius proprium ipsius¹⁴ civitatis: quod vero naturalis ratio inter omnes homines constituit, id apud 30 omnes¹⁵ peraeque custoditur vocaturque ius gentium, quasi quo iure omnes gentes utuntur.
10 ¹⁶ULPIANUS *libro primo regularum* Iustitia est constans et perpetua voluntas ius suum cuique tribu-
1 endi¹⁷. Iuris praecepta sunt haec: honeste vivere, alterum non laedere, suum cuique tribuere.
2 Iuris prudentia¹⁸ est divinarum atque humanarum 35 rerum notitia, iusti atque iniusti scientia.
11 PAULUS *libro quarto decimo ad Sabinum* Ius pluribus modis dicitur: uno modo, cum id quod sem- 3, 1 per aequum ac bonum est ius dicitur, ut est ius naturale. altero modo, quod omnibus aut pluribus in quaque civitate utile est, ut est ius civile. nec minus ius recte appellatur in civitate nostra ius honorarium. praetor quoque ius reddere dicitur etiam cum inique decernit, relatione scilicet facta non ad id quod ita praetor fecit, sed ad illud quod praetorem facere 5 convenit. alia significatione ius dicitur locus in quo ius redditur, appellatione collata ab eo quod fit in eo ubi fit. quem locum determinare hoc modo pos-

---

(1) *Sab.* 1. 3. 4. 6. 8...*11. *12; *Pap.* *2. *5. *7. — *Inst.* est: legum aliae scriptae, aliae non scriptae (11) *sic*
1, 1. — *Bas.* 2, 1 (2) = *Inst.* 1, 1, 4' (3) *sic dett.* FR, ab honore *dett.* (12) *Gai.* 1, 1 = *Inst.* 1, 2, 1
cum B, constitit *FR* (4) = *Inst.* 1, 2 *pr.* (5) = *Inst.* (13) *civitatis om. Gaius* (14) *ipsius om. Gaius* (15) po-
1, 5 *pr.* (6) a iure *S* (7) *sic S cum B,* introducta *F* pulos *ins. Gaius et Inst.* (16) = *Inst.* 1, 1 *pr.* § 3. 1
(8) eius *Brenemannus cum B* (9) = *Inst.* 1, 2, 3 (10) *id* (17) tribuens *Inst. cum B* (18) iuris prudenti *F*

Corpus Iuris Civiles Vol. I (second part). *Digesta*, ed. by Theodor Mommsen and Paul Krueger. 15th stereotype edition. Berlin: Weidmann 1928–1929

First **Page** of the Digest of Justinian

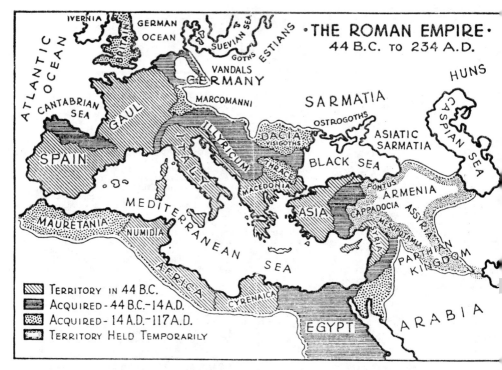

·THE ROMAN EMPIRE·
44 B.C. TO 234 A.D.

IVERNIA
GERMAN OCEAN
BRITAIN
SUEVIAN SEA
GOTHS
ESTIANS
HUNS
VANDALS
GERMANY
ATLANTIC OCEAN
CANTABRIAN SEA
MARCOMANNI
SARMATIA
GAUL
OSTROGOTHS
ASIATIC SARMATIA
CASPIAN SEA
SPAIN
ILLYRICUM
DACIA
VISIGOTHS
BLACK SEA
ITALY
THRACE
MACEDONIA
PONTUS
ARMENIA
MEDITERRANEAN
ASIA
CAPPADOCIA
ASSYRIA
MESOPOTAMIA
MAURETANIA
NUMIDIA
SYRIA
PARTHIAN KINGDOM
AFRICA
SEA
CYRENAICA
ARABIA
EGYPT

▨ TERRITORY IN 44 B.C.
▨ ACQUIRED — 44 B.C.–14 A.D.
▨ ACQUIRED — 14 A.D.–117 A.D.
▨ TERRITORY HELD TEMPORARILY

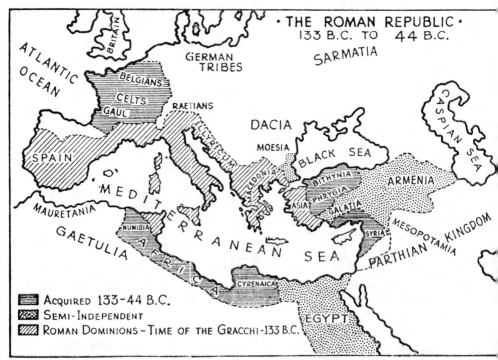

·THE ROMAN REPUBLIC·
133 B.C. TO 44 B.C.

BRITAIN
GERMAN TRIBES
SARMATIA
ATLANTIC OCEAN
BELGIANS
CELTS
GAUL
RAETIANS
DACIA
CASPIAN SEA
SPAIN
ILLYRICUM
MOESIA
BLACK SEA
BITHYNIA
ARMENIA
MACEDONIA
PHRYGIA
MEDITERRANEAN
ASIA
GALATIA
MESOPOTAMIA
MAURETANIA
NUMIDIA
SYRIA
PARTHIAN KINGDOM
GAETULIA
AFRICA
RRANEAN SEA
CYRENAICA
EGYPT

▨ ACQUIRED 133–44 B.C.
▨ SEMI-INDEPENDENT
▨ ROMAN DOMINIONS – TIME OF THE GRACCHI – 133 B.C.

INTRODUCTION

M. Rostovtzeff declares that classical Roman law was thoroughly adequate to the requirements of the most complicated business life.[1] Yet, it is generally acknowledged by students of legal history that the classical Roman legal system was highly formalistic and rigid. These characteristics, the heritage of a relatively simple, primitive agrarian society, would ordinarily tend to hamper dynamic commercial enterprises and variegated business activity. Thus, for example, the ancient law of the Romans, with its high degree of formalism, demanded the direct involvement of the parties concerned for every transaction into which they entered. By declaring, "There cannot be acquisition for us through a third party" and "No one can make a contract [*stipulatio*] on behalf of another", Roman law negated the possibility of agency and representation. Indeed, traditional Roman law lacked as basic an institution as agency. The Roman legal system did not operate with the principle that an authorized agent could conduct a transaction with a third party on behalf of his principal, and that the rights and liabilities created by said transaction could take effect between the principal and the third party without, however, similarly affecting the agent himself.

The convenience of carrying out transactions, commercial and non-commercial, legal and non-legal, through agents, intermediaries, and messengers is so obvious to modern students of the law that they

---

1   Rostovtzeff, II, 625, n. 54.

find it virtually impossible to conceive of a society managing without them. When one considers the distance between commercial centres within the Empire and the slow means of communication in antiquity, one is led to inquire how the Romans could carry on their intensive and far-reaching business enterprises without a developed concept of agency. The closest approximation to the modern institution of agency to be found in Roman law are the express and implied contracts of *mandatum* and *negotiorium gestio*, respectively; but, in view of the importance of commerce in the Roman Empire, these contracts were too limited in scope and application to have facilitated commercial activity. Rostovtzeff's declaration, grounded in indisputable historical fact as it is, demands, therefore, an explanation.

This explanation is to be found in the remarkable role non-contractual agency played in Roman life and law. In other words, the reason that the concept of agency was not fully developed in ancient Rome is that there were a sufficient number of people who performed the various services subsumed under the concept of agency who were, however, not bound to the people they thus served by the contractual bonds of agency and representation. Thus, for example, the Roman legal rule that one could not acquire through third parties did not necessitate the personal act of acquisition on the part of purchasers, borrowers or receivers of gifts, for there were subordinates in their power who could perform the act of acquisition on their behalf. Inasmuch as the legal exclusion of acquisition through third parties was never regarded as applying to slaves and children in one's power and since such subordinates were possessed in abundance, transactions involving acquisitions were nowhere so hampered as they would seem to have been by this rule superficially understood. The Roman *familia*, an institution which included not only one's wife and children, but slaves as well, was therefore a significant source of non-contractual agents.

An authority on Roman economics has described the Roman *familia* in the following manner:

> The Latin *familia* had a wide spectrum of meanings: all the persons, free or unfree, under the authority of the *paterfamilias*, the head of the household; or all the descendants from a common ancestor; or all one's property; or simply all one's servants .... The *paterfamilias* was not the biological father but the authority over the household, an

authority that the Roman law divided into three elements (I state this schematically), *potestas* or power over his children (including adoptees), his children's children and slaves, *manus* or power over his wife and his sons' wives, and *dominium* or power over his possessions.

This three-way classification is a precise account of a peasant household; the head manages and controls both the personnel and the property of the group, without distinction as to economic or personal or social behaviour, distinctions which could be drawn as an abstract intellectual exercise but not in actual practice.[2]

The crucial role of the Roman family as an inestimable source of agency cannot be understood properly, however, without reference to the law of the praetor, one of the most potent factors making for the flexibility of Roman law and for its applicability to a world far removed from the rustic scene of the pre-classical City. Praetorian law (known in Latin as *ius honorarium*) developed into a legal system parallel to the ancient law which the Romans had inherited from their ancestors. In practice, this supplementary system, with its amenability to substantive and procedural innovations necessitated by the changing economic and social conditions, prevailed. The praetor was the judicial magistrate of Rome, and, when the occasion arose, he would accommodate the legal machinery to new situations mainly through the creation of procedural remedies. He would, for example, recognize injustices arising out of new conditions that were not covered by the ancient law, and grant relief by providing for new actions to be brought in order to rectify the resultant inequities.

A case in point is the very question of agency which we address. The ancient civil law of the Romans, although it allowed members of the family to perform acts of acquisition on behalf of the head of the family, strictly limited such permission to acts which benefited the latter. It insisted that persons in one's power, i.e., slaves and children, had no legal power to worsen the condition of the head of family. In other words, they could not enter into any transaction or contract which would create liabilities for their respective master or father. Thus, a subordinate in power could neither create obligations for his master nor render him liable to suit. In effect, then, the head of a

2   Finley, 18–19.

family could not utilize the services of his slaves or sons as business agents, for no one would agree to contract with such persons since their principal could normally not be sued on the contracts into which they entered, and they, in principle, could own no property which could be seized in case of default or breach of contract. At this point, praetorian law intervened and made a whole series of actions available to third parties contracting with slaves and sons. These actions, available against the head of family, thereupon enabled subordinates in power to function effectively as agents of their principal, their master or father. In this manner, the judicial magistrate of Rome was able to accommodate the legal system to new situations and to the new needs they engendered. The main thrust of his innovations was to facilitate the employment of the members of the family as agents of the family by removing the cumbersome obstacles placed in the way by the archaic civil law.

The method of inquiry into the role of the non-contractual agent in Rome, therefore, entails an examination of Roman society. The purpose of this examination is to discern the social and legal relationships that existed in Roman society which enabled its citizens to fulfil the demands of business which in other societies were satisfied by the creation and operation of the institution of agency. These social, economic and legal relationships were contained within the Roman *familia*, and lessened the need for the law to develop fuller forms of agency. Moreover, beyond the periphery of the immediate *familia*, there were friends and relatives who served as agents, bound to their principals not by bonds of contract, but by a sense of duty and by ties of affection.

This study, then, is an attempt to indicate how a complex business world could operate without a system of agency (as the modern student of law and economics understands it). It shall attempt to document the multifarious roles fulfilled by sons, slaves, freedmen, friends, and relatives in Roman trade and shall show that these non-contractual agents filled the role which formal agents serve in other societies. Thus, there was no pressing economic need for the Roman civil law to go beyond the undeveloped forms of agency it possessed. The institution of slavery and the existence of a tightly-knit family as an economic unit made formal, contractual agency largely unnecessary. Conversely, the loosening of the family unit and the abrogation of slavery make a developed system of agency indispensable to the economic life of a society.[3]

Inasmuch as no monograph on this subject exists in English, the author has striven to give a complete and comprehensive treatment of the relevant provisions of Roman law even where he does not offer much that is original. He has often been compelled to reproduce the legal rules in rather great detail, occasionally presenting the conflicting opinions of scholars on some points of particular significance. Moreover, it was necessary to set much of the non-legal data about the position of slaves, sons-in-power, freedmen, and friends alongside the legal rules so as to bring out the social meaning and function of those rules.

Specifically, this book consists of a detailed description and analysis of the creation and operation of agency and representation in Roman classical life and law through those inter-personal non-contractual relationships that were characteristic of the Roman *familia* and those who were its extension. The first chapter describes how these non-contractual agents could be utilized in transactions involving property. The second chapter is devoted to a thoroughgoing discussion of the institution of the *peculium*, the name given to funds and items of property granted to slaves and sons by their respective masters and fathers; this *peculium* functioned as the patrimony of the subordinate slave or son, although legal title thereof was retained by the master. The purpose of describing the *peculium* arrangement at length is to assess it as an instrument of agency. The third chapter concerns itself with the various types of commercial transactions that could be carried out under the Roman legal system by authorized, non-contractual agents.

The fourth and concluding chapter deals with acts of agency performed by persons on the periphery of or outside the *familia* circle. Wives, freedmen, friends, and relatives in Rome, as elsewhere, performed innumerable acts of agency under circumstances and in a manner which indicates that the essential bond between agent and principal was not that of contract but of loyalty, indebtedness, friend-

---

3 *Cf.* Riccobono, Rec., 271–279. It is our fervent wish that this study will constitute a modest contribution to the task described by that great Romanist at the conclusion of his article.

ship, and kinship. The chapter, however, emphasizes those phases of Roman relationships which gave rise to mutual duties and services that were markedly different from those obtaining among members of a modern society. We regard the portrayal of such activities, where principals and agents acted with no thought of formal contractual obligations and with no intention of resort to court action in cases of failures and disappointments, as the key to the uniqueness of the operation of non-contractual agency in Roman life.

This is basically a legal study. Nevertheless, constant reference has been made to social and economic conditions that influenced the law and society in Rome. The sources used are both juristic and non-legal. Although the central task is the jurisprudential analysis of these sources, excursus on philological, textual, and historical problems have been introduced wherever they were deemed necessary. The frame of reference throughout has been the Roman law and society of classical times, i.e., from the late Republic through the Principate, with occasional references to their pre-classical antecedents.[4]

---

4 Adequate justification for placing prime focus on the classical law may be found in Pringsheim, Un., 60–64.

CHAPTER 1

TRANSACTIONS INVOLVING PROPERTY

A. THE ACQUISITION OF OWNERSHIP AND POSSESSION[1]

1. *The Rules Governing Acquisition Through Others*

a. *Acquisition Through Slaves and Sons*

Formulating the basic rule governing the acquisition of the ownership or possession of property, Gaius stated, "Acquisitions come to us not only by our own acts, but also through those whom we hold in *potestas*."[2] The term *potestas* refers to the power of the head of a family, the *paterfamilias*, over his children and his slaves.[3] Thus, an act of acquisition performed by a son or by a slave means that the article or piece of property acquired was thereby automatically added to the estate of the head of the family. The increase of one's property through acquisitions made "through those whom we hold in *potestas*" was recognized from ancient times, and Gaius' rule goes back at least to the time of the Twelve Tables.[4]

---

1 On ownership and possession generally, see Kaser, Con., 38–48.
2 G. 2.86: *Adquiritur autem nobis non solum per nosmet ipsos, sed etiam per eos quos in potestate . . . habemus.* Cf. ibid., 89; Ulp. 19.18; Inst. 2.9 pr. and 3; Gaius, D. 41.1.10 pr. and 2. For general understanding, Salkowski is still most helpful.
3 *Cf.* Sachers, 1046–1175.
4 Jolowicz, Hist. Introd., 118 and 135.

Examples of acquisition of property through one's sons and slaves abound in the legal literature. Thus, if a son or a slave found a treasure, it was as if the head of the family had found it.[5] If the person in *potestas* was instituted heir or granted a legacy by a Roman citizen, both the inheritance and the legacy belonged to the father or master in whose *potestas* he was.[6] If the subordinate received a gift, the gift was the property of his *paterfamilias*.[7]

Similarly, a purchase made by a slave was regarded as the legally acquired property of his master. In the event that the slave or the master subsequently lost possession of that property, there was available to the master the normal remedy for recovery known as the *actio Publiciana in rem*. By means of this action owners of a thing whose possession had been lost could reclaim it by merely proving that they had originally acquired it under conditions which put them in a position to acquire it legally by prescription.[8] Indeed, prescription *(usucapio)* itself could have been accomplished for the head of a family by persons in his power.[9]

In the case of acts of acquisition performed by a slave, however, there were three considerations which modify the automatic increment in the master's estate:

(1) If the ownership of the slave was in suspense, then the ownership of the acquired article remained in suspense. If a slave, for example, was given by a husband to his wife as a gift in contemplation of death *(donatio mortis causa)*, or if a slave was constituted as part of a legacy and the legatee had as yet not made the formal

---

5 Tryphoninus, D. 41.1.63 pr.; see Schultz, Fr., 95, 97–98.
6 Since, according to Roman law, an inheritance had to be formally "entered into" by the designated heir and a legacy had to be accepted by the legatee, if a slave were named heir or legatee, the inheritance or legacy would be subject to the approval of his master; G. 2.87; Ulp. 19.19.
7 Ulpian, D. 7.1.22. For the historical development inherent in this passage, where possession through one's slave represents the earliest stage, see Watson, Ac.P.E.P., 38.
8 This remedy for recovery was created by the law of the Praetor *(ius honorarium)*; Ulpian, D. 6.2.7.10. For the problems of the dating of this *actio*, see Watson, Prop., 104–107.
9 Paul, D. 41.3.8. pr.; see Nicosia, A., 223–233, and Watson, Ac.P., 214–222.

act of acceptance, the ownership of any acquisitions made by such slaves remained undetermined.[10]

(2) There were two sets of rules governing the manner in which a Roman citizen could acquire ownership. One set of rules was derived from the ancient civil law of the Romans, called *ius Quiritium*, which was a rigorous formalistic legal system of a primitive rural community; the other set of rules was the product of numerous praetorian modifications which gave rise to a more informal type of ownership, known as "bonitary" ownership, which was recognized by, and under the protection of, praetorian law. The rule of ownership governing acquisitions through others was that when property was acquired by a slave, it vested in his bonitary and not his Quiritarian (civil law) owner, when this was not the same person.[11]

Thus, if the civil law owner of a slave sold him and transferred the slave by delivery *(traditio)* to the purchaser, inasmuch as the ancient civil law did not recognize delivery of slaves as a formal transfer whereas the praetorian law did accept such delivery, the purchaser acquired bonitary ownership, and the vendor retained Quiritary ownership. This situation, where the slave was regulated by two kinds of ownership and had two different owners, persisted until prescriptive acquisition by the purchaser transformed the slave into his Quiritary property as well.[12] Again, if the Quiritarian owner of a slave, under duress *(metus)*, made a formal transfer[13] of the slave according to the Quiritarian law, then, although the receiver was recognized as the new Quiritarian, civil law owner, the original owner was regarded by praetorian law as the bonitary owner.[14] In all of these circumstances, anything acquired by the slave was recognized by the law as belonging to the bonitary owner.[15]

(3) If a slave was held in common by partners, any acquisition made by the slave belonged to each of his owners in proportion to

10 Iavolenus, D. 24.1.20; Julian, D. 30.86.2.
11 G. 2.88. On the earliest history of *ius Quiritium* and *in bonis esse*, see the summary of Diósdi, 166–179.
12 G. 2.41; *cf.* Solazzi, Scritti, VI, 204–207.
13 E.g., *mancipatio*.
14 Ulpian, D. 4.2.9.6. This passage, however, is regarded by some as Byzantine; see Schulz, Lehre, 200ff.
15 P.S. 1.7.6; see Huschke.

each one's share of ownership in him.[16] Whatever could not be acquired for all of the masters was acquired *pro solido* for him who could acquire it.[17] If he acquired something under an order from one master, he acquired ownership for that master alone.[18]

Through persons in one's power, ownership and possession could be gained by almost all modes of acquisition: by such natural, original acquisitions as the effective possession of ownerless or abandoned property *(occupatio)*, the process of addition whereby one thing became attached to and inseparable from a piece of property of the slave or the son *(accessio)*, and the gathering of fruit *(fructum perceptio)*; by the informal mode of delivery *(traditio)*; and by the formal, civil law ceremony of *mancipatio*.[19]

Any mode of acquisition, however, which involved the judicial process was closed to the slave, for the legal rule was, "A slave can neither be sued nor sue."[20] Thus, a slave could not acquire through the civil law transfer known as *in iure cessio*, which had the form of a (fictitious) trial before the magistrate wherein the transferee "sued for recovery" *(rei vindicatio)* and the transferer did not contest the "suit."[21] It follows then that the slave was incapable of acquisition through the adjudication of someone's property to him *(adiudi-*

---

16 G. 3.167. *Cf*. Bretone, Serv., 91, n. 111.

17 Julian, D. 26.8.12. *Cf*. Bretone, ibid., 60–61.

18 Pomponius, D. 45.3.6. *Cf*. Bretone, ibid., 87–79; Watson, Prop., 78–79.

19 G. 2.87; C. 4.27.1; *cf*. Solazzi, *Scritti*, VI, 353–356; Kaser, I, 286. As for *mancipatio*, the precise formulae that the slave could use are discussed in Buckland, Slavery, 712–713. Buckland's views, however, must be revised as the result of later studies (especially those of Kaser); *cf*. Prichard, 412–428.

20 Julian, D. 2.11.13: *Servus conveniri vel convenire non potest*. *Cf*. also G. 2.96: *Cum enim istarum personarum nihil suum esse possit, conveniens est scilicet ut nihil suum esse in iure vindicare possunt*. "For since such persons (among whom the slave is included – A.K.) can have nothing of their own, it obviously follows that they cannot vindicate in court anything as their own." Also Gaius, D. 50.17.107.

See now, however, Biscardi, 143–171, who successfully challenges the hitherto universally accepted notion that the judicial process was absolutely closed to the slave. Biscardi maintains that the older law, specifically among some of the Proculians, allowed for some exceptions.

21 G. 2.96; *cf*. Solazzi, *Scritti*, 360–362.

catio) in the so-called divisory actions.[22] A son, also, could not acquire property through these judicial modes of acquisition, for he, too, was not legally qualified to participate in the judicial process.[23]

Although we are here primarily concerned with transactions involving property, it should be pointed out in passing that a slave or a son could also serve as an instrument for the acquisition of rights on behalf of the *paterfamilias*. This may be illustrated by a few examples, briefly, as follows:

When a person in *potestas* was a party to the verbal contract known as *stipulatio*, the rights thereof derived vested in the master.[24] Although the subordinate acquired no rights for himself his individuality was material. "For instance, if a slave stipulates that he shall have a right of passage for himself *(iter)* or beasts and vehicles *(actus)*, it is he himself, not his master, who is not to be hindered from passing."[25] On the other hand, since the slave's capacity was derivative, he could acquire by *stipulatio* only for a master who himself was of legal capacity at least to acquire, if not to contract.[26]

Where a subordinate in *potestas* entered into a contract of sale, the master acquired thereby the right of suit against the vendor *(actio ex empto)*.[27] The same was true regarding the contract of mandate[28] and the gratuitous loan of a thing *(commodatum)*.[29]

---

22 *Actio communi dividundo* and *actio familiae erciscundae*; *cf.* Paul, V.F. 51.
23 See the sources cited in the two previous notes. On the capacity of the son to be involved in the judicial process, see Solazzi, Scritti, I, 1–74. The problem appears to be still *sub iudice*; *cf.* Longo, Ap., 393, n. 6; see further the brief critical remarks of Kaser, Rev. S., 419–420.
24 G. 3.111; Gaius, D. 41.1.10.1; Scherillo, 203–241.
25 Inst. 3.17.2: *Veluti si servus stipuletur, ut sibi ire agere liceat; ipse enim tantum prohiberi non debet, non etiam dominus eius.* This literal interpretation of the terms of the stipulation follows the rule, *Quae facti sunt non transeunt ad dominum*; Paul, D. 35.1.44 pr.
26 Pomponius, D. 41.3.28; Ulpian, D. 27.8.1.15; Buckland, Text., 439.
27 Julian, D. 21.2.39.1. The subordinate or his *paterfamilias*, of course, had to fulfil his obligations under the contract, e.g., they had to pay the purchase-price in full; Paul, D. 21.1.57 pr.
28 Paul, D. 17.1.22.8., citing Neratius.
29 Ulpian, D. 13.6.14. For details, see Buckland, Slavery, 154–158.

b. *Acquisition Through a Wife*

Whether legal title to property could be acquired through one's wife depended upon the status she had attained as the result of her marriage. In pre-classical times, when the formal *manus*[30] marriage prevailed, the woman at marriage became a kind of legal daughter of her husband or, if the latter himself was a son in *potestas,* of *his* father. In any event, the wife in *manus* was incapable of owning property.[31] Assuming that her husband was the head of the family, in which case she indeed occupied the legal position of his daughter, anything she acquired accrued to her husband's estate in the same way that anything acquired by a son belonged to his father's estate.[32]

In contrast to *manus*-marriage, there was the formless "free", consensual marriage, which, although also of great antiquity, came to prevail only in the classical period of Roman law. A "free" marriage had no legal effect on the wife's capacity to function as an agent of her husband. On the contrary, any act on her part which could be construed as having the quality of agency would be deemed to be that of her father, for free marriage did not remove a daughter from the *potestas* of her father. In accordance with the rules of the Roman civil law, therefore, a daughter continued to acquire real and personal rights for her father just as she had acquired such rights before her entrance into marriage. As far as her husband was concerned, she was juridically a total stranger, an individual like any other Roman.[33]

---

30 The word *manus* appears to have been used originally as a general term analogous to *potestas* and to have connoted the ruling and, simultaneously, protecting hand (Old High German *munt*). Later, it received a specialized meaning and was used only to denote the power over the wife if she belonged to the husband's house; Kaser, I, 56.

31 Zulueta, Gaius, II, 34–36; Corbett, 68–69, 108–109.

32 G. 2.86.

33 Zulueta, Gaius, II, 36–37; Corbett, 90–91, 112–114.

c. *Acquisition Through Independent Persons*

The following passage states that it is impossible to acquire property through persons not in one's power:

> From what we have said, it is evident that through free men who are neither subject to our power nor *bona fide* possessed by us, and through slaves of others of whom we have neither a usufruct nor a lawful possession, acquisition is impossible on any account. This is the meaning of the common saying that there cannot be acquisition for us through a stranger.[34]

The general principle embodied in the common saying, "There cannot be acquisition for us through a stranger" *(per extraneam personam nihil nobis adquiri posse)*, was that one could not acquire property through formal transfer *(mancipatio)* to, or other formal act of, any person who was not in one's power *(potestas* or *manus)*. Hence, one could not acquire property through one's emancipated son, one's manumitted slave, one's wife without *manus*, or any free Roman citizen. This was also true regarding the acquisition of an inheritance,[35] the acquisition of contractual rights, and the right to sue.[36]

The main exception[37] was the manumitted slave, a freedman, who continued to serve his former master as a kind of general agent, known as a *procurator*.[38] Concerning him, the rule was, "But through

---

34 G. 2.95: *Ex his apparet per liberos homines quos neque iuri nostro subiectos habemus neque bona fide possidemus, item per alienos servos in quibus neque usumfructum habemus neque iustam possessionem, nulla ex causa nobis adquiri posse. Et hoc est quod vulgo dicitur, per extraneam personam nobis adquiri non posse.* On the rule generally, see Buckland, Per., 188–210.

35 Modestinus, D. 41.1.54 pr.

36 G. 3.103; Quintus Mucius Scaevola, D. 50.17.73.4; Ulpian, D. 45.1.38.17: *Alteri stipulari nemo potest*, "Nobody may make a *stipulatio* on behalf of another."

37 Another exception was the *tutor*; Ulpian, D. 6.2.7.10; 13.7.11.6; Neratius, D. 41.1.13.1; Paul, D. 41.2.1.20.

38 For a long time, this type of independent person represented his principal without any clear contractual basis; much of Chapter Three below is devoted to this legal phenomenon. On the fact that the *procurator (omnium bonorum)* was invariably one's freedman, see below pp. 121–

a *procurator* possession can be acquired for us."[39]

It must be pointed out, however, that the principle that there could not be acquisition through "strangers" did not exclude acquisition through an independent person acting as one's agent where all that the agent did was carry out one's order to take or to receive a specified object *(corpus)* or where the acquisition was ratified by the principal subsequent to his agent's act of acquisition. In these cases the "agent" was little more than an instrument.[40] It was in cases where the authorization was *not* specific and the independent person himself *(animo suo)* had negotiated the transaction under which the act of possession had been accomplished that this principle negated the legal effectiveness of the agent's act. This, for example, was the general position both in the classical and in the Justinian law with regard to the acquisition of ownership through *traditio*, the informal delivery, to an *extranea persona* who received on behalf of the principal. There are, however, some variations on this general position. Whereas some jurists would allow such acquisition where the instrument was, as we have seen at the end of the previous paragraph, a *procurator*,[41] another tended to be more restrictive and did not allow acquisition of ownership through any free person even if he were nothing more than an instrument;[42] others allowed only acquisition of possession (and then only through a *procurator*) and, in exceptional cases, where possession and ownership could not be separated,

---

122. As to the extent to which the *procurator* could acquire rights on behalf of his principal, see Düll, Stell., 309–316.

39 P.S. 5.2.2: *Sed per procuratorem adquiri nobis possessionem posse . . .*; *cf.* G. 2.95. and Inst. 2.9.5. and commentaries. For a detailed textual and historical analysis of these passages, see Meylan, 105–114, and Watson, Ac.P.E.P., *passim*, as well as the studies cited in these two articles. Watson propounds the thesis "that before the end of the classical period one could acquire possession through any *extranea persona*"; ibid., 22, *contra* the generally accepted opinion as expressed, e.g., by Schulz, 438–349. The doubts expressed by Bretone, Ad., 280–292, have been effectively dispelled, to my mind, by Watson, ibid., and Nicosia, A., 189–195.

40 See below pp. 25–26.

41 And, probably, also a *tutor*; Neratius, D. 14.1.13 pr. and 1.

42 Callistratus, D. 41.1.59.

they would even permit acquisition of ownership (again only through a *procurator*).[43]

All of this, of course, was in marked contrast to an act of acquisition made through those in one's power, where no authorization was necessary for the validity of the acquisition.[44]

2. Acquisition Through Others Jurisprudentially Analyzed

a. Acquisition of Ownership Through Persons in Potestas

Do the rules of the acquisition of ownership through those in one's *potestas*, summarized above, add up to a concept of true agency? It appears not. Any human being has the necessary understanding (*intellectus*) and intention (*animus*) without which no act or transaction could have any status in the eyes of the law.[45] But Roman legal theory, as evidenced by its rejection of the possibility of independent persons acting as one's agents even though they possessed such understanding and intention, quite clearly did not recognize agency as the modern lawyer understands the term.

How did a slave's ability to acquire operate? As Gaius said, "A man acquires through his slaves even against his will on almost every occasion."[46] This statement indicates that the acquisition made by the slave accrued to his master *de facto*, by the mere fact that the master's chattel, the slave,[47] held another piece of property in "its" hands.

In principle, a slave consisted of two qualities: he was a human

---

43 C. 4.27.1 (Diocletian and Maximian). For details, see Watson, Ac. O., 189–209.

44 Mitteis, R.P., I, 212, n. 24, and 213, n. 31; Zulueta, Gaius, II, 82.

45 On *animus* see MacCormack, Role, 105–145.

46 Gaius, D. 41.1.32: *Etiam invitis nobis per servos adquiritur paene ex omnibus causis. Cf.* Inst. 2.9.3: *Hoc enim vobis et ignorantibus et invitis obvenit,* "for this takes place even without your knowledge and against your will." As for the force of the word "almost" in the Gaius passage, see Zulueta, 67.

47 In the eyes of the law, a slave can have nothing of his own; G. 2.96.

being *(persona)*, and he was a thing, a chattel *(res)*.[48] It was the human quality of the slave which accounted for his possession of the necessary understanding *(intellectus)* and intention *(animus)*. It was the human quality of the slave which made it possible for his very holding of property to achieve the status of "possession"; indeed, a slave in Roman law had the legal capacity to conduct a business transaction.[49] On the other hand, it was the chattel aspect of the slave that accounted for his lack of legal capacity and his total subjugation to his master; and it was this chattel aspect, the view that he was nothing more than a third arm of his master, which made it possible for the Roman law to accept the idea that his act could be construed, under prescribed circumstances, as the act of and/or for his master. Thus, it was paradoxically the slave in his "lower" status, as a thing owned or capable of being owned,[50] that was a major instrument in filling the need for something comparable to agency in Roman law.

Similarly, the ability of a son to acquire property on behalf of his father without the latter's knowledge and even against his will may also be regarded as a vestige of the chattel nature of the son in Roman law. Although the historic texts do not state so explicitly,[51] there are pre-classical indications that the son, too, was regarded as the chattel of his father. This is indicated, briefly, as follows: (1) The father had the power of life and death *(vitae necisque potestas)* over his children.[52] (2) The father could sell his children into permanent slavery, if sold to a foreign people, or into bondage *(in mancipio)*, if sold to a Roman. (3) The father had control over the children's marriage.[53] (4) Children in *potestas* lacked legal capacity in private law matters, such as the capacity to own property.

Moreover, there was a remarkable similarity, already found in the

---

48   Citations to this effect are numerous: e.g., G. 1.9. Ulpian, D. 7.2.1.1. = V.F. 75.2 *(persona)*; G. 2.13–14a. Ulp. 19.1 *(res.)*. *Cf.* Bonfante, I, 1948.

49   *Cf.* the title of D. 14.5: *Quod cum eo, qui in aliena potesta est, negotium gestum esse dicitur.* "Dealings alleged to have been had with a person in the *potestas* of another"; the reference is to, among others, the slave.

50   A slave could be ownerless *(res nullius)* as, for example, when he was abandoned by his master *(servus pro derelicto)*; Julian, D. 41.7.2.1.

51   Unless one is inclined to press the word *dominium*, used by Ulpian, D. 50.16.195.2, inordinately.

52   On *ius vitae necisque* generally, see Sachers, 1084–1089.

53   For details, see Corbett, 2–5, 53–67, 122–175, 239–243.

Twelve Tables, between the liability of a father for the delicts of his son and the liability of a master for the damage done by his animal. In both cases, the liability was alternative: either to pay the damages or to surrender the offender (usually) to the person injured.[54] Again, in both cases, the rule was "Noxal liability follows the person of the offender," so that if the animal were sold or the son passed into someone else's *potestas* by adoption, the liability attached itself to the purchaser or *adoptator*, respectively, and if the delinquent died the liability was extinguished.[55] And again, there were great similarities between the status of the son and the status of the slave.

These points of correspondence, many of which will be enumerated in the course of this study, are themselves strong indications that there must have been a time in primitive Roman history when a son, like a slave, was regarded as chattel of his father as long as the latter was alive.[56]

We may conclude, therefore, that the ability to acquire property through those who were in one's power was a vestige of the ancient view that such persons were regarded as proprietary extensions of the head of the *familia* to which they belonged.[57] This derivative nature of the subordinate's power of acquisition accounts for the rule that limited such power to the capability of his master. Thus, one who could not acquire anything by prescription in his own name could not acquire it by his slave; and one who was in the hands of the enemy could not acquire possession through the medium of his subordinate.[58, 59]

---

54 This type of liability for the delict of a subordinate is called "noxal", and the father of the delinquent son was liable to the *actio noxalis*: Table XII.2; G. 4.75–77; Inst. 4.8.1–5; D. 9.4; C. 3.4. See Buckland, Slavery, chap. V. The owner of the delinquent animal was liable to the *actio de pauperie*: Table VIII.6; Inst. 4.9. pr.; D. 9.1. See Zulueta, Gaius II. 273–274, and Buckland, Text., p. 603, n. 3. For details and bibliography, see Kaser, I, 162, n. 65, 163–165, 287, 630–634.

55 G. 4.77; Ulpian, D. 9.1.1.12.

56 *Cf.* Koschaker; Longo, Ap., 394–396; and the literature therein cited. More recently: Kaser, Eig., 1–6, 180–194; and Gallo, 17–58.

57 On the organic nature of the *familia* and of the place of the son and slave therein, see Kaser, Wes., 333ff. and 343ff.

58 Paul, D. 41.3.8.1 and 11.

59 For a summary of the basic theories regarding *potestas* and *mancipium* in earliest Roman Law, see Diósdi, 50–61, 180–185.

b. *Acquisition of Possession Through Persons in* Potestas

The theory underlying the ability of citizens to acquire possession through subordinates in their *potestas* has long occupied Romanists. The most acceptable explanation would appear to be the "thesis of possession." This thesis has been aptly formulated by Ihering, *"Recht erzeugt Recht; Besitz Besitz,"* with the second clause declaring that it was the *dominus'* very possession of his slave or son which enabled these latter to acquire possession of property on his behalf.[60]

In contradistinction to acquisition of ownership through slaves, however, acquisition of possession through them without one's knowledge and consent appears to be the subject of numerous contradictory opinions in the Digest. Papinian, for example, said, "Possession is not merely a matter of physical fact but also of right."[61] In other words, possession was not merely physical deten-

---

60 Nicosia, L., Chapter II. Note how this is corroborated by the jurists' consistent citation of the fact of the *dominus'* possession (or lack thereof) of the subordinate as being the crucial factor in determining the latter's ability to acquire possession on his behalf: G. 2.90, 94; Pomponius, D. 41.1.21 pr., citing Proculus; Julian, D. 41.1.37 pr., and Paul, D. 41.2.1.15, citing Julian; Nicosia, ibid., pp. 27–34. Nicosia's theory of possession is, it would appear, superior to that which seeks to find the basis of the subordinate's ability to acquire possession on his master's behalf in his ability to own property. After all, regarding persons *in manu* and *in mancipio*, who were totally incapable of owning property (G. 1.123), the possibility *is* entertained that they, too, could have been instruments for the acquisition of possession; Nicosia, ibid., pp. 21–23. Nor is the key explanation to be found in *potestas* which enabled the subordinate — who otherwise was incapable of ownership — to acquire on behalf of his master rather than not to acquire at all. But this theory of *potestas* would appear to be effectively refuted by the facts that a *bona fide* possessor of a slave who by rights was a free man and a citizen who had a usufruct in his neighbour's slave could both acquire possession through these subordinates (G. 2.92.84) though the elements of *potestas* and *dominium* were lacking; Nicosia, ibid., pp. 25–27, 72–78. Cf. Benöhr, Besitz, 18–20, for a summary of the main theories explaining the acquisition of possession through persons in *potestas*.

61 D. 41.2.49.1: *Possessio non tantum corporis sed et iuris est.* According to Benöhr, ibid., 20–72, summarized on 78–82, the fact of physical possession is a function of the view held in common by the members of a specific society; hence it may vary from time to time or from place to

tion, but rather detention by a person who had legal capacity of possessing *(ius possessionis)*. Hence, this same chattel nature of the slave and the vestiges thereof with regard to the son, both in *potestas*, which enabled them to acquire ownership for the *paterfamilias*, was the very factor which prevented them from acquiring possession on his behalf unless he had assented.

On the other hand, Ulpian declared, "My slave will also acquire possession for me without my knowledge."[62]

Various attempts have been made to resolve this and similar contradictions. A number of scholars accepted Papinian's statement, which denies the slave the power to accomplish an act of possession without his master's assent, as the definitive rule of the classical law. They disagree, however, as to the correct interpretation of Ulpian's conflicting remarks. Since many a slave was granted a sum of money or some property, known as his *peculium*, which he was free to administer at his own discretion,[63] one opinion is that the Ulpian passage refers exclusively to the slave's *peculium*; it is to be understood as saying, "My slave will also acquire possession for me without my knowledge through the enlargement of his *peculium* [*ex peculiari causa*]," for the owner of the slave always retained legal title to the *peculium*, and, therefore, any increment in the *peculium* was regarded as acquisition of possession for the master.[64] Another scholar agrees that, according to the classical law, a slave could perform an act of possession without his master's knowledge only if the act was in connection with the business of his *peculium*. However, inasmuch as the statement of Ulpian does not refer to a slave administering a

place. On the other hand, the legal elements of *possessio* are stable. Thus, a slave could not achieve *possessio* for himself, for he was incapable of bearing legal rights; he could not do as he wished with the article he held; his master could always deprive him of it. To accomplish *possessio* on behalf of his master, the slave, at the very least, would have had to constitute some part of the master's business, some organic element in the latter's enterprise.

62 D. 41.2.34.2: *Servus quoque meus ignoranti mihi adquiret possessionem.*

63 The *peculium* will be treated in detail in Chapter Two.

64 Buckland, Slavery, 200, n. 1. The main text which supports this interpretation is Paul, D. 412.1.5; see Francisci, 1002ff.; Micolier, 555ff.; and Bonfante, III, 329ff.

peculium, it may well contain a post-classical interpolation. Thus, it may represent a tendency on the part of Justinian to abolish the limitation to *peculium* and instead to allow unlimited acquisition of possession by a slave for his master.[65] A third opinion regards Ulpian's statement as based upon the mistaken notion that just as an owner could have acquired possession through his slave if he had known about said acquisition or had authorized it, so could he have acquired possession if the slave had performed the act of possession in his owner's name.[66]

A second group of scholars attempts to resolve the contradiction between the two passages by declaring that, on the contrary, it is not the Papinian passage, but rather the statement of Ulpian, which represents the classical law. From time immemorial, masters acquired possession through their slaves and sons just as they acquired ownership through them, whether or not the former were aware of the latter's acquisitive act. Gaius, for example, knew of no special requirement of knowledge and consent on the part of the head of the *familia* when persons in his *potestas* acquired property on his behalf.[67] Paul's requirement that an act of possession had to consist of the physical holding of the object being acquired coupled with a volitional intention to possess *(possessio corpore et animo)*[68] could have been fulfilled by the subordinate himself.[69] In this view, it was

65 Riccobono, Term., 356–361, esp. 358, n. 3.
66 Buckland, Slavery, 132–133. For details and elaboration of the views of this group of scholars, see the literature cited by Watson, Ac.P., 205, n. 1.
67 G. 2.86–96.
68 P.S. 5.2.1; D. 41.2.2.1. See some general remarks regarding *animus* in possession and ownership in Pringsheim, G.A., I, 308ff.
69 Nicosia, L., 87–114. Thus, contrary to the view of Bonfante, III, 332, that a subordinate in *potestas* was merely an "intelligent tool", e.g., like a messenger-boy who turns up for delivery at the conclusion of a legal transaction, the *subiectus,* according to Nicosia, should be regarded as a true representative of his *dominus* and of his will. On this very important point in the dogmatics of the question, we cite the following weighty words of Wieacker, 374–375: "Always admitting that the sources have the last word, it seems to us that the conventional doctrine (and not that of Nicosia) should be preferred. The *animus adipiscendae possessionis* is, in accordance with its historic origins, directed towards one's own possession, i.e., the conscious will to acquire and to possess

the post-classical law that introduced the need for the assent of the master and limited the older ability of subordinates to acquire possession on their own to those acquisitions that were connected to a *peculium*.[70]

The most significant case in point was the role of delivery *(traditio)* as a mode of acquisition. We have already seen that a citizen could have acquired ownership over something by its delivery being made to a slave or a son in his *potestas*. Now, the informal mode of delivery known as *traditio* was in essence an act of possession; hence it was impossible to acquire ownership by *traditio* without also acquiring possession. Inasmuch as *traditio* to a person in *potestas* gave his master ownership even without the latter's knowledge, it is clear that acquisition of possession could also have been accomplished

---

the property as one's own (or in accordance with one of the few other legal relations which give rise to civil possession, e.g., as creditor holding a pawn or as a receiver under an order of sequestration). The *subiectus* as such is incapable of having the will *rem sibi habere* and can therefore not represent the *dominus* as having such a will. For purposes of acquisition of possession by the *dominus*, he can only function as a mediating, albeit intelligent tool, as *minister*, insomuch as he transmits to him the (social) control of goods which we call *corpus possessionis*. To that end, it is essential that the *subiectus* should be in physical possession of the object *(tenere, detinere)*; admittedly, he controls it only if he also wills to be in possession, and to possess it as belonging to another, namely the *dominus*. Such a will is not the will to possess for oneself, no *animus adipiscendae possessionis*, but 'natural will'; it does not derive from the *subiectus'* ability to act, but from his natural ability to will. This is the situation to which the sources, in the case of *subiecti* as in the case of a procurator or other *extraneus*, refer as *alieno nomine possidere*; D. 41.2.18 pr. shows that this situation excludes civil possession by the intermediary himself. It follows that acquisition of possession *ignaro domino* was in principle impossible. If it were admitted, even if only for *peculiaris causa*, we should have to show the particular *ratio essendi* of this exception."

70 Beseler, Beit., IV, 61ff.; ibid., Misc. 417–418; Schulz, 438. The most comprehensive treatment in recent times of the problems related to the acquisition of possession through persons in *potestas* is by Nicosia, L., *(passim)* and Watson, Ac.P., 205–213, who are in general agreement with this second group of scholars. See further their treatment of the following passages: Gaius, D. 41.2.15., Javolenus, D. 41.2.23.2., and *idem* D. 41.2.24.; Nicosia, ibid., pp. 301–305, 375–376, and Watson, ibid., 205–209.

through *traditio* without the master's knowledge — without said acquisition being *peculiaris causa.*[71]

The divergence of opinion as to whether the classical law recognized the validity of acts of possession performed by a slave without his master's knowledge and consent[72] affects a number of related problems. For example, to be valid, acquisitions must have been made in good faith *(bona fide).* The question then arises as to whose good faith was required, that of the slave when he took possession or that of his master when he was informed of the act of possession. The Digest indicates both. Those, however, who maintain that, according to the classical law, the master's knowledge and consent were not necessary at all consider those portions of the Digest passages that do require the master's good faith to be post-classical

---

71   Nicosia, ibid., 115–136; *traditio* follows the same rules as *mancipatio* (ibid., 120–122). Nicosia's thesis, that *traditio* has its basis in possession and that it is impossible to acquire ownership by *traditio* without also acquiring possession, has been defended by Gordon, 279–300, against the attacks of Watson, ibid. Gordon himself, however, maintains that although the thesis is correct, it is irrelevant for the classical period. He contends that those passages in the Digest which indicate that ownership could be acquired through *traditio* even without the master's knowledge and consent do not reflect the classical law; they are the product of the policy of the (Justinian) compilers to substitute regularly *traditio* for *mancipatio.* In classical times, acquisition of ownership for the master was indeed accomplished without his knowledge if it was done through the formal act of *mancipatio.* "That acquisition was automatic can be explained on the rather primitive principle that pronunciation of appropriate ritual words of acquisition by a person who is an appropriate instrument of acquisition leads to acquisition" (Gordon, 282). This did not hold true with respect to the informal *traditio.* Gordon thus joins the first group of scholars, mentioned *supra,* who are of the opinion that acquisition of possession through a son or a slave could not be accomplished without the master's knowledge and authorization unless it was done for the subordinate's *peculium.*

72   Benöhr, Besitz, 83–86, has refined the controversial opinions into *four* ways of interpreting the various contradictory passages in the sources. The divergence of opinion persists, as can be seen by the reaction of Romanists to Nicosia's book (see above, n. 68). Compare, for example, the laudatory review of Wieacker, 371–386, to the total rejection expressed by Sella, 432–462.

interpolations.[73] Again, a slave administering a *peculium* could always have acquired for his *peculium (peculiari nomine)* without his owner's knowledge.[74] His discretionary ability to acquire on behalf of his master's estate *(domini nomine)* without such knowledge, however, would have depended on the opinions cited in the above-described dispute.[75]

Reference has been made to the chattel nature of the slave and the vestiges thereof with regard to the son, both in *potestas*, and the role of this aspect of their nature in enabling them to serve as a means of acquisition of ownership and possession. This requires further elucidation.

Paul declared:

> Through a slave over whom a man has an usufruct he can get possession, according to the ordinary rule of acquisition. It does not matter that he is not in possession of the slave himself, for neither is he in possession of a son.[76]

Thus, that which was questioned in Gaius' time[77] and was sustained

73 Paul, D. 41.4.2.11, citing Celsus and Pomponius. See Buckland, Text., 244, and Beseler, Beit., IV, 67–68. As to the problem of good faith, we prefer the view of Benöhr, Irrtum, 9–32, according to which the organic unity of master and slave is such that the *mala fides* of either negates the legality of the slave's act of possession. Similarly, error on the part of the master is ineffective in destroying the act of possession if the slave is aware of the true nature of the item being possessed, or, *vice versa*, error on the part of the slave does not impair the transaction if the master is aware of the true circumstances.

74 Paul, D. 41.2.1.5; 32.2. See Zulueta, Gaius. Even those scholars who maintain that in the classical law the master's knowledge was necessary for the slave's acquisition readily accept this exception *peculiari nomine*. A master who hands over a *peculium* to his slave and leaves him in actual possession of it, has implicitly given his general consent to acquisition on his behalf.

75 Thus, in all cases except the acquisition of possession, the slave or son could determine whether the acquisition was directly that of the master *(domini* or *patris nomine)* or indirectly so *(peculiari nomine)*.

76 D. 41.2.1.8: *Per eum in quo usum fructum habemus possidere possumus, sicut ex operis suis adquirere nobis solet: nec ad rem pertinet, quod ipsum non possidemus: nam nec filium.*

77 G. 2.94; *cf.* Solazzi, Scritti, VI, 356–357.

by Papinian,[78] was stated by Paul as a matter of fact, namely, that slaves (in *usufruct)* and sons, who themselves were, strictly speaking, not in the possession of their masters, could nevertheless serve as a means of acquiring possession. This conclusion, which contradicts the formal logic of the classical law, was based upon a concept of *possessio naturalis ("naturaliter teneatur")*[79] which the fructuary was understood as having over the slave and was opposed to the normal *possessio;*[80] it then, interestingly enough, draws upon an analogy from the *filiusfamilias ("nam nec filium").* In other words, the archaic formal law understood that the master was able to acquire possession through slaves and sons because of the fact that they were in his possession. As a result of the later development of the law, the ability of sons and slaves to acquire possession on behalf of the master was retained despite the fact that the latter no longer was in full *possessio* of them — as far as slaves in usufruct and sons were concerned. The fact that sons, for example, were no longer in the full *possessio* of their fathers may be adduced from the changes that had taken place in the noxal liability of fathers for the torts of their sons, in the remedies available to protect *patria potestas* from dissolution, in the type of compensation a father could sue for in the case of his son having been kidnapped. Indeed, it is clear that in the classical law a son was no longer the chattel of his father. But, although the *patria potestas* in which he was held had changed, as long as it existed, he was viewed as being capable of acquiring possession for his father; and, analogously, a slave in the usufruct of someone, although only *naturaliter teneatur*, could have done the same.[81]

---

78 D. 41.2.49 pr. "... since both the slave is as a matter of fact in the possession of the fructuary *(naturaliter a fructuario teneatur)* and possession borrows a great deal from right *(plurimum iure possessio mutuetur* [i.e., judicial consequences derive from possession])."

79 Regarding the classical nature of this expression, see Nicosia, L., 39, n. 46.

80 Normal *possessio* is retained by the *dominus.*

81 All the foregoing is based upon Maschi, 467–478. *Cf.* Nicosia, ibid., 27–31, 36–41, 49–56.

c. *Acquisition Through Independent Persons*

By declaring, "There cannot be acquisition for us by a third party," and, "No one may make a contract [*stipulatio*] on behalf of another," Roman law negated the possibility of true agency. The reasons for this negation are buried in hoary antiquity, for it was an unchanging feature of the *ius civile* from its inception, i.e., from the times which yield us its earliest formulations. Rather than enter into the sphere of speculations,[82] we prefer to accept this rejection of direct representation as a datum, describe it as "repugnant to the Roman juridic conscience,"[83] and let it go at that.

The ancient civil legal tradition, however, did arrive at the point of admitting that a factual situation or a legal situation could come about by means of a person who had been placed in an intermediary position in the sense that the will or intention necessary to accomplish an act of acquisition could have been physically expressed through some other person *sui iuris*.[84]

In setting forth the rules governing acquisitions through independent persons, a distinction was made between the physical act of acquiring a specific object *(corpus)*, on the one hand, and the intention or will of a person to conclude a transaction of acquisition *(animus)*, on the other. The legal rule which declared that one could not acquire ownership through the agency of persons outside of one's *potestas* referred to those acts where the intention to acquire as well as the physical taking of the object must have been provided by the

---

82 For a summary of the theories of the nineteenth century, when such speculation was in vogue, see Mitteis, 9–13. Mitteis himself, 13–25, rejects any one facile, general explanation; and correctly refuses to attribute the lack of agency to the extreme strict formalism of the ancient Roman law with its external solemnity and emphasis on ceremony. Daube, Text, and, following his lead, MacCormack, Form, 439–468, argue convincingly against the stereotyped views of the ancient *ius civile* as rigidly formalistic and of the ancient Roman legal procedure as ritually magical. Although these authors do not mention the problem of agency explicitly, their conclusions do tend to corroborate Mitteis' analysis made almost a century earlier.

83 Biondi, 7.

84 Ibid.

agent. Where, however, the principal had expressed his intention to acquire and the agent was called upon merely to perform the physical act of taking the object, agency then was limited to persons in one's power. This distinction helps clarify the differences between two types of agents and to delineate their respective roles.

If one wished to conclude a transaction, but could not do so because of physical reasons alone, he could avail himself of the services of another who, like a letter, helped him overcome the external obstacle of distance. It was the principal who concluded the juristic act; his agent was merely the instrument whereby the principal expressed *his* will. This type of representative was properly called a messenger *(nuntius)*, for his role was to convey the expression of his sender's will. In cases involving acquisition of property, the expression of the sender's will (i.e., his *animus*) was essentially manifested in the physical taking or giving of a specified object (the *corpus*).

However, where the principal had no intention of concluding the transaction himself, where the principal authorized another to act on his behalf and in his name, in other words, where the agent was empowered to decide as to the will to be expressed and then to express that will and thereby conclude the juristic act — this type of representative was properly called an agent. In cases involving acquisition of property, the agent not only performed the physical act of taking or delivering, he negotiated the transaction under which the act of possession was accomplished.[85]

In line with this analysis, it is correct to say that Roman law recognized the use of free persons as messengers, not as agents. In contrast, the acquisition of ownership through others when those others were in one's power referred to the intention to acquire *(animus)* as well as to the physical aspect of acquisition *(corpus)*. Persons in *potestas*, being extensions of the head of family, were sufficiently identified with him to have been enabled to perform juristic acts on his behalf. Strangers, i.e., persons free from his *potestas*, were not sufficiently identified with him to have been en-

---

85 Sohm, 243–245.

abled to do so.[86] The role of these latter was limited to that of a mere messenger.[87]

B. ALIENATION OF PROPERTY

A slave could work very effectively as an instrument of his master to transfer property to someone else. For example, he could sell a fellow slave.[88] He could alienate anything.[89] He could give his creditor a pledge *(pignus)* for his debt; indeed, the pledge might be the slave himself.[90] Further, he could hand over items for the gratuitous use of others *(precarium)*; those, too, might include himself.[91]

There was, however, one major limitation upon the power of a slave to alienate property: The agreement of his owner was required. Inasmuch as alienation diminishes the owner's estate, the basic rule that declared, "Our slaves can better our condition, but can not make it worse,"[92] applied. The express agreement of the owner was therefore required for all acts performed by the slave disposing of the property.[93] This agreement could have been an expression of consent *(voluntas)* given prior to the transaction, as in the passage we have cited above; it could have been in the form of a statement of ratification *(ratihabitio)* subsequent to the transaction; or it could have been part of a general authorization *(permissio generalis)* granted to the slave by his master for such dealings.[94]

---

86 Except the *procurator* and *tutor*.
87 Watson, Ac.O., 189, 207–209, *q.v.* for the slight variations of this generalization as it is formulated by each jurist.
88 Julian, D. 21.2.39.1a.
89 Ulpian, D. 6.1.41.1.
90 Paul, D. 12.6.13. pr. and 20.1.29.3.
91 Julian, D. 43.26.19.1.
92 Gaius, D. 50.17.133: *Melior condicio nostra per servos fieri potest, deterior fieri non potest*; cf. Savigny, III, 93, note e.
93 If a slave acted *bona fide*, under a reasonable, but mistaken, notion that his acts had been authorized by his owner, they were nevertheless invalid; Proculus, D. 12.6.53. It follows that if the slave was unaware of the fact that the authorization had expired, his acts of disposition were also invalid; *arg.*, D. 12.1.11.2.
94 *Cf.* Julian, D. 43.26.19.1. and Paul, D. 15.1.46.

Thus, without the consent of his master, the slave could not transfer ownership of anything to anyone.[95] If he sold something, the sale was invalid. If delivery had taken place with the purchaser's awareness that the slave was acting without his owner's authorization, not only could the purchaser not acquire by adverse possession, i.e., prescription *(usucapio)*, he was also liable to delictual action for theft *(furum)*.[96] The same was true if a slave executed a gratuitous loan to a borrower who was aware of the master's objection thereto. The owner had the choice of proceeding against the borrower with a suit for recovery on the loan *(actio commodati)*, on a delictual action for theft with an *in personam* action for unjust enrichment on the ground of theft *(actio et praeterea condictio ex causa furtiva)*.[97] Similar rules could have been applied to any unauthorized loan of money made by the slave and to any payment of money made by the slave on the basis of his unauthorized acceptance to act as a surety for a debtor.[98]

Since the slave's ability to act as an agent for his master to transfer property to others stemmed from the *potestas* relationship between master and slave, all the foregoing was equally true with regard to one's son and, at least theoretically, one's wife in *manus*. These latter, too, could perform transactions involving the alienation of property from the estate of the head of the family, providing, of course, that the head had given his consent to said transactions. Thus, for example, a gift *(donatio)* authorized by the father could have been carried out through the agency of his son.[99] The ability of the son to dispose of property on behalf of the head of the family equalled that of the slave, for the formal mode of alienation known as *cessio in iure*, closed to the slave, was also closed to him.[100]

95   Proculus, D. 12.6.53.
96   C. 4.26.10.
97   Ulpian, D. 13.6.14.
98   Ulpian, D. 12.1.11.2., and Julian, D. 46.1.19. "Unauthorized", incidentally, also includes those acts of the slave in which he exceeded his authority; Julian, D. 15.1.37.1.
99   Ulpian, D. 39.5.7 pr., 4.
100 Inasmuch as the most widely-used mode of delivery, the informal *traditio*, was open to him, the slave's effectiveness on behalf of his owner was not seriously weakened by his inability to engage in the *iure in cessio* and, according to some, to transfer by *mancipatio*.

As for persons outside of the power of the head of a family, acts of alienation on his behalf were limited to the mere physical transfer of the object. In other words, their role was limited to that of messenger. The classical Roman law did not recognize the legality of any act of agency which was the product of the arbitrary will and intention *(animus)* of an agent who was not in the *potestas* of his principal.[101]

C. LOSS OF POSSESSION

Ulpian declared:

> An owner is considered to have possession of property which is held by his slave...; and therefore if [the slave] is forcibly deprived of possession, he [i.e., the owner] himself is also considered to be dispossessed, even if he did not know that those by whom he held possession had been ejected.[102]

Just as the head of a family gained possession of property through those in his power, so might he have lost possession through them. Since a person in *potestas* was a "third arm" of the *paterfamilias,* if said person was deprived of a piece of property, the "third arm" was in fact no longer holding it, i.e., the *paterfamilias* had lost possession. Thus, for example, a slave's *de facto* holding of land was construed as an act of possession on the part of his master, and, conversely, his *de facto* relinquishment of the land was as it should have been, for, in contradiction to ownership *(dominium)*, which was the legal title to a thing, possession *(possessio)* was essentially the factual, physical control over it. Buckland put the matter succinctly:

> [O]nce *possessio* was acquired, the slave's personality was immaterial: he was a mere receptacle. If a thing fell from the slave's hand, it was much as if it had fallen from the master's pocket. And *possessio* was a question of fact.[103]

---

101 *Cf.* Buckland, Inst., 166–174.
102 D. 43.16.1.22: *Quod servus ... tenent, dominus videtur possidere; et ideo his deiectis ipse deici de possessione videtur etiamsi ignoret eos deiectos per quos possidebat.*
103 Buckland, Text., 203.

Moreover, since possession was a question of fact, Gaius' famous statement, "Our slaves can better our condition, but cannot make it worse,"[104] which was concerned with the *juridical* condition of things, is inapplicable. Loss of possession by a slave did make his master's condition worse.

The factual, physical nature of possession through persons in *potestas* affected the rules governing remedies for recovery in cases of forcible dispossession. When someone was ejected from his land, Roman law provided the victim with a possessory interdict, known as *interdictum de vi*, to enable him to recover it. In the passage cited at the beginning of this section, Ulpian indicated that if a slave was dispossessed *(deiectus de possessione)*, the interdict was available for the master whether he was aware of the act by which he was dispossessed or not. Moreover, as long as the slave was left in possession, the owner was *not* considered as having been dispossessed *(deiectus)*, even though he, the owner, had been ejected; for the physical holding of the land by the slave was regarded as an alternative form of the master's retention of possession.[105]

---

104 D. 50.17.133.
105 Hence, the possessory interdict is not available to the owner; Ulpian, D. 43.15.1.45. Interestingly, if the slave of the original owner, as he holds the land, is bound by or acts at the behest of the dispossessor, then he, the slave, passes into the possession of the dispossessor and, with him, the land he is holding; ibid., 46.

CHAPTER II

THE PECULIUM ARRANGEMENT

A. INTRODUCTORY DESCRIPTION OF THE *PECULIUM*

1. *The* Peculium *and its Role in the Economic Life of Rome*[1]

In the period of the classical Roman law, commerce was to a great extent in the hands of the slaves; they were the true middlemen of the city. A significant number of them were endowed with business acumen and commercial savoir-faire. Moreover, trade had not yet lost its traditional stigma, and Romans of noble birth were forbidden by law to engage in commercial activity.[2] Agents, particularly slaves

---

1 The following works served as the basis of the General Remarks made in this section: Baldsdon, Life, 106–115; Barrow; Brewster; Buckland, Slavery; Carcopino, Life; Duff, J.W.; Finley; Frank, Ec. Survey I and V; Gummerus; Loane; Oertel; Rostovtzeff; Staerman; Westermann, Sk.; *idem.*, Slave.

The *peculium* remains one of the most problematic subjects of Roman law. From Cuiacius (*Ubi est peculii nomen, ibi semper nodus vel scrupulus aliquis*, quoted by Solazzi, Scritti I, 161) to Kaser (I, 287, n. 47, and 344, n. 26), scholars have complained about its intricacies and confusions. It is hoped that this chapter will contribute toward a better understanding of the role of the *peculium* in the area of non-contractual agency.

2 The *lex Claudia de senatoribus* (218 B.C.E. ?) hindered aristocrats from engaging in maritime commerce, for example, by forbidding them to

and freedmen, afforded a convenient method whereby a Roman could maintain the air of an aristocrat while his feet stood firmly on the solid ground of gold derived from business and trade.[3] In addition, slaves were psychologically best suited to serve as managers and agents for the following reasons: self-respecting free men were unwilling to accept positions in which they had to obey the orders of an employer; employers preferred to utilize the services of men whose character they knew and on whose obedience they could rely; slaves could be chastised if they disobeyed instructions; and slaves had formed the habit of executing their masters' orders.[4]

But the facts, (1) that a number of slaves had come from a background of training in business and trade and (2) that they were not inhibited by any restrictions, legal, social or psychological, which implied that such activities were lowly and unworthy, are insufficient in and of themselves to explain the singular success of so many slaves in a multitude of commercial activities. Since all the profits derived from the slave's business ventures belonged to his master, what motive could there have been for a slave to exert himself? Why should he have extended himself for the benefit of another? The coercion applied to a slave working in mines, on farms or in factories could exact labour, not initiative; it could produce physical exertion, not the shrewdness necessary to conceive and execute a profitable transaction.

The mental agility and psychological enthusiasm indispensable for the successful pursuit of business ventures found their much-needed incentive by reason of the *peculium* arrangement, already in exist-

---

possess sea-going vessels except for the transport of their own produce, and (probably) by prohibiting them to engage in banking and high finance. It remained in force under the Principate; Rotondi, 249; Mommsen, Staats., III, 898–899; Huvelin, 30. See also Cicero, *De officiis* 1.150–151, which summarizes the conventional Roman attitude to money-making until Rome progressed beyond its limited, early-classical economy; Wiseman, 77f. Wiseman points out that although the prejudice against senatorial participation in commerce was neither universal nor applied in practice, it did encourage the employment of slaves (and freedmen) as a "discreet camouflage."

3 See Arms, 1–71, especially with regard to freedmen.
4 Jones, 186.

ence in the time of Plautus (254–184 B.C.E.).[5] Rooted in custom,[6] the institution of *peculium* was an ever-present feature of Roman economic life and served, among other things, as the basis for a type of agency in Roman society in a unique way.[7]

Our earliest juristic definition of *peculium* was recorded by Celsus (early second century C.E.) in the name of Tubero,[8] a jurist who flourished toward the end of the Republic. It reads as follows:

> Tubero, however, defines *peculium* thus, as Celsus reports (*Digest*, bk. 6): what the slave, by the master's permission, holds distinct from the master's accounts,[9] there being deducted from it, if anything, that which is owed to the master.[10]

But as it developed, the *peculium* was not only a sum of money. It was very often a commercial establishment, an industrial shop or factory, or some separate piece of property — each of these of any size. Indeed, derived from the word *pecus*, which means cattle, the *peculium* in the earlier agricultural stage of Roman history must have consisted of a flock of sheep or other domestic animals.[11] It was granted by a master to his slave for the latter's utilization,

5 Costa, Dir., 104–108.
6 Savigny, I, 77, note a, and Volterra, 521, n. 1.
7 Wallon, II, 119–120, 181–183, 207–209.
8 Jolowicz, Hist. Introd., 90–91 (Tubero) and 389, 394 (Celsus).
9 The keeping of separate accounts was indispensable for the legal validity of the *peculium* arrangement; Pomponius, D. 15.1.4 pr.
10 Ulpian, D. 15.1.5.4: *Peculium autem Tubero quidem sic definit, ut Celsus libro sexto digestorum refert, quod servus domini permissu separatum a rationibus dominicis habet, deducto inde si quid domino debetur.*
11 Kaser, I, 64; *cf.* Plutarch *Publicola* 9.4. Traces of the existence of a *peculium* in the hands of a slave have been detected in the Twelve Tables (7.12), where it is stated that the condition of payment of a sum of money for manumission could be fulfilled by the slave even if he had been alienated. Whereas in most ancient legal systems, the slave was regarded as capable of owning property, the Roman slave was not (Taubenschlag, 87). Hence the assumption therein that a slave could possess money can be understood only if we predicate his holding a *peculium*: Kaser, ibid., 114. On the significance of the term *pecus* for the earliest Roman notions of property, see Diósdi, 19–30. On the probable connection between *pecus* and *pecunia*, wealth, property, riches, *cf.* Ernout; also Zeber, 9–10.

development and enlargement through labour, transaction, and manipulation.[12]

Legally, the slave-owner always retained title to the *peculium*;[13] in actual, everyday life, however, the *peculium* was regarded as the *de facto* property of the slave[14] which was normally reincorporated into the estate of his owner only at the death of the slave.[15] Thus, the profits derived from the slave's business operations on the basis of his *peculium* belonged, in legal theory, to his master, and in economic reality, to the slave. The practical implications of this arrangement as a means of profit-making for the slave and as an instrument of agency for the master will be discussed at length at various appropriate points throughout the remainder of this chapter.

Legally, the *peculium* was generally described as resulting from an outright grant of property or money by the master to his slave. In fact, it originated from or was augmented by gifts, wages and tips either from the master himself when he was pleased by certain acts of the slave or from the master's friends and relatives in whose eyes he had found favour, usually because of some service he had performed for them.[16] It was a general practice to permit a slave to sell the remains of a banquet for his own profit.[17] Voluntary economy on the part of the slave, such as frugality with an allowance[18] or skimping on food ("cheating the stomach"),[19] was another method of increasing the *peculium*. In other cases, he was allowed to earn money for himself either (1) by turning his leisure to profit by hiring himself out or (2) by working for others — paying his master for the time of employment out of his wages and pocketing the surplus. Farm slaves were allowed to cultivate a plot or graze an animal, and they were permitted to keep the profits as their own. Sometimes the

12 On the creation of the *peculium*, see further: Zeber, ch. III.
13 G. 2.86–87; Papinian, D. 41.2.49.1; Gaius, D. 41.1.10 pr.-i.
14 Florentinus, D. 15.1.39; Ulpian, D. 15.1.32 pr. at end; Paul, D. 15.1.47.6. See also Ulpian, D. 15.1.63 and 50.16.182.
15 Arg., D. 15.1. and 2, *passim*.
16 Plautus *Mostellaria* 252; *Persa* 192; Juvenal *Saturae* 3.189; Florentinus, D. 15.1.39.
17 Appuleius *Metamorphoses* 10.4.
18 Florentinus, ibid.: *parsimonia sua*; see also Mandry, II, 26f.
19 Seneca, *Epistulae* 80.4: *ventre fraudato*.

master would set the slave up in a bank, a business establishment, or over a ship with the arrangement that the slave pay a fixed return, retaining income and profits for the continued operation of the enterprise.[20] A *peculium* could also have arisen, or been augmented, when a master recognized the ill-gotten gains of his slave.[21]

This assortment of gratuities, petty savings, rewards and gains were for the personal enjoyment of the slave. If the slave was astute, capable and farsighted — qualities which he undoubtedly possessed to have obtained such sums and gifts in the first place — he would utilize them for investment and business ventures. Thus, numerous slaves succeeded in amassing a fortune in land, houses, shops, rights, claims and even other slaves *(vicarii)*.[22]

Many were the times that the *peculium* would be surrendered wholly or, more usually, in part by the slave in return for his freedom.[23] Most slaves, having obtained their freedom through their *peculium*, seem to have taken with them some capital of their own.[24] This capital then served as the basis for fresh economic activity

---

20 Ulpian, D. 2.13.4.3. and 17.2.63.2; also D. 15.1 *passim*. If the arrangements were converse, i.e., if the slave received a wage or a commission and turned over all the income and profits to the master, there would usually not be a *peculium*. The relationship would then be subsumed under the institorian arrangement to be discussed in the next chapter.
21 Slaves, of course, were well-known for their dishonesty and adeptness at theft, common themes in the comedies of Plautus; see also Dionysius of Halicarnassus *Antiquities* 4.24.
22 Ulpian, D. 15.1.7.4–5 and 33.8.6 pr.; Tryphoninus, D. 15.1.57.2; Celsus; D. 33.8.25. The claims might include monies which the master himself had borrowed from his slave; Ulpian, D. 15.1.7.6; *cf.* Zeber, ch. IV. On the *vicarius*, see Erman, 391–527; Schneider, 2044–2053; *cf.* Berger, Nota, 122–125. In post-classical literature, the terms *peculium adventicium*, for peculiary property acquired by a person in *potestas* through his own labour or by gifts from third persons, and, in contrast, *peculium profecticium*, for that which had been granted to him by his master, were found useful; *cf.* Zeber, 7–9.
23 Examples of slaves who were permitted to accumulate money in order to purchase their freedom may be found in Ulpian, D. 33.8.8.5. and in Marcellus, D. 37.15.3; see also Buckland, Slavery, 640–646 and Roby, I.320.
24 Papinian, V.F. 261; Paul, D. 15.1.53; Ulpian, D. 23.3.39 pr. See also Micolier, 205.

leading to new financial successes; this time, however, all the profits accrued to themselves. The best illustration of the shrewd business ability of an Oriental slave, as well as of the extent to which a *peculium* could be acquired, expanded and exploited, is the story of Trimalchio, the freedman whom Petronius made famous.[25] Other sources show us one slave building a temple and another helping to finance the construction of religious statues for a municipality.[26]

Thus, the true source of the incentive by which the *peculium* arrangement spurred the slave on to make an all-out effort on behalf of his master's enterprises was the attraction of the profits which the slave himself stood to gain from assiduous and industrious application of his business talents. This arrangement was more beneficial to the master, in one way, than that based upon a direct agency relationship, for it relieved the master of the burdensome necessity of keeping a close watch over the slave and his activities.

The incentive created by the institution of the *peculium* would have been fatally vitiated, however, if masters were wont to renege on their arrangements with their slaves. The success of the system was due to the dependability and trustworthiness of the Roman master, to the confidence he inspired in his slave that he would not suddenly assert his legal rights and take the entire *peculium* for himself. There were, of course, exceptions, cases where this trustworthiness failed and confidence was betrayed.[27] But such cases were rare and did not occur frequently enough to disturb the system. In the earlier, formative years of the *peculium* arrangement, an unjustified withdrawal of funds from the *peculium* or of the *peculium* itself evoked strong social disapproval and condemnation.[28] In later times,

---

25 *Satyricon*, pp. 75–77. We are, of course, aware of Petronius' tendency to over-colour the picture here and there. Nevertheless, the over-all result of his account is essentially accurate. Proof: Trimalchio is by no means unique, *cf.* Carrington, 111–115. Veyne, 213–247, has written an excellent description of the economic and socio-psychological insights into the life of slaves-turned-freedmen in Rome as reflected in and derived from the *Satyricon*. See also: Arms, ch. 5.

26 I.L.S., 3581 and 3611. See further: Arms, ch. 6.

27 See, for example, Terence *Phormio* 43ff. The *paterfamilias'* legal power of revocation or withdrawal of a *peculium* is known as *ademptio peculii*; *cf.* Pomponius, D. 15.1.4 pr.

28 Ihering, II, 211–212, note 324, and Kaser, Inh., 85–86.

the self-interest of the slave-owner was a most powerful stimulus for him to respect the integrity of the *peculium*. The goodwill of his astute and capable slave, the prestige he derived from the activities of his affluent slave, and the advantages of agency that a *peculium* holding slave afforded him — all these assets buttressed the moral and social considerations that dissuaded a master from capriciously and avariciously taking the *peculium* to himself.[29]

The *peculium* arrangement, however, was not limited to the master-slave relationship. Sons, also, were granted *peculia* by their fathers. For, inasmuch as the rule of the Roman private law was that a man's children were in his power as long as he was alive and had not emancipated them, mature men who were themselves fathers of children[30] were generally under their fathers' legal power and, in the eyes of the law, could not possess any property.[31] Thus, in addition to the numerous slaves administering *peculia*, many Roman citizens had their economic lives organized on the basis of a *peculium*.[32] Just as slaves could not be construed as having rights in their *peculium*, so these freemen, too, had no rights in their *peculium*. Viewed juridically, the *peculium* of a freeman was the property of his father. The following two passages from the Digest state the matter succinctly:

> Those who are in the *potestas* of another can hold a thing in *peculium* but cannot possess it, since possession is not merely a physical fact but also a right.
> A *filiusfamilias* is construed as neither retaining, recovering, nor acquiring possession of his *peculium*.[33]

29 Costa, Dir., 104–105. The possibilities of real affection and intimacy between slave and master must not be underestimated; *cf.* Veyne, 215–221.
30 Ulpian, D. 15.3.7.5, for example, deals with a case where a son *(filiusfamilias)* borrowed money and gave it as a dowry for *his* daughter.
31 G. 2.86–88 and its parallel, Gaius, D. 41.1.10 pr., 1.2. The one exception, the *peculium costrense* acquired from or during military service, has no relationship to agency, neither conceptually nor practically.
32 D. 15.1. *passim* and Papinian D. 41.3.44.4.
33 Papinian, D. 41.2.49.1: *Qui in aliena potestate sunt, rem peculiarem tenere possunt, habere possidere non possunt, quia possessio non tantum corporis, sed et iuris est.* Marcellus, D. 50.17.93: *Filiusfamilias neque retinere neque reciperare neque apisci possessionem rei peculiaris videtur.* These citations are specific manifestations of the general rule that

We hasten to add, however, that although the son in power resembled the slave in that neither could own property, he differed from the latter in that he was regarded by the law as a person. He could therefore institute claims in his own name whereas the slave could not do so.[34] We shall have occasion to utilize this distinction when we describe the details of peculiary transactions as an instrument of agency for the head of the *familia*.

Despite the fact that legal title to his *peculium* was vested in his father, the son found sufficient stimulus to carry on the business of the *peculium* carefully and industriously. Fathers, after all, invariably had their sons supporting themselves and their families out of the proceeds of the *peculium*, and sons lived with the expectation that, after their fathers' death, they would be heirs to the state, a share of which was undoubtedly the *peculium* itself.[35]

But the economic significance of the *peculium* lay not only in that it was (1) the source of stimulus for dynamic commercial activity on the part of capable and clever slaves and (2) the device whereby numerous sons could support themselves by pursuing a variety of business activities. Possession of a *peculium* by a slave or a son encouraged people to deal with these persons. According to the theory of the law inherited by the classical jurists from ancient times, a person in *potestas* could not worsen the condition of the head of family economically or legally. Thus, a subordinate in power could neither create obligations for his master nor render him liable to suit. Moreover, since a slave could not be hailed into court and a son legally had no assets to speak of, it was useless to bring an action against either of them on any transaction that had gone wrong. Therefore, if the principles of the civil law had been applied consistently, all transactions by third parties with persons in power would have been stifled, and a considerable part of the commerce of Rome would not and could not have taken place.[36] It was chiefly

all persons held in power *(personae alieni iuris)*, in the eyes of the law, own nothing; see Mandry, I, 9f.

34 For details see Roby, I, 66.

35 See Daube, R.L., 75–91, for a vivid picture of the economic realities of the *filiusfamilias* and his *peculium*.

36 Savigny, III, 93, note e; Girard, Man., 106–108, 707; Buckland, Slavery, 702.

because of the *peculium* arrangement that people did not hesitate to do business with slaves and sons. Since the *peculium* was regarded in the market-place as *de facto* property of sons and slaves, the courts held that it was only fair and reasonable to hold citizens liable for the business undertakings of their subordinates, at least to the extent of the assets of their *peculium* (details to follow). In addition to engendering a sense of security for third parties by providing them with an avenue of legal redress, the *peculium* itself was evidence of the trust the *paterfamilias* placed in his slave[37] or son, and it acted as a kind of endorsement of the subordinate's moral character.

Thus, the *peculium* was a major financial arrangement through which slaves and sons acted as business agents of their respective masters and fathers; it was the source of stimulus and incentive for a slave to conduct such business to the best of his ability; and finally, it was the guarantee to third parties of the good faith of citizens, of the trustworthiness of slaves and sons, and of the stability and dependability of the transactions of people who themselves could not be sued with any effectiveness.

2. *The Administration of the* Peculium

We have seen that all assets in as well as those acquired by the *peculium* belonged legally not to the slave or son administering the *peculium* but to the master or father. This held true even for those things that had been acquired without these latter's knowledge and authorization. Considerations of general economic facility and convenience resulted in the act on the part of a citizen establishing the *peculium (concessio peculii)* being construed as his general authorization which validated all subsequent acts of acquisition performed for the *peculium* by his slave or son.[38]

Thus, the acquisition of real assets or rights was the most obvious way in which the *peculium* arrangement served as a means whereby

---

37 As early as the times of Plautus it seems to have been a mark of unusually bad character for a slave not to have been entrusted with a *peculium*; Pernice, I, 123, n. 45.

38 Paul, D. 41.2.1.5; see Zulueta, *ad loc.*

slaves and sons performed those services on behalf of their respective masters which were ordinarily subsumed under the heading of agency in modern systems of law, for such acquisitions clearly resulted in the enrichment and enlargement of a master's estate. The multifarious activities of trade and business that were associated with the institution of the *peculium*, and which we shall have occasion to allude to throughout the remainder of this chapter, serve as eloquent testimony to its flexibility and effectiveness in enabling it to fulfil this role. But such activities also included, of necessity, acts of alienation, transactions in which rights were surrendered, and contracts in which obligations were undertaken. Now, since these transactions disposing of property or surrendering rights appear to lessen the assets of the *peculium* or to place the estate of the master under obligation, they had the effect of nullifying the rule that masters' (or fathers') legal and economic conditions could not be affected adversely by transactions entered into by subordinates in their power.

From a plain reading of the relevant texts in the Digest, it would appear that to validate any act of alienation of property within the *peculium* on the part of a slave or a son, such as the payment of debts incurred in the course of carrying on its operation, prior authorization by the *paterfamilias* or subsequent ratification was necessary. The more usual procedure was for the master to make a grant of full (*plena* or *libera*) *administratio*, a general authorization that served as a blanket manifestation of his agreement to and endorsement of all the acts of alienation which might be performed by the slave or the son.[39]

This requirement of *administratio*, i.e., that there had been a specific grant of blanket authorization, seems to have been already recognized by the early classical jurists, specifically by Proculus, of the first generation after Augustus.[40] Pernice, however, takes the first century passage recording this requirement as representing a *change* in the rules governing the administration of a *peculium*.

---

39 Ulpian. D. 6.1.41.1. and Paul, D. 15.1.46; see Mandry, I, 87ff. The expressions for "full", *libera* or *plena*, appear to add nothing of legal significance to the word *administratio*; Mandry, II, 103–106; Micolier. 487, n. 3; Serrao, 27.

40 D. 46.3.84.

According to Pernice, the old rule was that a slave could alienate property from his *peculium* without having ever been granted the specific right of *administratio*.[41]

This interpretation has been taken up and modified by a number of twentieth century scholars who have sought to demonstrate, by a careful review of the relevant passages, that in the classical Roman law, the concept of *administratio* was inherent in the very act establishing the *peculium (concessio peculii)*; only in the law of Justinian did the two concepts become separated. According to these scholars, what happened was that the classical *concessio*, as referring to any grant of power of management, encompassed the power to carry out dispositive acts by the person to whom the administration had been entrusted. This power gradually lessened in late classical, post-classical, and Justinian times until it was reduced to mere acquisitive acts. As a result, *concessio peculii* and *administratio peculii*, originally implying the same thing, became two separate concepts. Thus, the administrator of any estate under the law of Justinian needed a special mandate or, at least, an explicit grant of *libera administratio* in order to carry out those acts disposing of property which, under the classical law, the administrator had been able to carry out as a matter of course since they had been inherent in the concept of administration. Similarly, the very explicit grant of *libera administratio* was necessary for anyone who received a *peculium* under Justinian law in order for him to carry out those acts disposing of property which in the classical law had been inherent in the *concessio peculii*.[42] This interpretation of Pernice and its modifications have not, however, received unanimous approval. There are those who maintain that a deliberate grant of *administratio* was the standard requirement of the classical law.[43]

Bearing in mind this difference of opinion as to whether the classical law required a specific grant of *(libera) administratio* over and above the mere granting of the *peculium* itself in order to validate

---

41 I, 135–136. Pernice cites Julian, D. 46.1.19, as representing a minority opinion among the later jurists who still maintained the "old rule".

42 Longo, Con., 184–203; Albertario, I, 137–156; Longo, Lib., 29–49; and Longo, Ap., 411–422.

43 *Cf.* Micolier, 487–533, and Watson, Per., 179–181.

acts alienating property, the following transactions may be taken as falling within the scope of the administration of a *peculium*:

(1) A debt paid to the son constituted the legal discharge of the obligation *(solutio)*, i.e., it extinguished the debt and liberated the debtor. Similarly, a deposit *(depositum)* returned to the slave conducting business on the basis of a *peculium* released the depositee.[44]

(2) The grantee of a *peculium* was legally empowered to conclude a pact whereby he assumed the obligation *not* to sue the debtor of the *peculium* for non-payment or for non-fulfilment of his obligation toward it. Subsequent suit in the name of the creditor could then be blocked by an affirmative defence.[45]

(3) A slave could come to terms with someone who stole something from his *peculium* and effectuate a compromise with the thief so as to avoid an action on the theft brought by the slave's owner.[46]

(4) A slave operating a *peculium* had the power to effectuate a *novatio* of a debt due to it whereby the old debt was cancelled and rewritten as a new one. According to the Digest, the law was that a slave or son could not validly do this unless he had a special grant of *administratio* (although payment to the slave or son constituted a valid discharge of one's obligation to the *peculium*). This law of the Digest, however, may reflect the law of Justinian. The classical law may have empowered the slave or the son to effectuate a *novatio* without the necessity of a specific grant of *administratio* in much the same way as it declared a debt paid to them as legally discharged.[47]

(5) If, in the event of a divorce, the dowry *(dos)*, which had originally been paid from the *peculium* of the *filiafamilias*-bride herself, was returned to the *peculium*, the groom was considered to have

---

44 Ulpian, D. 12.6.26.8 and 16.3.11. On the latter passage, as well as the other passages cited on this and the following page, *cf.* the articles by Longo *(passim)* that are cited in note 42.

45 Gaius, D. 2.14.28.2; see Albertario, I, 142–143, and Micolier, 499 and 501, n. 17. The pact referred to is called *pactum de non petendo*, and the affirmative defence is known as *exceptio pacti*.

46 Ulpian, D. 47.2.52.26; see Albertario, I, 143; Jolowicz, Dig.; and Micolier, 499, n. 13, and 500, n. 15.

47 Gaius, D. 12.2.21. and Celsus, D. 46.2.25. See Robinson, 39, n. 1; and Micolier, 499, n. 13, 501, n. 16, and 509 — who regard the requirement of a specific grant of *administratio* as classical. See, however, Albertario, I, 143–144, who regards this requirement as post-classical.

validly discharged his obligation. Thus, both the act of constituting a dowry and the act of returning a dowry might have been accomplished through the *peculium.*[48]

(6) Subordinates in power could lend money from their *peculium.*[49]

(7) A grantee of a *peculium* could validly administer or accept an oath that was due to the *peculium.*[50]

(8) Sale of peculiary possessions *(res peculiares)* was, of course, one of the most essential powers invested in a subordinate conducting the business of a *peculium.*[51]

(9) Peculiary possessions could be given as sureties or pledges *(pignora)* on obligations.[52]

(10) The slave or son could pay debts with *peculium* money.[53]

An examination of the above-enumerated acts reveals that they either diminished the rights of the master or alienated assets of the *peculium.* In the first five acts, the right of suit on the transactions had been vested in the head of family by the valid contracts entered into by the subordinates in his power. However, by the rules of good faith *(bona fides)*, when the party contracting with the subordinate had rendered his performance to the subordinate himself, the obligation was regarded as legally discharged and the right of suit on the part of the head of family was destroyed. Thus, all ten acts, viewed narrowly, represented a "loss" to the legal owner of the *peculium,* the *paterfamilias.* Nevertheless, since they were performed as part of the business in which the *peculium* was involved, they were regarded as conducive to its viability and proper functioning, and, as such, were granted legal recognition.

48 Pomponius, D. 23.3.24; also, Alfenus Varus, D. 46.3.35. See Albertario, I, 144, and Micolier, 501 and 510.

49 Paul, D. 12.1.2.4; see Beseler, Beit., IV, 126. *Cf.* Ulpian, D. 12.1.11.2, concerning which see Albertario, I, 144–145, and Micolier, 502–504.

50 Paul, D. 12.2.20; see Albertario, I, 146, and Micolier, 501, n. 18, and 509, n. 38.

51 Venuleius, D. 44.3.15.3; Paul, D. 41.2.14 pr.; Ulpian, D. 6.1.41.1; C. 4.26.10. See Albertario, I, 146–148, and Micolier, 504, nn. 27–31.

52 Paul, D. 12.6.13 pr. and 13.7.18.4; see Albertario, I, 149, and Micolier, 500.

53 Paul, D. 12.6.13 pr., and Proculus, D. 46.3.84; see Albertario, I, 149–150, and Micolier, 505–508.

3. *The Jurisprudential Nature of the* Peculium

The Digest records the following description of the *peculium*:

> The *peculium* comes into existence, grows, diminishes and dies; and thus Papirius Fronto justly said that the *peculium* resembled a man.[54]

With this observation by Papirius Fronto[55] as the point of departure, the *peculium* has been described as an artificial person, as a kind of corporation.[56] This legal fiction would explain rather neatly the unusual phenomenon of a slave, himself bereft of personal status and legal capacity, entering into legal transactions and creating legal relationships between himself on the one hand and third parties as well as his own master on the other. With this approach, the law of the *peculium* was regarded as focusing its attention not upon the slave, but rather upon the corporately personified *peculium* itself; the slave was viewed merely as an administrator of the *peculium*, nothing more.[57]

Another interpretation is that, although the *peculium* depended upon the head of family for its creation and its (economic, non-legal) transfer to the person in his power and although the *peculium* remained legally subject to the control of the head of family, nevertheless jurisprudentially the *peculium* was a manifestation of the general capacity of every subordinate in power to possess and to administer such a fund. Students of Roman law have traditionally formulated this view as follows: *Intellectu iuris*, the *peculium* is to the *persona alieni iuris* what patrimonium is to the *persona sui iuris*.[58]

A third view is that the *peculium* must be regarded as simply a portion of the property of the head of family, what may be called a sub-*universitas*. Setting this portion up as a separate fund, the *pater-*

---

54 Marcianus, D. 15.1.40 pr.: *Peculium nascitur crescit decrescit moritur, et ideo eleganter Papirius Fronto dicebat peculium simile esse homini.*
55 Second century, C.E.; see Berger, Pap., 1059.
56 *Eine juristische Person, une personne fictive.*
57 This theory of the *peculium* is cited in the name of Muehlenbruch by Mandry, II, 20 and Micolier, 227, n. 1.
58 Dietzel and Kuntze cited by Micolier, 228, nn. 2–4; this view is also found in Mandry, II, 6ff. The expression used by Dietzel is *Pekuliumfaehigkeit.*

familias allocated it to his slave or son for a specific purpose. It was the creation of the head of family and related constantly to his allocation *(concessio)* for its legal existence.[59]

Gabriel Micolier rejects the first theory as foreign to the thinking of the classical Roman jurists.[60] He points out that, if the second theory were true, an element of necessity would attach itself to the *peculium*, namely that just as legal theory views *patrimonium* as a necessary attribute of every citizen so would *peculium* have to be regarded as a necessary attribute of a subordinate in power. On the other hand, according to the third theory, the act *(concessio)* manifesting the will, intention, and agreement *(voluntas)* of the head of the family was the sole element necessary for the creation of the *peculium*, and the *peculium* could not survive the failure of the very *voluntas* that created it.[61] Micolier himself accepts the two latter theories: the third one for the earlier classical period and the second one for post-Hadrianic times.[62]

In canvassing the history of the *peculium*, it can be shown that the earlier jurists required the consent of the head of family for the establishment of the *peculium* itself.[63] The subsequent expansion of an already existing *peculium*, however, was in need of his specific ratification only if it was brought about by additions from the master's estate or by the exploitation of the master's property *(ex re patris)*. But if the expansion of the *peculium* was accomplished through acquisitions made from third parties *(ex re aliena)*, the consent of the head of family was not necessary.[64] The later classical law, on the other hand, did not require the consent of the *paterfamilias* even for the very establishment of the *peculium*, except when the *peculium* was being set up *ex re patris*.[65] Micolier traces this later

---

59 This view is cited by Micolier, 228, n. 5, as that of Bekker.
60 Micolier, 228, n. 5.
61 Ibid., 229.
62 I am indebted to Kaser, Rev. P., 392–402, and to Longo, Ap., 392–422, for a goodly number of the critical observations included in the summary that follows.
63 Ulpian and Celsus, D. 15.1.5.4.6.7 pr. and Paul, D. 41.2.1.5; see Micolier, 233ff.
64 Micolier, 251ff.
65 *Idem.*, 264ff.

development from Proculus, who was its lone forerunner in pre-Hadrianic times,[66] through Marcellus,[67] to the jurists of the high classical period.[68]

Thus, in the later classical law, avers Micolier, a slave could hold a *peculium* even though it had not been granted to him consciously and purposefully by his master, and subsequent acquisitions could be added to the *peculium* without any need of ratification on the part of the master — as long as the original grant and the subsequent expansion had been brought about through gifts, grants and payments made to the slave by persons other than the master *(ex re aliena)*. This interpretation of the later law tends to corroborate the second view mentioned above, namely that the power to hold a *peculium* was theoretically an attribute of any subordinate in *potestas*. It would seem, however, that this theoretical attribute of "power to hold a *peculium*" was an artificial creation of a modern scholar, not the operative concept of the later Roman jurists. The innovation of the later jurists may be explained simply by assuming that these same jurists found it both wise and expedient to allow persons in power a general right of acquisition *of* a *peculium* and thereafter acquisition *for* the *peculium* as long as such acquisitions were not expressly forbidden by the head of family.[69]

Micolier's "proof" that the peculium could and did exist as a creation of jurisprudence, sometimes even devoid of economic reality,[70] is equally unconvincing. The text upon which he relies, namely the Digest statement that an *actio de peculio* lies "even though there is nothing in the *peculium* at the time of suit,"[71] does not necessarily imply that the *peculium* was an artificial creation of juristic theory.

---

66 Paul, D. 14.3.17.4. Kaser, Rev. P., 396, n. 2, is of the opinion that the reference to enrichment in the Paul passage is inappropriate for an *actio de peculio*.

67 Ulpian, D. 15.1.7.1.

68 *Idem.*, D. 15.1.7.1; 3.4; 7.3; Pomponius, *h.t.*, 49 pr. These citations are challenged by Kaser, Rev. P., 396, nn. 3 and 4; see also Longo, Ap., 404–408, and Albertario, I, 140–141.

69 Kaser, Rev. P., 396.

70 Micolier, 193–201.

71 Ulpian, D. 15.1.30 pr., citing Proculus and Pegasus: *etiamsi nihil sit in peculio cum ageretur*; *cf.* also D. 15.2.1 pr. where Ulpian cites the praetor in this connection.

It may very well be that the passage was referring to a *peculium*
which was very much in existence, perhaps even one in possession
of a large amount of capital; inasmuch, however, as its indebtedness
to the head of the family as well as prior claims against it registered
by other creditors surpassed this amount of its capital, the text
regards the present plaintiff as bringing suit against a *peculium* which
has "nothing in it."[72]

We shall have occasion to deal with a number of other topics
treated by Micolier in the development of his thesis that the
juridical nature of the *peculium* was changed by the latter-day
classical jurists. Professor Max Kaser, who has subjected this thesis
to a brief but competent review, remains unconvinced of such a
change. He accepts the third view of the *peculium*, namely that it is
a separate fund granted by the head of family to his subordinate,
that it relates constantly to this grant *(concessio)* for its existence,
and that it depends upon his (implied) consent for its continued
operation. He insists, moreover, that the *peculium* as an artificial
juristic creation *(iuris intellectu)*, which is alleged to have served as
the general concept for the innovations of the second half of the
classical period, was unknown to the Romans. It is very doubtful,
he concludes, that the later jurists were really motivated by and
operating with a single underlying and pervading principle; the
pragmatic basis of their decisions must never be underestimated.[73]

B.   THE *ACTIO DE PECULIO* AND AGENCY

1.   *The* Actio de Peculio *and the Nature of the Liability of the Head of Family*

For third parties who were wronged by breach of contract on the
part of persons in *potestas* conducting a business by means of a
peculium, the Roman praetor introduced the remedy of an *actio de
peculio* against the head of family in whose power the subordinates

---

72   Kaser, Rev. P., 395, n. 1. For additional passages adduced by Micolier
and their effective refutation, see Longo, Ap., 398–400.
73   Kaser, Rev. P., 402; further: Zeber, ch. V.

were. By making this action available, the praetor transformed the *peculium* arrangement from a *de facto* economic reality to a *de iure* legal institution. This action on the *peculium* has been aptly summarized in the Institutes of Justinian as follows:

> The praetor has introduced the action *de peculio* against fathers and masters because, although they are not, according to civil law, bound by the contracts of their children and their slaves, yet they ought in equity to be bound to the extent of the *peculium*, which is a kind of patrimony of sons and daughters and of slaves.[74]

The distinguishing feature of this action was that it limited the liability of the head of family to the extent of the assets of the *peculium*. In other words, it was the transaction *(negotium)* of a slave or a son administering his *peculium* that served as the basis of the action.[75] Hence, *every* action *de peculio* was really similar to any standard action that obtained between two

---

74   Inst. 4.6.10; *Actionem autem de peculio ideo adversus patrem dominumve comparavit praetor, quia licet ex contractu filiorum servorumve ipso iure non teneantur, aequum tamen esset, peculio tenus, quot veluti patrimonium est filiorum filiarumque item servorum, condemnari eos.* In connection with the last clause, *cf.* Ulpian, D. 15.1.32 pr., and Paul, D. 15.1.47.6. Included among the daughters mentioned in the Institutes passage was the wife *in manu*, for with regard to her husband such a wife had the status of a *filiafamilias*. Thus, according to the rules of the civil law, any obligations arising out of any contracts into which the wife *in manu* had entered could not bind her husband. Had her husband granted her a *peculium*, however, he could be held liable to the action *de peculio* for any obligation arising out of a transaction that had been made on the basis of her *peculium* in the same way any head of family could be held liable for the peculiary transaction of his slave, son or daughter (G. 3.104; F.V. 294; Ulpian, D. 13.6.3.4; Pomponius, D. 23.2.24; Paul, D. 25.2.3.4.). In any event, the availability of such actions to third parties who had business dealings with a wife *in manu* must be relegated to the realm of speculation and theory. "We have no record of such proceedings against a husband on obligations assumed by a wife, but there seems to be no reason in principle why they should not have been possible," writes Corbett, 111. If the woman had contracted a "free" marriage, as, it will be recalled, most women were wont to do in the classical period, there could be no *peculium* arrangement between herself and her husband. *Cf.* Plautus (Casina 198), where a woman *in manu* possesses a *peculium*.

75   Ulpian, D. 15.1.1.2.

Roman citizens. Thus, the action on the *peculium* might be a suit to recover a deposit *(actio depositi)*, a suit for fraud *(actio doli mali)*, a suit on breach of mandate *(actio mandati)*, and the like,[76] against the head of family, with the distinguishing proviso, however, that the defendant's liability was limited to the extent of the *peculium* which his subordinate was administering. This limitation on the liability of the head of the family was contained in the condemnation clause of the formula according to which the action was framed.[77] Thus, for example, if a slave administering a *peculium* was withholding a deposit from its rightful owner without sufficient justification, the latter could bring an *actio depositi* against the slave's owner. The formula, according to which the suit was framed, would be the normal formula for a suit on a deposit; in the condemnation clause, however, the judge would be instructed, if he found for the plaintiff, to limit the award to no more than the extent of the assets of the *peculium*.

In legal theory, the action was, strictly speaking, predicated upon the existence of a *peculium*.[78] Thus, as long as the slave and the son were in the power of their respective master and father and were conducting their business enterprises on the basis of a *peculium*, the availability of the *actio de peculio* was without limitation of time. If, however, the *peculium* was extinguished by either the non-fraudulent exhaustion of its capital and stock, or the death, alienation or manumission of the slave, or the death or emancipation of the son, the legal grounds for the action were thereby lost. But in order to protect the "security of transactions," this could not be allowed to happen. Therefore, liability was extended by the praetor for one year after the extinction of the *peculium*.[79]

In a note discussing the liability of the defendant in an *actio de peculio*, Buckland points out that the liability was not attached to

---

76 E.g., Gaius, D. 15.1.27 pr. and Africanus, D. 15.1.38 pr., Buckland, Slavery, 211, n. 7, gives a comprehensive list of such actions and the references to them in the Digest.

77)Lenel, E.P., 282. The condemnation clause containing the words limiting the liability *(dumtaxat de peculio)* is known as *condemnatio cum taxatione*.

78 Paul, D. 21.1.57.1; *cf.* Gaius, D. 15.1.27.8.

79 Ulpian, D. 15.2.1. pr., 3.4; Lenel, E.P., 277.

the *peculium* but rather was placed on "the *dominus* as holder of the *peculium*."[80] This formulation is set forth on the basis of the following Digest passage:

> If the master or the father declines the action on the *peculium*, he is not to be listened to, but should be compelled to join issue, as in the case of any other personal action.[81]

In other words, the *actio de peculio* was not an *in rem* action on the *peculium*, but an *in personam* action against the head of family with regard to and to the extent of the *peculium*. This means that the liability of the head of family was not confined to the objects in the *peculium*. Rather the *peculium* served as the source of the liability and as a kind of yardstick which determined the maximum limit of this liability. The award to the plaintiff could be collected from any part of the property of the *paterfamilias*. Moreover, if the slave were sold and his *peculium* transferred to the purchaser, the latter became liable to all suits on the *peculium*, even those arising out of transactions concluded before the sale and transfer.[82] Thus, again, it was not the master *per se* who was liable to the action *de peculio*, but the master who was the holder of the *peculium*.

It has already been indicated, at the beginning of this section, that the distinguishing feature of the *actio de peculio* was that it limited the liability of the head of family to the extent of the assets of the *peculium*. This 'extent of the *peculium*' was measured by adding up all the assets therein and subtracting from the total anything owed to the head of family or to any other member of the *familia* from the *peculium*.[83] Also included in the total assets of the *peculium* were debts owed to it by the head of family, by other members of the *familia*, or by any outsider,[84] *plus* anything the *paterfamilias* had removed fraudulently from the *peculium*.[85] Similar to the debts and

---

80 Buckland, Slavery, 207; see also Inst. 4.6.8.

81 Ulpian, D. 15.1.21.3: *Si dominus vel pater recuset de peculio actionem non est audiendus, sed cogendus est quasi aliam quamvis personalem actionem suscipere.*

82 Ulpian, D. 15.1.32.1.2.

83 G. 4.73; Ulpian, D. 15.1.5.4. in the name of Tubero as cited by Celsus; Ulpian, D. 15.1.9.3.4, citing Servius.

84 Ulpian, D. 15.1.7.6.

85 Ulpian, D. 15.1.9.4. and D. 15.2.1 pr., citing the Edict.

claims of third parties, these deductions of claims and additions of debts, vis-à-vis the head of the family and other members of the *familia*, were not merely fictitious accounting adjustments made in order to compute the value of the *peculium* for the specific purpose of the *actio de peculio*. Although obligations between members of one *familia* were theoretically not recognized by the law, the courts, in calculating these "claims" and "debts" were merely recognizing the economic reality, namely that within the *familia* unit there were, in fact, economic transactions among the various members each one of which possessed a separate fund. Thus, a person in power could owe something to his head of family and vice versa, and similarly one person in power could owe something to another person in power even though both were in the power of the same head of family. The basis for determining these natural obligations were the same rules which held true for dealings between independent citizens *(personae sui iuris)*.[86]

No deductions were made for monies owed to any other creditor or possible claimant. Priority of right of collection among creditors and claimants outside the circle of the *familia* was determined by priority of possession. "He who holds a thing is in a better position"[87] was the rule. Once the *peculium* was exhausted of its assets, creditors could no longer successfully bring suit.

This practice of including the claims against and the debts owed to the *peculium* in calculating its size was a fully developed feature of the classical law. Indeed, it has been shown that already from the time of Servius of the first century B.C.E., claims of a subordinate in power against the head of his family, of a head of family against his subordinate, as well as claims against third persons, were items reckoned with in calculating the extent of the *peculium*.[88]

As indicated, it is the business transaction of the subordinate with

---

86 Micolier, 737ff.

87 Gaius, D. 15.1.10: *occupantis melior est condicio*; the rule referred to the better procedural situation of the holder of a thing, i.e., the claimant who first obtained a favorable judgment, when other persons claimed the same thing. See also Paul, D. 15.1.52 pr. Exception was made, however, in favour of privileged creditiors; Paul, D. 15.1.52, and Ulpian, D. 24.3.22.13.

88 Micolier, 148–186; Kaser, Rev. P., 394–395; and, especially, Watson, Ob., 189. These scholars are opposed to the view that this practice was the product of the late classical development, see Tuhr, 259–282.

peculium which gives rise to the *de peculio* action,[89] not his delict.[90] The proper remedy for the torts of sons and slaves in power could be obtained through three actions: (1) A noxal action *(actio noxalis)* available from ancient times, whereby the party injured by a son or slave in power sued the head of family for damages, and the latter had the option of paying or surrendering the person of the offender.[91] (2) A *condictio (furtiva)*, the standard remedy against unjustified enrichment. In the context of the liability for torts of subordinates in his power, this *condictio* was an *in personam* action against the head of family to recover from him "that which had come into his hands."[92] Its justification was that "it is most unjust that, by the slave's theft, the master should be enriched without incurring any liability."[93] A number of cases are cited in the Digest in which victims of illegal acts of subordinates in power had recourse to this *condictio furtiva*: e.g., a daughter had illegally removed goods belonging to her husband, a son had committed an act of theft, and a slave had committed an act of theft.[94] (3) A praetorian action *in factum* known as the *actio rerum amotarum*, granted against a father whose married daughter absconded with her husband's property before a divorce.[95]

It seems to me that one more consideration must not be overlooked, namely that of torts committed by the subordinate in connection with the business of his *peculium*.[96] A delictual act com-

---

89 Ulpian, D. 15.1.1.2, citing the Edict; see Levy, Pauli, on P.S. 1.4.5.

90 Ulpian, D. 9.3.1.7.8; see Girard, Man. 707, n. 1.

91 For details see G. 4.75–79; Inst. 4.8; D. 9.4; C. 3.41; and the literature cited in Kaser, I, 630f, nn. 3ff.

92 Ulpian, D. 13.1.4; *Id quod ad eum pervenit*; see the discussion on this passage in Levy, Konk., 438–445.

93 Ulpian, D. 15.1.3.12, citing Labeo: *iniquissimum est ex furto servi dominum locupletari impune*; see Levy, ibid., 440–441. Concerning the relationship between an *actio de eo quod pervenit* and the noxal action, see Betti, Ist., 1369ff.

94 Paul, D. 13.1.19; Ulpian, D. 15.1.3.12; African, D. 19.1.30 pr.

95 For details, see D. 25.2. and C. 5.21; and literature cited in Kaser, I, 618, nn. 54–55.

96 An outright criminal act on the part of a subordinate, even one committed in connection with the operation of a *peculium*, would certainly not render the head of family liable to the *actio de peculio*; Ulpian, D. 50.17.58, *q.v.* Micolier, 682, n. 55.

mitted by a subordinate in power in connection with contracts entered into and transactions accomplished in the course of managing a *peculium* created a tort liability on the part of the head of family for which the *actio de peculio* served as the normal avenue of redress.[97] For example, Ulpian made the following statement:

> The father or master is liable to be sued on account of a deposit only to the amount of the *peculium* and so far as I may have been defrauded by any fraudulent act on his part.[98]

In this statement, the liability of the head of family was not measured by the extent to which he gained from the fraudulent act but rather by the extent of the *peculium* and the extent of the fraud because the delict was not merely a wrongful act of a subordinate but rather an act of fraud perpetrated as part of the business operations of the *peculium*.

To summarize, in the classical Roman law the tort liability of the head of family for general delictual acts committed by persons in his power was covered by resort to the noxal action supplementing, or supplemented by, the *condictio furtiva* on the basis of the profits gained by the head of family from the delictual act. The exact applicability of these remedies is variously interpreted by modern scholars,

---

97 *Arg.*, Ulpian, D. 4.3.9.4a, citing Labeo. Micolier, 685, n. 63, regards the passages as interpolated. I have followed Buckland (Slavery, 209), who accepts it as classical. *Cf.* Ulpian, D. 4.9.3.3, and Paul, D. 4.4.24.3; the latter is also regarded by Micolier as interpolated, 685, n. 65. On Paul, D. 47.2.42 pr., see further in Micolier, pp. 686ff, and Jolowicz, Dig., 51–52.

98 D. 15.1.4 pr.: *Depositi nomine pater vel dominus dumtaxat de peculio conveniuntur et si quid dolo malo eorum captus sum.* The word *eorum* referring to *pater vel dominus* should not be taken seriously, for if the act of fraud were indeed perpetrated by the head of family and not by the subordinate *in potestas*, the regular action on fraud *(actio doli)* would be appropriate, not the action on the *peculium* *(actio doli de peculio)* with its limited *(dumtaxat)* liability. Even sale of the *peculium*, which usually transfered the obligations thereon attached to the purchaser (Gaius, D. 15.1.27.2), and did not free the head of family from the consequences of his fraudulent art. Fraud was sufficiently delictual-criminal to create a strictly personal liability for its perpetrator, a liability which, although incurred in connection with the operations of a *peculium*, was and remained legally separate from the *peculium* (see Ulpian, D. 15. 1.21.2).

but the general consensus among them is that the relationship of the *condictio* to the *peculium*, if classical, was nominal, not essential. In limited, specific cases, an action on absconded property was also available. However, liability of the head of family for the delicts of a person in his power committed in the course of administering a *peculium* entrusted to him was covered regularly by the *actio de peculio*.

But if the head of family was liable to the *actio de peculio* for the delicts of his son and slave which they committed in the course of administering their *peculium*, it follows that he might have been rendered liable to the action on the basis of acts the knowledge of which he never had and the consent to which he never granted. Indeed, in order to understand the role of the head of family as the principal in the *peculium* arrangement more fully, we must supplement our discussion of the nature of his liability with an examination of the extent to which his knowledge and consent were required to validate the transactions of the subordinate who was acting as his agent in administering the *peculium* and operating its business.

In the remarks opening our description of the main features of the *peculium*, we indicated that peculiary acquisitions and alienations could be carried out by the subordinate without the knowledge *(scientia)* and consent *(voluntas)* of his master. Generally speaking, the action on the *peculium* lay on any contract of the subordinate, even on one which was based on a transaction which was not closely related to the ordinary business of the *peculium* or which had no reference to the head of family,[99] for the very act of establishing the *peculium* (called *concessio peculii*) by the head of family was construed as a general authorization on his part for all such acts. But no matter how loosely we construe the *concessio peculii* as a general authorization on the part of the head of family to his subordinate, the liability of the former for the acts or transactions the subordinate carried out before he came into his power or prior to the actual creation of the *peculium* could never be viewed as lying within the intent of the head of family when he created the *peculium*. Such liability was the subject of disagreement among the earlier classical jurists, but it became later to be the accepted law.

99 Ulpian, D. 3.5.5.8; Gaius, D. 15.1.27.8.

To begin with, the formula of the *actio de peculio*, as evidenced by its language, requires or at least presupposes that the transactions on the basis of which the action was brought were necessarily entered into while the subordinate was in the power of the defendant.[100] This undoubtedly reflects the earlier classical law. Ulpian, however, recorded the following controversy:

> Some authorities rightly think that an action on the *peculium* should be given against an arrogator, though Sabinus and Cassius consider that an action on the *peculium* ought not to be given on account of earlier dealings.[101]

Sabinus and Cassius required that the *potestas*-relationship should have been in existence before the transaction had been entered into. In their opinion, the pre-existence of the *potestas*-relationship was a condition for the availability of the *actio de peculio* because only a head of family who himself had set up his subordinate with a *peculium*, in other words who himself had given the general authorization implied in every *concessio peculii*, could be rendered liable on the *peculium*.

In opposition to this requirement, "some authorities" were of the opinion that the head of family could also be held liable on account of dealings which *preceded* the entrance of the subordinate into his power *(ex ante gestis)*. Among these anonymous authorities who

---

100 Lenel, E.P., 282, n. 4.
101 D. 15.1.42: *In adrogatorem de peculio actionem dandam quidam recte putant, quamvis Sabinus et Cassius ex ante gesto de peculio actionem non esse dandam existimant.* Buckland, Slavery, 213, interprets this passage as dealing with an *adrogatus* who had a slave with a *peculium*. The liability of the *adrogator* on the slave's contracts which were made before the *adrogatio* is the point of the controversy. This interpretation strikes one as forced. A plain reading of Ulpian's words yields the interpretation we have presented in the text. Attention should also be called to the fact that the word *adrogatio* refers exclusively to the entrance of a person *sui iuris* into someone else's *potestas*. This adrogated person, therefore, could not have possessed a *peculium* at all when he entered into the transaction for which his present *paterfamilias* is being held liable. This extremely unusual case of an action on the *peculium* based upon a transaction of a person *sui iuris* apparently motivated Buckland in interpreting the Ulpian passage in the forced manner he did.

disagreed with Sabinus and Cassius, we may in all probability include Proculus.[102] Whether one postulates a concept of the *peculium* as a theoretic entity *(iuris intellectu)* which served as the basis of this liability[103] or whether one sees in this opinion another example of Proculus' general practice of holding himself within the literal wording of the formula,[104] his ruling vitiates any possibility of interpreting the role of the subordinate operating a *peculium* as that of a true agent of his head of family. In terms of agency, how can a principal be held responsible for the acts which the person who is now his agent performed before the principal-agent relationship began? Indeed, a half-century later, the jurist Neratius negated the idea that the liability on the *peculium* could stem from a meeting of minds between the principal, *i.e.*, the head of family, and third parties when he ruled that if a slave were sold and his *peculium* transferred to the purchaser, the latter became liable for all suits on the *peculium*, even those arising out of transactions concluded before the sale and transfer.[105]

Julian and Gaius also ruled that the head of family may be held liable for transactions concluded by his subordinates before they came into his power.[106] Now, we know from other sources that these jurists recognized that slaves were subject to natural obligations just as sons in power were subject to civil law obligations. This has led a modern student of Roman law to surmise that Julian and Gaius allowed the liability of the head of family for the earlier transactions *(ex ante gestis)* because, even after his subordinates had entered into his power, they were still under obligation to the plaintiff. Thus, it is the *present* obligation of his subordinates that lay at the bottom of their master's liability *ex ante gestis*.[107]

Even more striking was the liability of the head of family *de peculio* which arose out of transactions that were expressly forbidden by him.

102 See Paul, D. 15.1.47.3.
103 Micolier, 296ff.
104 Kaser, Rev. P., 397.
105 Ulpian, D. 15.1.32.1.2.
106 Julian, D. 15.1.37.2, and Gaius, *h.t.*, 27.2.3.
107 Micolier, 299ff; *cf.* Kaser, Rev. P., 397. On some of the more important points made above, see further Solazzi, Scritti, I. 161–206.

Even though a master prohibited dealing with his slave, an action on the *peculium* will lie against him.[108]

The only way a citizen could prevent dealings with his slave's *peculium* was by removing it.

Thus, the liability of the *paterfamilias* for (1) the delicts of his subordinate committed in the course of conducting the business of the *peculium*, (2) the transactions of subordinates that preceded the very *potestas*-relationship upon which the action on the *peculium* was based, and (3) transactions that he expressly forbade, clearly show that the knowledge and consent of the head of family, *i.e.*, his authorization, express or implied, were not necessary for the availability of the action to third parties as a remedy for tort and breach of contract on the part of his son or slave.

2. *The* Actio de Peculio *and the Nature of the Liability of the Subordinates*

The following scheme reduces the law of agency as conceived by modern lawyers to its barest essentials:

1. The agent performs an act which creates for his principal (a) rights and (b) liabilities;
2. By performing said act, however, the agent has *not* created for himself any (a) rights or (b) liabilities.[109]

Analyzing the *peculium* arrangement in the light of the above schematic outline, we find that, with regard to the creation of rights and liabilities for the head of family, the subordinate operating a business establishment on the basis of a *peculium* was in a position analogous to that of an agent. Legal title to the *peculium* was vested in the head of family. Following the general rule of acquisitions made by persons in *potestas*,[110] legal title to everything acquired through the *peculium*, real estate, chattels and contractual rights,[111]

---

108 Gaius, D. 15.1.29.1: *Etiamsi prohibuerit contrahi cum servo dominus, erit in eum de peculio actio; cf.* Paul, D. 15.1.47 pr.
109 Hunter, 609.
110 G. 2.86.89; Inst. 2.9 pr. 3; Gaius, D. 41.1.10 pr., 2.
111 G. 3.163; Inst. 3.28.

also belonged to him. Then again, although modern scholars disagree whether the classical law required a specific authorization or ratification on the part of the head of family for his subordinate's act of possession or whether said act was automatically valid, all are agreed that there was no such requirement in the classical law if the subordinate performed his act of possession in connection with the business of his own *peculium*; the grant of a *peculium* itself was construed as a general authorization by the head of family, applying to all acts of possession in everything acquired as part of the *peculium*. Moreover, in addition to the ability of the subordinate to acquire physical acquisitions and to create contractual rights on behalf of the head of his family, he was also capable, in the course of administering his *peculium*, of creating legal liabilities — albeit, liabilities whose financial measure could not exceed the extent of the *peculium* itself — on the part of his head of family.

It is, however, in the realm of rights and liabilities for himself that the subordinate in power, operating with a *peculium*, departed most significantly from the status of a true agent as modern law understands it. According to the Roman legal tradition which the classical jurists inherited from their predecessors, the primary parties to a contract were the persons immediately involved and not those whom they represented. Thus, when a person in *potestas* concluded a transaction or entered into a contract, it was he, and not his *paterfamilias*, who was regarded as the person primarily involved with the third party. With regard to these primary contracting parties, the subordinate and the third party, rights and obligations were created between them. Although these rights and obligations were partly void and partly either not enforceable at all or, if enforceable, only within narrow limits,[112] they are nevertheless of great significance for a proper understanding of the status of the subordinate as a true agent.

If the subordinate who administered the *peculium* was a *filius-familias*, the civil law regarded his transactions as those of any citizen. They were binding; the rights and obligations incurred by both contracting parties were recognized by the judicial authorities;

---

112 A summary of these rights and obligations and their limitations is found in Kaser, I, 286–288, 330–331, 343–345, 605, upon which the following three paragraphs, unless otherwise noted, are also based.

and in theory, even suit could be brought against the son for breach of contract.[113] Inasmuch, however, as title to all property in the son's possession was vested in his father, successful execution upon a judgement was usually impossible.[114] The daughter in power and the slave, however, were accorded no such recognition by the civil law. The daughter was probably altogether incapable of creating any primary contractual liabilities between herself and third parties, and a slave could certainly neither bind himself nor be a party in legal proceedings under civil law rules.[115]

But in contrast to the traditional refusal of the classical Roman law to recognize any civil law obligation as binding daughters and slaves, Iavolenus and Julian, jurists of the high classical period, did give formal recognition to the ability of these persons to become subject to what was called a "natural obligation."[116] Although this natural obligation was not actionable,[117] it did create certain practical consequences. Debts of persons in power, because they were natural obligations, could be secured by securities or by pledges; anything that had already been given in performance of such obligations could not be recovered by a *condictio*, the remedy against unjust enrichment;[118] on the basis of them new obligations could be substituted by the legal process of *novatio*; and they served for claims against slaves after manumission and against sons and daughters after emancipation.[119]

113 Indeed, under certain circumstances, a son in power could also *bring* an action in his own name; Ulpian, D. 5.1.18.1. See Mandry, I, 200ff.
114 "Usually," not "always," for the son may possess a *peculium castrense.*
115 Julian, D. 2.11.13; see above p. 5.
116 Julian, D. 46.1.16.4; Iavolenus, D. 35.1.40.3. I am following Micolier, 620ff, *contra* Vážny, 144ff.
117 Julian, ibid.; Schulz, 461. For details, see Micolier, 609ff.
118 Julian, D. 41.1.16.3; Paul, D. 12.6.13 pr.; Papinian, D. 15.1.50.2; and G. 3.119a. Concerning the last passage, Schulz (461) writes, "This term [*obligationes naturales*] comes as a surprise, since we find it in the *Institutes* only in this place, and Gaius does not explain it. The decisive words *at ne . . . adiciatur* look like an addition, but Gaius himself may have written it. Gaius was probably the first to apply the term *obligatio naturalis* which in post-classical times was in general use."
119 Ulpian, D. 46.2.1; 44.7.14: "Slaves . . . may not be obligated according to the *ius civile*, but according to the *ius naturale* they both are obligated

It was these natural obligations which served as the basis for the bookkeeping of the debts and assets of a *peculium* with regard to the head of family and the other members of the *familia*, who, according to the rules of the civil law, could never be regarded as creditors or debtors of the subordinate and his *peculium*.[120] This practice, although formalized by Javolenus and Julian in the high classical period as we have indicated, was standard procedure long before. Indeed, the earliest reference to the *actio de peculio*, going back to the times of the late Republic, gives ample evidence for this.[121]

The primary obligation falling upon the subordinate administering a *peculium*, then, depended upon whether said subordinate was a son or a slave. If he was a son, the obligation was civil; if he was a slave, the obligation was natural. This difference, depending upon the status of the subordinate as a legally recognized person (the son) or not so recognized (the slave), caused Roman classical jurisprudence to view the son as having a relationship to his *peculium* different from that obtaining between a slave and his *peculium*. This distinct view of the relationship of the subordinate to his *peculium* comes to the fore when we examine the decisions of the classical jurists with regard to transactions by a subordinate for the benefit of persons other than himself and his superior *(i.e. donandi animo)*.

and obligate others"; African, D. 12.6.38 pr.; G. 4.78. There was, however, a certain praetorian protection for the son or slave who became *sui iuris*; Ulpian, D. 14.5.2 pr., and Lenel, E.P., 278.

120 G. 4.73; Ulpian, D. 15.1.41. See Micolier, 175ff.

121 Ulpian, D. 15.1.5.4; 9.3; 17. Micolier, 151ff. (esp. 162), *contra* Tuhr, 275ff. Generally on *obligatio naturalis* see Buckland, Slavery, 683–701; for bibliography, Didier, 239–273 esp. n. 2. Special mention should be made of Longo, Ric. I have avoided Longo's doctrine of the "*de facto* coercibility" of *obligationes naturales* in the classical law and his thesis of the post-classical introduction of "incoercible" *obligationes naturales*; they do not appear to be warranted by the sources. Moreover, Longo's attempt (1) to make the creation of *obligationes naturales* contingent upon the existence of a *peculium* and (2) to limit them to debts which the slave owed the master (and to exclude debts which the master owed the slave) are equally unconvincing. See Donatuti, 310–317. Nevertheless, Longo's study remains a most important one for the understanding of the Roman legal concept of *obligatio naturalis*.

If a subordinate, in the course of administering a *peculium*, became a guarantor *(fideiussor)*, a voluntary surety *(intercessor)*, a voluntary defendant *(defensor)* on behalf of someone, or mandated (as a mandator) a loan on behalf of someone, the jurists declare the head of family liable to an *actio de peculio* on these transactions only if the subordinate was a son. If, however, he was a slave, then the liability of the head of family was limited to those obligations arising only out of those acts which could be shown to have been undertaken for the advancement of the business of the *peculium* — a requirement that was not laid down with regard to similar transactions entered into by the son.[122] The obvious inference is that a *paterfamilias* was rendered liable to an action on the *peculium even if such obligation was purely personal to the son and in no wise related to the business of the peculium.*

As a matter of fact, Papinian and Marcellus went even further by declaring that even if the son created a liability that ordinarily could not lead to an action on the *peculium*, such as on an obligation created by the oral, solemn contract known as *stipulatio* which was independent of the business of the *peculium* or in an action on a judgement-debt *(actio iudicati)* which had been based upon an award against the son for tort which had nothing to do with the *peculium*, the father was held liable to the extent of the *peculium*. The reason for this ruling is that "not the origin of the action, but the actual liability on the judgement, is to be taken account of as the source of the obligation."[123]

These decisions lead to the conclusion that there was a basic distinction between the legal status or, to be more precise, the juristic understanding of the relationship of a slave to his *peculium* and that of a son to his. Inasmuch as a slave was not a legally recognized person, his *peculium* was not only legally the property of his master, it was essentially so. The slave in the eyes of the law was regarded

---

122 Gaius, D. 2.14.30.1, citing Julian; Ulpian, D. 15.1.3.5.6.9. and Paul, *h.t.*, 47.1, citing Celsius, Julian, Sabinus and Cassius; Labeo, D. 16.3.33; Papinian, D. 17.1.54 pr. Julian's statement, D. 46.1.19, must be understood this way. As for Paul, D. 13.7.18.4, which appears to contradict our thesis, see Albertario, I, 149.

123 D. 15.1.3.11.: ... *non originem iudicii spectandam, sed ipsam iudicati velut obligationem.*

as a mere tool of administration. Hence, all liability is not only limited to the extent of the *peculium*; it could arise exclusively out of those obligations that were incurred while operating the business of the *peculium* and were related to said operation. On the other hand, a son was a person sufficiently recognized by the civil law that the *peculium* may be viewed as essentially his, though formal title thereof was vested in his father. Thus, *all* obligations, peculiary or otherwise, had to be answered by the son and his patrimony, the *peculium*. It was only *pro forma* that the father's name was entered into the condemnation clause of the formula when the action was brought.[124]

If we bear in mind, then, (1) the civil law obligation which bound a son in power who entered into a contract, (2) the natural obligation which bound any subordinate in power who did so, and (3) the difference in their respective relationships to their *peculia*, Paul's characterization of the liability of the head of family in such transactions as "superadded" is immediately understood. "For no transfer of any action," he explained, "is effected by this edict, but one is added."[125] His meaning is clear: The civil law insisted that the liability for a contract always attached primarily to the contracting party himself. When the praetorian Edict gave third parties the right to sue the head of family who stood behind the slave or son who concluded a transaction, the former's liability did not supersede the primary liability of these subordinates but was supplementary to it. The son or slave, filling the role of agents, nevertheless remained liable to the civil law obligation and could, in the case of the son, be sued directly on the contract (by an *actio directa*), or, in the case of the slave, at least be held responsible for the natural obligation incurred.

---

124 When it came to outright gifts, however, even the son's powers were curtailed. He would not be allowed to preside over the liquidation of even a part of what the law still considered his father's property; Ulpian, D. 39.5.7 pr. Although he does not cite the Ulpian passage, Daube, R.L., 83–85, rightly emphasizes this curtailment of the son's power. (He also offers a most convincing explanation of the feasibility and tenacity of these rules; ibid., pp. 85–87.) There were, nevertheless, some few special cases in which the son could make gifts from his *peculium*; see Ulpian, ibid., 1. As for the textual problems in these passages of Ulpian, see Albertario, I, 153–154.

125 D. 14.1.5.1: *hom enim edicto non transfertur actio sed adicitur.*

The father or master, equivalent to principals, were rendered liable under the praetorian law *(ius honorarium)* and could be sued by an action modelled on the direct action against the primary, contracting subordinate (called an *actio utilis*). This latter action was added *(adiectus)* to the former. This addition, explained in the formula itself,[126] accounted for the (non-classical)[127] nomenclature by which the *actio de peculio*, among other actions, was known: *actiones adiecticiae qualitatis*, which in paraphrase means, "Actions against the principal bearing the quality of being added to the primary actions against the agent himself."

A distinguished writer on Roman law summarized the matter as follows:

> Roman law remained with the point of view that a contract concluded by an agent obligates, in principle, the agent (the contracting party), and not the one whom he represented (the principal); in other words, that the obligation of the person represented is in all cases an obligation (or liability) for the act of *someone else*, i.e., for the act of the agent.[128]

In contrast, true agency, to the modern lawyer, looks upon the obligation of the principal *as his own*. Thus, any idea that the action on the *peculium* and the other actions considered *adiecticiae qualitatis* represent a praetorian institution of agency is without basis. These actions presuppose economic services which we associate with agency; they do not, however, presuppose the legal concept of agency.[129]

This lack of true agency meant that there was open to the plaintiff the choice of one of two defendants whom he could sue: the head of family or the subordinate in power. For the purpose of formulating the jurisprudential relationship between the head of family and his subordinates *as defendants*, it would be helpful to utilize some concepts popular among students of jurisprudence during the last century. The Romanists of the nineteenth century divided

---

126 Lenel, E.P., 278f.
127 Jolowicz, Hist. Introd., 269, n. 2. The term was coined by the Roman Glossators of the early Middle Ages; Kaser, I, 605. See generally Guarino, 270–272.
128 Sohm, 474.
129 Ibid., 472–474; de Zulueta, Gaius, II, 268.

the phenomenon of a plurality of litigating parties into three basic categories. Their schematic analysis was approximately as follows:[130]

The ordinary rule is: (1) when there is a plurality of plaintiffs *(creditores)* or a plurality of defendants *(debitores)* in an obligation, the object of the obligation is correspondingly divided. Each *creditor* (or *debitor*) is entitled to recover (or bound to bear) only a proportional fraction of the advantage (or burden); in other words, a divided or partial *(pro rata)* power (or liability) exists among them. Thus, the *creditores* would be only *jointly* entitled to receive the whole object (or the *debitores* would be only *jointly* bound to discharge the obligation).

On the other hand, (2) penal law, concerned with actions generated by delicts, is based upon a rule of multiple or cumulative liability. For example, if several persons combine to commit a theft *(furtum)*, they are all severally liable to suit for the whole penalty, and payment by one does not discharge his fellow delinquents. Again, if a person is guilty of an outrage *(iniuria)* which wounds the honor of several victims, they are all *creditores* for the penalty, and recovery by one does not extinguish the claims of the rest.

Between the extremes of (1) and (2) lies the concept of correality.[131] In correality, each *creditor* (or *debitor*) is *severally* entitled to receive (or bound to discharge) the whole object or performance of the obligation. Hence, correality denotes a total or integral claim on the part of the *creditor* (or a total or integral liability on the part of the *debitor*). The right of action against the remaining co-*debitores* (or by the remaining co-*creditores*) is extinguished by the joinder of issue *(litis contestatio)* in an action against or by one of the parties, for the only basis of the suit (as framed in the *intentio*-clause of the formula) that would have been available to them is identical with that already used, and thereby consumed, by the party who brought the action. The correal *debitor* who pays does not have the right to proceed against his co-*debitores (regressus)* for their contribution and his proportional reimbursement.

To the student of jurisprudence, the praetorian institution of liability of the head of family on the *peculium* presents a curious

---

130 I am indebted to Poste, 353–358, for the material presented in the three following paragraphs.

variation on the theme of correality. In common with the other
actiones adiecticiae qualitatis[131] (i.e., *actio quod iussu, actiones institoria et exercitoria*, and *actio de in rem verso*, some of which will be
discussed fully below), the *actio de peculio* represents the *paterfamilias* and his son as correal *debitores*: The father was liable as
a "superadded" defendant,[132] and his son was liable directly as the
contracting party in accordance with the rules of the civil law. In
the case of a slaveowner and his slave, the natural obligation of the
latter created no more than a theoretic correality, of decidedly
limited practical value, as explained previously.

However, Ulpian makes us aware of the fact that the head of
family and his subordinate were not identical *debitores*. In the following passage he was careful to point out that:

> If anyone has contracted with a *filiusfamilias*, he has two debtors, the
> son for the whole debt and the father to the extent of the *peculium*.[133]

In other words, the object of the obligation (the *debitum*) of each of
the correal *debitores*, head of family and subordinate, may have
been theoretically identical, but the *legal liability was not*. Thus, as
correal *debitores*, discharge of the obligation by either one released
the other; and this release took place even if it was the head of
family who was being sued. Although he is required to pay no more
than the extent of the *peculium* and may therefore not have covered
the entire civil law obligation of his subordinate, the latter is thereby
released totally. This comes as no surprise, for the right of action (as
expressed in the *intentio*) which the creditor of the *peculium* originally had available against the son was consumed at the moment of
joinder of issue in the action he brought against the father. The
ability of each of these correal *debitores* of unequal liability to

---

131 A useful, though non-classical, term; see Schulz, 827–830 (bibliography,
   505). For an exhaustive treatment of the subject in English, see Wylie.
   My preference for the non-classical term is motivated by the desire to
   present a conceptual analysis and to avoid involvement in historical
   questions that are irrelevant as far as the *actiones adiecticiae qualitatis*
   are concerned.
132 Paul, D. 14.1.5.1: *adiectus*.
133 D. 15.1.44: *Si quis cum filiofamilias contraxerit, duos habet debitores,
   filium in solidum et patrem dumtaxat de peculio.*

release the other by discharging the specific obligation under which he was found, even when it was less than that of his colleague who was thereby released, was further shown by a ruling of Paul that the oral formal statement, known as *acceptilatio*, made by a creditor to dissolve an obligation due to him by a subordinate in power barred the action on the *peculium* against the head of family.[134]

This slight variation on the theme of correality did not trouble the Roman jurists, nor did it disturb business transactions or upset business relationships, for businessmen could be careful in their dealings with persons in power never to have debts or other obligations that were due them exceed the assets of the *peculium*.

3. *The Institution of the* Peculium *as an Instrument of Agency*

In order to understand the institution of the *peculium* as an instrument of agency in the economic life of Rome, we propose to synthesize the many details we have hitherto presented and to create a unified picture of the *peculium* arrangement in terms of modern business relationships.

In modern business, we speak of a general agent as one who is authorized to assume charge of his principal's entire business, of the entirety of some line of the business, or of the totality of his principal's business at some particular place. In this sense, a slave or son in power who had been granted or who had accumulated a lump sum of money or other property as his *peculium* and thereby had been set up or had set himself up in a business enterprise whose accounts are separate from those of his head of family could have been viewed as a general agent of his master akin to one in modern times who manages a branch establishment of his principal. Legal title to this branch was vested in the principal, yet people dealing with the general agent, the son or the slave, had the right to assume on the basis of the establishment of the *peculium* (or, as others maintain, by a special grant of powers of administration) that he was authorized to do anything that was usually done in such a business. They may have assumed that he had wide powers in his

134 **D**. 46.4.11.1.

particular line or at his particular branch, and they did not need to make any inquiry as to the extent of his authority.

The agent differs from the ordinary employee in that he represents the principal and, in the eyes of the law, acts for the principal, whereas the ordinary employee has no such authority. This representation is most apparent at times of suit. Should the son or slave, having administered the *peculium* as an agent of the head of family, have desired to bring suit against a third party for breach of contract, the right of suit was that of the head of family, and it was in the name of the head of family that the action was brought. Similarly, had third parties wished to sue the son- or slave-agent, it was the master-principal who was named as defendant, and it was the master-principal who, by the acts of his agent, had been rendered liable — albeit in a limited liability.

It is the last point of the previous paragraph that distinguished the son and slave as agents, marking them off from the independent contractor; for the latter, carrying out certain work which he was employed to do, had no authority to put his employer-principal under any obligation.

Then again, the agent does not fulfil the same role as a trustee, although agent and trustee do have certain characteristics in common. Although agency involves a trust or fiduciary relationship in the sense that it requires of the agent a high degree of loyalty and fidelity to the interests of his principal, nevertheless in contrast to agency the title to the property involved is vested in the trustee. In an ordinary agency relationship, as in the *peculium* arrangement, title to the property, estate, or company is vested in the principal, the head of family, and not in the agent, the son or slave. Furthermore, the law always viewed the slave or son as acting in the name of the *paterfamilias* exactly as an agent acts in the name of his principal, whereas the trustee acts in his own name. A still further distinction is that a *peculium*, like an agency, could be revoked legally at any time; whereas a trust may be terminated only by the fulfilment of the purposes for which it was established (unless a specific power of revocation was retained by the creator of the trust).

But it is precisely in our examination of the role of a subordinate in power administering a *peculium*, as an agent of his head of family as opposed to an employee, a contractor and a trustee, that we must be mindful of the limitations of the subordinate as a true agent in the modern sense. The facts are (1) that the liability of the master-father could not exceed the assets of the *peculium*, (2) that said liability was created by transactions of the slave-son entered into with the knowledge and consent of the head of family, and (3) that the transactions upon which the liability was based need not be closely related to the business of the *peculium* and need not have any reference to the head of family. These facts, it is true, in and of themselves do not negate a concept of agency in defining the relationship between the head of family and his subordinate. Indeed, the very act of establishing the *peculium* on the part of the *pater-familias* may be construed as his general authorization for all such transactions. But, on the other hand, the liability of the head of family for acts or transactions of his subordinate (1) before the latter came into his power, (2) prior to the actual creation of the *peculium*, and (3) against his express will, makes it abundantly clear that agency and representation are not the operative concepts underlying the institution of *peculium*.[135] We must constantly bear in mind the distinction between the factual, day-to-day rendering of economic services which, akin to that which is accomplished by agency in modern legal systems, was performed by persons in *potestas* administering *peculia*, on the one hand, and the legal concept of agency which was lacking in the praetorian action on the *peculium*, on the other.

The discrepancy between economic function and legal concept in the description of the institution of the *peculium* as an instrument of agency is further shown by an examination of the nature of the liability of the subordinate. According to the principles of true agency, once the agent has performed his duty, he recedes into the background. The contract he has concluded with third parties on behalf of his principal creates rights and liabilities for the third parties and for his principal. The agent himself withdraws from the scene bereft of any rights and unencumbered with any liabilities. Not so the subordinate who administered a *peculium* and concluded contracts based thereupon. If he was a son of his principal, he was

135 See Buckland, Slavery, 212.

under the same civil law obligations as a result of the contract he had concluded as if he were a citizen *sui iuris*. If he was a slave of his principal, not recognized by the civil law as a person, he was bound by the "natural" obligations he had thereby engendered. But whether he was son or slave, the liabilities and obligations he had created were viewed by the praetor as "superadded" to his own. In legal theory, he never receded into the background. The acts he had performed remained his own, never those of his principal. Jurisprudentially, he and his principal were regarded as co-real *debitores* with regard to the obligations and liabilities created by the contract he had concluded with third parties.

The evidence we have assembled to prove that the *peculium* arrangement was not based upon an agency relationship between the head of family and the subordinates in his power helps us to interpret more accurately the case of contracts entered into on the basis of an undisclosed *peculium*. Having seen that the established classical law considered the head of family liable on account of dealings which preceded the entrance of the subordinate into his power, indeed that there was a possibility for an action on the *peculium* to be available on a transaction carried out by a subordinate even before he was granted a *peculium*, we may infer that third parties need not have had any knowledge of the existence of a *peculium* at all in order for this liability to arise. Although the Digest does contain a few passages which speak of third parties as contracting with a view toward the *peculium*,[136] there are others which give the impression that such knowledge was lacking.[137]

The liability of the head of family on the transactions with third parties accomplished by the subordinate without revealing to them the existence of his *peculium*, i.e., without revealing to them that he was a slave and that the capital with which he was conducting his business was peculiary, is a legal phenomenon not foreign to the modern institution of agency. It is akin to the liability of an un-

---

136 Ulpian, D. 15.1.19.1, citing Marcellus, and *h.t.*, 32 pr. at the end.
137 Ulpian, D. 15.1.3.8, and African, D. 15.1.38 pr. Even with regard to the *condictio furtiva*, nominally associated with the *peculium* in the classical law, one cannot apply the notion of reliance on the *peculium* as the basis for the availability of the *actio de peculio* to third parties; Buckland, Slavery, p. 213.

disclosed principal to third parties. If an agent acts within his authority, the third party, upon discovering the identity of the principal, may elect to hold the principal instead of the agent. The principal is very properly held liable because the contract was, in reality, made for him and under his instructions. The same, of course, may be said with regard to a *paterfamilias* whose subordinate did business with a *peculium*. Thus, without having other evidence that the agency function of the *peculium* arrangement was *not* based upon a legal concept of agency, we might have been inclined to assume that the liability of the head of family on transactions carried out with an undisclosed *peculium* should be explained in terms of the liability of an undisclosed principal in modern jurisdictions where agency is the operative concept. However, taken in the context of the data which we have presented above which preclude the concepts of agency and representation as integral to the Roman classical law, it would be more correct to explain this liability, with Buckland,[138] as based upon the principle that one who provided the slave or son with the means of entering into business transactions generally and obtaining credit should have taken the limited risk engendered by such transactions.

Similarly, one may not assume that the jurist was motivated by concepts of agency and representation, implied or otherwise, as underlying the *peculium* arrangement when he excluded those acts performed by the subordinate which appear to be principally for the benefit of third parties *(donandi animo)* from constituting sufficient grounds for a suit *de peculio*. Rather, his refusal to grant third parties an action on the *peculium* on the basis of the subordinate's guaranteeing their debts, his acting as a voluntary surety or voluntary defendant for them, his mandating a loan for them, or his making an outright gift to them — his refusal in these cases was based upon the feeling that it was reasonable to protect the head of family from liability for what were in effect gifts or acts of possible collusion between strangers (*i.e.*, the third parties) and his subordinate.[139]

Thus, although in comparison with an employee, an independent

138 Buckland, Text, p. 534.
139 Buckland, Slavery, 214; Walker, 68. n. 3. On Marcellus, D. 42.8.12, and its relation to our remarks, see Albertario, I, 152.

contractor, and a trustee, the subordinate with a *peculium* most closely approximated an agent, the approximation is essentially functional not conceptual. The reason for the wide discrepancy between the subordinate as agent and the modern agent must be sought in the non-contractual nature of the former's agency. The term that characterizes the relationship between principal and agent in the *peculium* arrangement was not contract but *potestas*, the power Roman law vested in a father over his son *(patria potestas)* and in a master over his slave *(dominica potestas)*.[140] There were no contractual terms of commission, reimbursement, scope of agency, etc., between subordinate and head of family. In the *peculium* arrangement, the agent's obligations of obedience and the limitations of his powers, as well as the principal's powers over and obligations, if any, to his agent, were all subsumed under the rules of *potestas*.

But the high degree and fidelity to the interests of the principal generally associated with the proper discharge of the duties of an agent were usually not sufficiently met by the demands of filial piety implicit in the *potestas* relationship and certainly not by the demands of servile obedience and devotion. As pointed out at the beginning of this chapter,[141] the crucial source of incentive that motivated subordinates to pursue the business of the *peculium* effectively and dynamically was the self-interest of the subordinate agent. Although the *peculium* was *de iure* the property of the head of family, it was treated *de facto* as the property of the subordinate to whom it was granted. The son or slave had the use of the profits derived from many a *peculium*, transforming them to his own needs as he wished. There were severe restrictions, not legal but rather moral and social, that prevented the *paterfamilias* from rapaciously plundering the *peculium* of his subordinate.

The character of the *peculium* as the *de facto* property of the subordinate, to the point of even restricting the head of family from deriving direct use and benefit from it, would appear to vitiate the

---

140 A convenient, though non-juristic, term.
141 In section A 1, "The *Peculium* and its Role in the Economic Life of Rome — General Remarks." Review the discussion in Costa, Dir., 104–105. Further confirmation of the points that follow drawn from non-juristic literature may be found in Norden, 72–73.

institution of the *peculium* as an instrument of agency. This is partially correct insofar as the *filiusfamilias* was concerned. We found that the *peculium* of the son may be viewed as *essentially* his though formal title was vested in his father. Thus the granting of a *peculium* to a son was the method whereby his father arranged for him to support himself and his family. Here indeed not only was a theoretic concept of agency and representation lacking; functionally, also, an agency relationship between father and son was minimal.

As far as the slave with the *peculium* is concerned, however, the function of agency was greater. Although slave-owners would normally not appropriate the assets or profits of the *peculium* for themselves, the enlargement and enrichment of the *peculium* did accrue to their benefit. This took place in a number of ways. At the death of the slave or when the slave surrendered the *peculium* in whole or in part in return for his manumission, it was the master who reaped the harvest of its increments and profits. But of overwhelmingly greater significance was the fact that very often the profits derived from the business enterprise operating on the basis of a *peculium* were applied to the accounts of the head of family on a more or less *regular general agency basis*. This regular general agency procedure was also applied occasionally to the *peculium* of a son as well. It is this role of a slave and, to a lesser extent, of a son, as general agents which brings us to a detailed study of the *actio de in rem verso*.

C. THE *ACTIO DE IN REM VERSO* AND AGENCY

1. *A Juridical Analysis of the* Actio de in Rem Verso

In conjunction with the action on the *peculium*, the praetor rendered the head of family liable to an action based upon the business transaction *(negotium)* of his subordinate if and to the extent that the former had profited from said transaction *and* had applied such profits to his own purposes or registered them in his own accounts.[142]

---

142 The extension of this action to include the liability of principals for transactions of agents *sui iuris*, which is found in C. 4.26.7.3., is the

Thus, in every action on the *peculium*, if, as a result of a preliminary investigation, it was determined that the proceeds from the transaction of the subordinate had not been incorporated into the *peculium* but had rather been applied by the *paterfamilias* for his benefit, the latter's liability became personal and was no longer limited to the extent of the assets of the subordinate's *peculium* but rather to the extent the *paterfamilias* had been enriched.

This aspect of the action on the *peculium* was provided for by an additional statement in the condemnation clause of the formula to the effect that, as an alternative to the liability of the master that was limited to the assets of the *peculium*, there lay a liability based upon and measured by the profits which the master had derived from the transaction.[143] Thus, in Roman legal literature the action was generally called *actio de peculio et de in rem verso*.[144] Despite this nomenclature, in the everyday operation of the law, the *de in rem verso* aspect of the action preceded the *de peculio* alternative as a source of remedy for the aggrieved party. It was only in the event that the head of family had been found *not* to have applied the profits to his own benefit, or that the plaintiff lacked sufficient proof to that effect, that the plaintiff would invoke the *de peculio* part of the condemnation clause.[145]

The texts provide numerous examples of what is meant by the application of the proceeds or profits of a transaction to the purposes or desires of the head of family. We cite a few by way of illustration: As a result of a transaction concluded by a subordinate, said subordinate came into possession of wheat and then made use of this same wheat as food for the slave-force of the head of family; the slave or son entered into a transaction, making a loan or a purchase, in order to pay the debts of the head of family or to buy

---

result of interpolation and is not part of the classical Roman law; Mitteis, 224, n. 70. For an analysis of this Code passage, see Lenel, Zur., 354–362. For an earlier discussion, see Mandry, II, 460–465.

143 Compare Ulpian, D. 15.1.9.2.3, with Alfenus, D. 15.3.16; and see the remarks of Watson, Ob., 185–189.

144 On all of the foregoing, Inst. 4.7.4; Ulpian, D. 15.3.1 pr. – 2; P.S. 2.9.1; Lenel, E.P., 279. *Cf.* C. 4.25.1.2 and 4.26.7.

145 Ulpian, D. 15.2.1.2, in the name of Pomponius citing Julian.

food for his slaves or animals;[146] the slave borrowed money and loaned it to a third party — this, too, rendered the head of family liable to the *actio de in rem verso,* "for he has acquired an obligatory right," namely the right to sue his slave's debtor.[147]

Several rules are helpful in further delineating the liability of the principal. Generally speaking, liability to the action *de in rem verso* was created if the subordinate had made the type of application of the profits to the uses of the head of family which, had such application been carried out by a *procurator,* would have rendered the principal liable to an *actio mandati,* or, had such application been carried out by an unauthorized person, would have rendered him liable to an *actio negotiorum gestorum.*[148] This rather complicated rule will be explained and discussed below.

Another general rule is that the availability of the *actio de in rem verso* was determined by the ultimate disposition of the profits. Therefore, not only was the action denied if the profits were incorporated into the *peculium* and remained there; even if the profits were first applied to the accounts of the head of family and only subsequently returned to the slave's *peculium,* here, too, the action would be denied unless, of course, such return was a payment releasing the head of family from a debt he had owed the *peculium.*[149] Conversely, "the rule of law is that there may be an *actio de in rem verso* even though the son or the slave applies it at first to the

146 Ulpian, D. 15.3.3.1. For the further elucidation of this passage and of the passage cited in the following note, see Gay, 190–199.
147 Ulpian, D. 15.3.3.5.
148 Ulpian, D. 15.3.3.2–4; see also *idem.* D. 15.3.1.2 and 3.5 both passages citing Pomponius. *Procurator,* explains Ulpian, is "one who administers another's affairs under his authorization" (D. 3.3.1 pr.). This authorization was known as *mandatum.* Hence, the consensual contract by which a person assumed the duty to conclude a legal transaction or to perform a service gratuitously in the interest of the one who authorized the transaction or service *(mandator)* or of the third party in behalf of whom the authorization was given was also called *mandatum.* Relations between mandator and mandatory were governed by the *actio mandati.* In the event that the transaction or service had *not* been authorized, there was between the one who performed the service and the one on behalf of whom it had been performed a relationship of implied agency governed by the *actio negotiorum gestorum.*
149 Ulpian, D. 15.3.10.6.7.

peculium and afterwards to his master's affairs."[150] The ultimate disposition of the profits which determined the availability of the action referred to the accounts into which they were entered, not to the subsequent use to which they were put or to the final fate which may have befallen them. Thus, once the profits had been applied to the advantage or to the account of the head of family, their subsequent loss or damage did not affect the legal rights of the plaintiff, and an *actio de in rem verso* was still available as a remedy for a third party who incurred a loss unjustifiably as a result of his transaction with the subordinate.[151]

In any event, it was the direct enrichment of the head of family that was the source of his liability, not his indirect enrichment via the *peculium*.[152] This statement, which was the conclusion yielded to us from the general rule documented in the previous paragraph, means that one and the same transaction carried out by a subordinate with *peculium* and a third party could have served as the basis of alternative remedies. Moreover, the determination of which of the alternative remedies was available for the plaintiff was made not on the basis of any of the terms of the contract, but by the ultimate disposition made of the profits which proceeded from the transaction.

Thus, it was not merely a matter of nomenclature that brought the *actio de peculio et de in rem verso* together. The actions were framed in one formula. Otto Lenel, in his monumental work on the praetorian Edict, has reconstructed the formula as it would have been used in an action on a deposit involving a slave and his *peculium* as follows:

> [*Intentio*] Whereas A. Agerius deposited with Stichus, who is in the *potestas* of N. Negidius, a silver table, on which there is a suit,
>
> [*Condemnatio*] whatever for this reason Stichus, were he free by Quiritarian law, ought in good faith to give or do to A. Agerius, do you iudex condemn N. Negidius [to pay] A. Agerius of his property
>
> [alternative 1:] to the extent of the *peculium* and, if anything was done in bad faith by N. Negidius, to the extent that the *peculium* was [thereby] diminished, or
>
> [alternative 2:] if anything was converted therefrom to the advantage

---

150 Ulpian, D. 15.3.3.1, at end.
151 Ulpian, D. 15.3.3.7.8, and African, D. 15.3.17 pr.
152 See Ulpian, D. 15.3.3.5, citing Pomponius, and Paul, D. 15.3.11.

of N. Negidius [then do you iudex condemn the latter to pay the extent of said conversion even if it exceeds the extent of the *peculium*].

If it does not [so] appear, dismiss.[153]

Note that the introductory *intentio* is formulated with reference to the subordinate in power who, with the plaintiff, was the primary contracting party. The fiction, "were he free by Quiritarian law [the ancient, formalistic law of the Romans, used synonymously with the civil law]" is appended immediately thereafter. Thus, formally speaking, we have here a direct action *(actio directa)* between the slave and the third party. The intimate relationship between the head of family and the subordinate in his power may be deduced from the ease with which the suit *(iudicium)* may be transferred at the death of the subordinate and transformed into a direct action against the master.[154]

In discussing the relationship between the alternative remedies provided for in the condemnation clause of the formula, the jurists attribute to the second one, that of the *de in rem verso*, a number of advantages for the plaintiff over the first one, that of the *de peculio*. We have already seen that the liability covered by the *de in rem verso* alternative was not limited to the assets of the *peculium*, but rather to the extent to which the profits had been applied to the direct advantage of the head of family. If this latter amount was the greater one, the superiority of the *de in rem verso* remedy was obvious.[155] Furthermore, since the action was not limited to the *peculium*, the plaintiff was in a position superior to any other cre-

---

153 Lenel, E.P., 282: *Quod A⁰A⁰ apud Stichum qui in N¹N¹ potestate est, mensam argenteam deposuit, q.d.r.a., quidquid ob eam rem Stichum, si liber esset ex iure Quiritium, A⁰A⁰ dare facere oporteret ex fide bona, eius iudex NᵐNᵐ A⁰A⁰ dumtaxat de peculio et si quod dolo malo N¹N¹ inde versum est c.s.n.p.a.* Intentio is the introductory clause of a formula in which the basis for the action is described. *Condemnatio* is the condemnation clause. *A(ulus) Agerius* is the stereotyped, fictitious name for the plaintiff, from the verb, *ago, agere,* to bring an action, to sue. *N(umerius) Negidius* is the stereotyped, fictitious name for the defendant, from the verb *numero, numerare,* to pay, and *nego, negare,* to deny. *Stichus* is the standard name for a slave.

154 See Ulpian, D. 5.1.57; Lenel, E.P., 281.

155 Inst. 4.7.3, parallel to the illegible G. 4.72a; Ulpian, D. 15.3.1. pr.

ditors who might have been proceeding *de peculio*.[156] Moreover, the *actio de in rem verso* was perpetual. It was available even though the *peculium* had been extinguished or removed without fraudulent intent, even after the death or alienation of the slave, and also after the lapse of the additional year thereafter (*annus utilis*) which the praetor allowed for suits on the *peculium*.[157] In addition, the *actio de in rem verso* was also available against the heirs of the head of family, and in this case, too, all the aforementioned advantages belonged to the plaintiff.[158]

The historical relationship between the alternative remedies provided for in the condemnation clause is not clear at all and has been the subject of speculation among some modern scholars. There is, it is true, ample evidence that the *actio de peculio et de in rem verso* was an established remedy provided by the law already in the first century B.C.E. Servius and his pupil, Alfenus, were concerned with the extent of the *peculium* and with the ability of a plaintiff to recover by means of this action.[159] The definition of the *peculium* made by Tubero, another republican jurist, which we have already quoted at the very beginning of this chapter, reveals the fact that the *actio de peculio* was an established remedy in the first century B.C.E. Inasmuch as Tubero's definition was cited by Celsus in book VI of his *Digesta* which deals with the action on the *peculium*, it may be safely assumed that his definition was originally formulated in connection with that action.[160] But the internal relationship of the component parts of the condemnation clause at this early time is unknown. The most plausible theory is that originally the *de peculio* sub-clause and the *de in rem verso* sub-clause were separate

156 Ulpian, D. 15.3.1.2.
157 Ulpian, D. 15.3.1.1, citing Labeo; C. 4.26.7 pr.; *arg.*, Ulpian, D. 15.2.1.10, citing Labeo. See also Julian, D. 15.3.14, citing Marcellus and Paul.
158 C. 4.26.7.1 and 2. See also Ulpian, D. 15.2.1.10, citing Labeo.
159 Ulpian, D. 15.1.9.3 and 17 (on the extent of the *peculium*) and Alfenus, D. 15.3.16 (on the ability to recover). The words relating to *de in rem verso* in the latter passage are suspect; Solazzi, *Scritti*, VI, 5. The full names of the jurists are, respectively, Servius, Sulpicius Rufus and P. Alfenus Varus.
160 Watson, Ob., 189. Watson, 186 and 189, n. 1, also points out that the passages citing Servius, Alfenus and Tubero are considered relatively free from interpolations.

condemnation clauses of separate actions and that the *actio de peculio* had been created earlier than the *actio de in rem verso*. It was only later, for reasons of efficiency and flexibility — i.e., to allow the plaintiff to find the path most advantageous to him: through direct suit of the head of family on the basis of the latter's profits, or through indirect suit of the head of family via the *peculium* — that an action framed around a formula containing two alternative condemnations was invented.[161] But the words, "to allow the plaintiff to find the path most advantageous to him," are an over-simplification. For included among the assets of the *peculium* were the debts due to it as well as the stock in its inventory. Now, any profits made by a slave administering a *peculium* which were appropriated by the slave-owner for his own advantage were also construed as debts owed by him to his slave.[162] Thus, it is more than likely that what was being sought in a *de in rem verso* action could usually be recovered by a *de peculio* action as well.

W.W. Buckland is of the opinion that the substantive advantages of the *actio de in rem verso* over the *actio de peculio* which we have described in the previous paragraph are not substantial enough to have warranted its creation on the part of the praetor. Buckland therefore seizes upon the thesis propounded by Pernice[163] to explain the need for the *de in rem verso* action.

According to this thesis, the *actio de peculio* was originally effective only with regard to the corporeal assets that were in the *peculium* stock, not with regard to the debts owed to it. Hence, any profits which had been applied to the uses and advantage of the head of family and which were recorded in the books of the *peculium* as "debts" owed by him to it were beyond the reach of a plaintiff suing *de peculio*. It was to cover this rather large area of possible injustice to creditors of the *peculium* that the praetor made the *actio de in rem verso* available. When subsequent jurisprudence construed debts which were owed to the *peculium* as also lying within the purview of the *de peculio* action and included within those assets of the *peculium* which determined the extent of the

---

161 Karlowa, II, 1155–1156.
162 E.g., Paul, D. 15.3.19.
163 I, 382–385; *cf.*, however, the dissent in Mandry, II, 32, n. 15.

principal's liability, the original, primary and substantial purpose the *actio de in rem verso* was supposed to serve faded; and the above-mentioned advantages alone remained.[164] This construction, whereby debts to the *peculium* were accounted as assets to be included in the calculations determining the limit of the master's liability, had already been made by the time of Servius.[165]

This speculation, concerning the origins of the *actio de in rem verso* and the relationship of the *de peculio* sub-clause to the *de in rem verso* sub-clause of the formula around which the combined action was framed, presupposes the essential independence of the two actions from each other despite the fact that the Digest invariably refers to them together. This presupposition would appear to be supported by a careful reading of the Digest's description of the praetor's Edict. Although the Edict records *one* formula for *one* action when it speaks of *actio de peculio et de in rem verso*, the words introducing the *de peculio* action in the Digest characterize the relevant edict as a "threefold" one *(edictum triplex)*. The Digest passage then proceeds to explain this characterization in the following manner:

> ...for there arises from it [i.e., from the Edict] either an action on the *peculium*, or one based on the application of profits to [the defendant's] concerns, or that based on authorization.[166]

The wording of this explanation seems to imply rather clearly that the *actio de in rem verso* could have been an action independent of the *actio de peculio*.[167] Certainly, if a plaintiff would have registered his desire to bring one action and not the other because he considered the second one futile, thereby separating the two actions, the praetor would hardly have objected.[168] Thus, the *essential* indepen-

---

164 Buckland, Slavery, 184–186.

165 Micolier, 148ff. The dating of this construction is contrary to the opinion of Tuhr, 267f., who regards it as the work of the late-classical jurists.

166 Ulpian, D. 15.1.1.1: *aut enim de peculio aut de in rem verso aut quod iussu hinc oritur actio.* For a critical examination of this passage, see Fabricius, 10–12.

167 A similar implication may be derived from the last sentence of Inst. 4.7.5. However, no such clear indication may be obtained from the parallel wording in G. 4.74.

168 Lenel, E.P., 279. See Ulpian, D. 15.2.1.10, and Paul, D. 15.3.19 where

dence of the two actions from each other is a reasonable assumption despite their *formal* unity.

Further analysis of the reconstructed formula around which the *actio de peculio et de in rem verso* was framed, however, not only indicates that the two actions were essentially and historically independent of each other. It reveals also that, although the condemnation clause was expressed with reference to — and to the extent of — the *peculium*, the introductory *intentio* clause which gives the background for the action made no reference at all to the *peculium*.[169] The absence of any reference to the *peculium* in the *intentio* clause of the formula leads to the conclusion that the *actio de in rem verso* was not necessarily predicated upon the existence of a *peculium*. It was available even against the head of family whose son or slave was doing business without a *peculium* — nay, even without the former's authorization — as long as the profits derived from the transactions of the subordinate were applied to the use, advantage or capital stock of his superior.[170]

The fact that the availability of an *actio de in rem verso* was independent of the existence of a *peculium* could serve as sufficient explanation for its survival after the *peculium* was extinguished or after the subordinate person administering the *peculium* had died or been alienated by manumission or emancipation. This independence could be the source of the perpetual liability to this action, that is, beyond the normal one year provided for by the praetor after the extinction of the *peculium* or after the death or alienation of the slave.[171] The invariable practice of the Edict of coupling the *actio*

the specific references to the *actio de peculio* preclude the *actio de in rem verso*. Although one may counter with reference to Scaevola, D. 15.3.20 pr. and 21, to prove that in the Ulpian and Paul passages a *de in rem verso* clause, though not mentioned, may have been included, this counter-argument fails when one realizes that, on the contrary, Scaevola's very use of the term *actio utilis de in rem verso* may itself refer specifically to an *actio de in rem verso* which is brought alone, unattached to the *actio de peculio*; Lenel, ibid., 279–280, n. 2, and Solazzi, Rev., 544.

169 Gay confuses these two questions: (1) the independence of the two actions, and (2) the independence of the *actio de in rem verso* from the existence of a *peculium*; see the criticism of Solazzi, Rev., 544.

170 Lenel, E.P., 280ff.

171 Mandry, II, 454–458.

de in rem verso with the *actio de peculio* and incorporating them in a unified formula may not be adduced as evidence to the contrary, namely that the *actio de in rem verso* was conditioned upon the existence of a *peculium*. It merely indicates that the praetor had taken cognizance of the well-known facts of Roman economic life, that people in their everyday business would not trust a slave who had not been entrusted with a *peculium* to administer or who had not been specifically authorized by his master.[172]

A word of caution, however. Certain passages have been cited as "proof" that the *actio de in rem verso* was available even where no *peculium* arrangement existed. Ulpian, for example, cited Proculus and Pegasus as ruling that the action on the *peculium* was available "even though there is nothing in the *peculium*,"[173] and, reasoning *a fortiori*, the same would hold true with regard to the action *de in rem verso*.[174] Indeed, Ulpian himself cited the praetor as granting the *actio de in rem verso* itself "if those who are in the *potestas* of another have nothing in the *peculium*."[175] These passages, however, hardly constitute proof that the action lay when no *peculium* arrangement existed between *paterfamilias* and subordinate. The distinction between a non-existent *peculium* and a *peculium* whose stock was depleted, albeit totally but nevertheless temporarily, is clear. The transfer of legal rules from one to the other is of dubious validity.[176]

The word of caution contained in the previous paragraph, however, does not constitute a refutation and does not warrant a rejection of the well-established thesis that the action *de in rem verso* was available equally against a head of family whose slave did *not* have a *peculium*.[177] Once this thesis is accepted, of course, no other proof

---

172 Buckland, Slavery, 184.

173 Ulpian, D. 15.1.30 pr.: *etiamsi nihil sit in peculio*.

174 Lenel, E.P., 280. Lenel's implied conclusion *a fortiori* is made explicit by Buckland, Slavery, 184.

175 Ulpian, D. 15.3.1 pr.: *si hi qui in potestate aliena sunt nihil in peculio habent*; see Mandry, II, 456.

176 Buckland, Slavery, 184, n. 15; Kaser, Rev. P., 395, n. 1. See also the analysis by Watson, Ob., 186, of the "proof" presented by Gay, 171, based upon Alfenus, D. 15.3.16.

177 In addition to the works of Mandry, Lenel and Buckland already cited concerning this question, see also Gay, 166–175, for a full exposition of

is needed for the assertion made above that the *actio de in rem verso* was independent of the *actio de peculio.*

Thus, although the formula upon which the *actio de peculio et de in rem verso* was a unified one — with *one* introductory clause *(intentio)* relating the cause of action and *one* condemnation clause *(condemnatio)* offering the plaintiff alternative remedies — this unification was a practical, not an essential one. In theory, the two actions could be separated, and, again in theory, the suit *de in rem verso,* based as it was upon the fact that the head of family had applied the proceeds of his subordinate's transaction to his own accounts, could be brought without reference to a *peculium,* nay, it could be brought even if the slave or son did not possess a *peculium* at all. In examining, therefore, the jurisprudential basis of the liability of the head of family for the dealings of his subordinate, we cannot resort to Buckland's explanation of the basis of his liability to the *actio de peculio,* namely that setting up one's subordinate with a *peculium* and thereby providing him with the wherewithal to conduct its business, with all that such business implies, is an act which made him responsible, in a limited fashion, for the dealings and transactions that resulted therefrom. This explanation, intimately associated as it is with the institution of the *peculium,* is, in theory at least, irrelevant with regard to liability to the *actio de in rem verso.*

Looking elsewhere, scholars have propounded two main theories in an attempt to explain the jurisprudential source of a citizen's liability to the *actio de in rem verso*:

First there is the *gestio* theory. If someone manages another's affair or affairs without authorization by the person interested, usually during the latter's absence in order to defend the absent party's rights and interests, the classical law defined the mutual rights and obligations of the principal and his (unauthorized) agent. The absentee principal is referred to as *dominus negotii* and the unauthorized agent as *negotiorum gestor*; the rights of the former were pro-

this thesis. Also in agreement are Perozzi, I, 218, and Niederländer, 51. The preponderance of scholarly opinion tends to agree with this position. The minority of scholars, who maintain that the liability to an *actio de in rem verso* did depend upon the existence of a *peculium* arrangement, are well represented by Tuhr, 238–259; Solazzi, Scritti, I, 247–267; VI, 1–13. See further Fabricius, 12–15.

tected by the availability of the *actio negotiorum gestorum*, and his obligations to the agent were enforced by his liability to the *actio negotiorum gestorum contraria*.[178] We have already cited the rule that any application by a subordinate in power of the profits accruing from his transactions to the uses of his superior which, had such application been carried out by a citizen on behalf of another without being authorized to do so would have rendered the principal liable to an *actio negotiorum gestorum contraria*, rendered the superior liable to an *actio de in rem verso*.[179] From this correlation of the liability of the head of family for transactions of his subordinate with that which was engendered by the *negotiorum gestio*, it has been inferred that a citizen's liability to an *actio de in rem verso* was derived from the general liability of anyone to cover the expenses and liabilities incurred by any *gestor* who had managed his affairs or enhanced his estate without his authorization. Any third person who had business dealings with a slave or son in power who had not been authorized by their respective master or father was, albeit unwittingly, in a position analogous to that of such a *gestor*. This held true if the profits accruing from those business dealings had been applied to the uses or had been entered into the accounts of the master or father.[180]

A detailed analysis of the passages supporting this theory would be of limited value and would occupy us with matters of tangential interest. Suffice it to say that the theory has been effectively attacked on grounds which may be summarized along three lines:[181] (1) The passages which tie the *actio de in rem verso* with *negotiorum gestio* must be construed as expressing a limit in order to produce this correlation. In other words, we are being asked to assume that the principle governing the action is that it applies only when a free person would have had a cause of action for a *negotiorum gestio*. This, of course, is an assumption that need not be made. The connection may be descriptive, not limitative. The analogy of the *paterfamilias'* liability *de in rem verso* to that of an absentee *dominus negotii* may

178 The rules of *negotiorum gestio* are found in D. 3.5 and C. 2.18.
179 Ulpian, D. 15.3.3.2; 5.3; Africanus, *h.t.*, 17 pr.
180 Karlowa, II, 1156.
181 Buckland, Slavery, 179f.

indeed help us understand many cases in which a slave-owner had to undertake and discharge those obligations which had been created by his slave's transactions. But the analogy must not be taken as indicating a condition *sine qua non*, i.e., that unless the act, had it been performed by a free person, would have rendered the principal liable to the *actio negotiorum gestorum contraria*, it could in no wise have rendered the slave-owner liable to the *de in rem verso action*.[182] (2) Passages which would tend to establish this theory may be easily, and preferably, interpreted in another fashion.[183] (3) Some Digest passages either are left without sufficient explanation by this *gestio* theory or actually contradict it.[184]

Because of these attacks on it, the *gestio* theory must be rejected in favour of the enrichment theory. The enrichment theory hinges upon the jurisprudential essence of the conversion of the profits to the benefit of the head of family. The opening words of the Digest Title 15:3 *De in rem verso* state clearly that citizens are liable to this action on the basis of transactions of their subordinates in power "if what was received has been applied to their [*i.e.*, heads of families] concerns, the contract being considered to have been, as it were, made rather with them."[185] On the basis of this and similar statements, the essence of this application *(versio)* is usually summarized by the concept of enrichment.[186] The praetorian creation of the *actio de in rem verso* thus came to provide

182 Windscheid, II, 483.
183 See, for example, Buckland, ibid., note 3, on Ulpian, D. 15.3.7 pr.
184 E.g., on Ulpian, D. 15.3.7.1, see Pringsheim, G.A., I, 271–273; Tuhr, 198ff; Buckland, ibid., note 7; and Gay, 180ff. On Javolenus and Ulpian, D. 15.3.2,3 pr., see Tuhr, 178ff, and Buckland, ibid., 180, n. 1. On Ulpian, D. 15.3.10.7, see Tuhr, 177, 225ff.
185 Ulpian, D. 15.3.1 pr.: *si in rem eorum quod acceptum est conversum sit quasi cum ipsis potius contractum videatur.*
186 Windscheid, II, 438; Dernberg, II, 14; Mandry, II, 467ff; Buckland, Slavery, 178–179. Tuhr, 188ff, combines the enrichment with the *gestio* theory. According to Tuhr, the action was originally based upon the idea of enrichment and was subsequently developed along the lines of *negotiorum gestio*. As for the difficulty for the enrichment theory raised by Ulpian, D. 15.3.10.2, citing Pomponius, see Buckland, ibid., 180, n. 3, and Beseler, Beit., III, 192ff. An important contribution to this matter is to be found in Niederländer, 42–51, where also the enrichment theory is favoured.

for the liability of a head of family on the transactions of his subordinate which would correspond to the enrichment the former enjoyed as a result of those transactions. The praetor thereby fulfilled the legal maxim *(regula)* that

> It is just in accordance with natural law that no one should be enriched at the expense and harm of another.[187]

The expression "should be enriched" *(locupletior fieri)* is not uncommonly associated with liabilities whose justification is enrichment.[188] Although Ulpian's opening statement does not explicitly base the obligation *de in rem verso* on any reference to enrichment, there are occasional allusions to it elsewhere.[189]

But enrichment as the basis for the liability *de in rem verso* cannot be accepted without certain reservations. We have seen, for example, that an addition to the *peculium*, even though the head of family had been enriched thereby, at least in the eyes of the law, did not constitute a basis for suit *de in rem verso*. Moreover, although in other cases of liability whose source was enrichment, destruction or loss by accident extinguished the claimant's right to recover, this did not hold true with the enrichment which served as the basis of the *actio de in rem verso*. Subsequent destruction or accidental loss did *not* deprive the claimant of his right of action.[190] These deviations

---

187 Pomponius, D. 50.17.206: *Iure naturae aequum est neminem cum alterius detrimento et iniuria fieri locupletiorem.*
188 Paul, D. 3.5.36 pr., and Pomponius, D. 12.6.14. This latter passage cites the *regula* as the basis of the *condictio* available for the recovery of money, which, though not due, had been paid mistakenly.
189 E.g., Paul, D. 14.3.17.4.
190 The following are some examples of cases of liability whose source was enrichment, yet should the gains have been destroyed subsequently by accident the claimant's right to recover was extinguished: (1) Someone managed the affairs of a ward without the authorization of his guardian, and the ward was thereby enriched. The estate of the ward became liable to an *actio negotiorum gestorum contraria* to compensate the *gestor*; this liability existed as long as the gains of the ward had not been destroyed by accident (Paul, D. 3.5.36 pr.). (2) A *bona fide* possessor who was enriched in the course of possessing the farm was liable to an actio for recovery on the part of the true heir. If his gains were destroyed by accident, the action for recovery (called *petitio her>iditatis*) was limited to the farm itself (Paul, D. 5.3.36.4). (3) If one gambled with a slave or a

do not, however, represent a serious challenge to the enrichment theory. "When it is remembered that the principles of this action [*de in rem verso*] are developed by the jurists from the scanty words of the Edict, and are not governed by those words [but by the desire of the praetor to cope with specific economic institutions], it will not seem strange that its rules should not exactly square with those of the *iure civili* remedy for causeless enrichment."[191] Thus, in making the *actio de in rem verso* available to third parties dealing with subordinates, the praetor was in effect declaring that one who reaps the profit of a transaction was responsible for any breaches of contract of anyone in his *potestas* through whom he had thereby become enriched.[192]

son and lost, he could bring an *actio negotiorum gestorum de peculio* against the head of family to recover his loss as long as the winnings had not accidentally been destroyed (Paul, D. 11.5.4.1).

191 Buckland, Slavery, 179.

192 The enrichment theory, in a modified form, is intimately connected with the jurisprudential analysis of the nature of the *peculium* which we have presented in the name of Micolier. Micolier, 307ff., adduces from the action *de in rem verso* further proof for his theory that in the later classical law the *peculium* was a juristic entity *(iuris intellectu)*. The theory itself is summarized above. Agreeing with the position taken by Tuhr who maintains that the actio *de in rem verso* was originally based upon the idea of enrichment and was, in classical times, subsequently limited to cases analogous to those in which *personae sui iuris* would have been able to recover along the lines of *negotium gestum*, Micolier seeks to protect this position of Tuhr against the attacks of other scholars mainly through different reconstructions and interpretations of the relevant texts. According to Micolier 242ff, the ability of third parties to recover on their claims by suing *de in rem verso* presupposes the existence of a *peculium* in the hands of the slave, which, in contradiction to one in the hands of a *filiusfamilias*, becomes encumbered by the payments made by these third parties; for these latter are analogous to a *negotiorum gestor*, and their payments are construed as *gestio*. (Recalling other distinctions between sons and slaves administering *peculia*, the reader will not look askance at the additional distinction described by Micolier). Holding the opinion that in later times a *peculium* could be acquired without a deliberate grant *(concessio)* on the part of the head of family, Micolier considers the existence of a *peculium* in the hands of a slave a condition necessary for the availability of the *actio de in rem verso*. He observes that, according to G. 4.74, a plaintiff in this action must prove the existence of the *peculium*, whereas

2. *Jurisprudential Implications of the* Actio de in Rem Verso

The discrepancy we noticed in the *peculium* arrangement between legal theory and economic practice was even more marked with regard to the *actio de in rem verso*. Theoretically and historically independent of the *actio de peculio*, it was, nevertheless, always brought in conjunction with it. Juridically free from the *peculium* and not even predicated upon the very existence of a *peculium*, it invariably involved a subordinate who was administering a *peculium*.

Thus, although we indicated in our assessment of the *peculium* arrangement that it could be instituted in the interests of and for the personal aggrandizement of the subordinate, our examination of the *actio de in rem verso* has shown us that it was equally available as an instrument of agency. Here indeed, the role of the subordinate with *peculium* as a general agent managing a branch establishment of his principal emerges in bold relief: The *peculium* was separate from the accounts and business enterprises of the principal; title remained vested in the *paterfamilias* principal; the profits or a share of the profits derived from the business operations of the subordinate with *peculium* or from his individual transactions were regularly or irregularly applied to the accounts or purposes of the head of family. The *peculium* arrangement thus took on the true character of agency in its economic, if not its strictly legal, role.

In legal theory, the liability of the head of family on the transactions entered into by his subordinate was derived not from agency but from enrichment. Having seen from our analysis of the *peculium* arrangement that the concepts of agency and representation were foreign to the minds of the classical Roman jurists, we found that the enrichment of the principal by the application of the proceeds

in Inst. 4.7.5. such a requirement no longer exists; for Justinian already follows the late classical development whereby every subordinate has a *peculium* as a matter of course. The two parallel Institutes passages, however, may be understood differently. Moreover, besides the doubts raised by Beseler against Tuhr's thesis, Kaser, Rev. P., 397–398, has pointed out that the conclusions to which Micolier arrived are not convincing — especially in view of the well-known inaccuracy of the Byzantine handling of the texts. See also Longo, Ap., 402–404.

of his subordinate's business transactions and contracts to his (the principal's) advantage offered the best explanation of his liability. When we learn, therefore, that the knowledge and intent of the third party that the proceeds of his transaction with the subordinate were to be applied to the accounts of the latter's principal were irrelevant with regard to the availability of the action *de in rem verso* and that the knowledge and consent of the principal himself were equally irrelevant, we need not interpret these rules as being based upon a theory of implied agency. The theory of enrichment affords us sufficient explanation.

Not so in economic practice. On the practical level, the availability of the action *de in rem verso* is most instructive in pinpointing the *peculium* arrangement as functioning as an implied agency. To put the matter in more exact and specific terms, let us translate the *peculium* arrangement into modern business terms. The action *de peculio et de in rem verso* which was brought against a citizen on the basis of the contract entered into by his subordinate agent was based upon a formula whose condemnation clause was composed of two parts: (1) liability *de peculio*, which implied the most common method of forming an agency, by appointment. The act whereby the head of family granted his subordinate in *potestas* a *peculium (concessio peculii)* or, as others would insist, plenary powers of administration *(libera administratio)* was essentially an act appointing a business agent. This act of appointment created a limited liability for the principal, limited, that is, by the extent of the assets of the *peculium*; (2) liability *de in rem verso*, which implied another method of forming an agency, namely by ratification. Ratification may be express or implied. It is express when the person for whom the agent is purporting to act makes a statement in writing or orally to the effect that he accepts or ratifies or will carry out the terms of the contract made in his name by the agent. Ratification is implied when the designated principal accepts any payments or other benefits under the contract or proceeds to carry out some of the terms of the contract. Thus, the liability *de in rem verso* predicates an agency formed by implied ratification. We must emphasize, however, that this analysis is functional; it is not meant to imply that jurisprudentially Roman law was operating with the concepts of agency and representation.

CHAPTER III

AUTHORIZED COMMERCIAL TRANSACTIONS

The utilization of persons in one's power as agents in commerce was a major accomplishment of praetorian law. According to the Roman civil law, "Our slaves can better our condition, but cannot make it worse."[1] The rule, formulated in terms of slaves, applied equally to all subordinates in the power of the head of the family. In effect, it stated that no master or father could be held liable for any transaction carried out by his slave or son. As already indicated in the previous chapter, if this principle of the civil law had been applied consistently, it would have stifled all transactions with slaves and sons, and a gigantic proportion of commercial activities would not have taken place. Recognizing, therefore, both the desire and the practice of the citizenry to utilize slaves and, to a lesser extent, sons as viable economic tools and motivated by a sense of equity and fairness, the Roman praetor gradually came to hold people responsible for acts concluded by persons in their *potestas*. Third parties, confident that the courts would henceforth entertain actions against citizens for the acts of persons in their power acting in their behalf, were no longer reluctant to deal with these subordinates. With the security of transactions thereby enhanced, commercial activity was greatly facilitated.

The responsibility of citizens for the business acts of their subordinates was limited, however, by two broad conditions: (a) that the head of the *familia* had authorized the act — specifically or generally,

---

1   Gaius, D. 50.17.133.

expressly or implicitly — by instructions beforehand or by ratification thereafter, or[2] (b) that the head of the *familia* had profited thereby.

In the previous chapter, we saw to what extent the *peculium* arrangement could be construed, juridically and economically, as a type of implied general agency: The citizen's grant of a *peculium* to a person in his power was viewed as analogous to an implied general authorization; and the conversion of the profits accruing from peculiary transactions to the accounts of the familial head, serving as the basis for the *actio de in rem verso*, was viewed as analogous to an implied ratification. In the present chapter, it is proposed to examine commercial transactions that were carried out by authorized agents *outside* of the institution of the *peculium*. As such, this investigation will not be limited to the acts of subordinates in power, although it is the acts of such persons that will dominate our study.

A. INTRODUCTION: THE EXERCITORIAN AND INSTITORIAN ARRANGEMENTS

A century and a half before the Roman Republic gave way to the Principate, the hegemony of Rome had been extended to all of Italy and its islands, to Carthage and to Macedonia. As a result, commercial activities took a markedly new turn.[3] Whereas the Romans had never before been attracted to sea-trade, mercantile undertakings now became the most prominent and desired means of amassing wealth.[4] At this time, business transactions were undertaken in much greater numbers; qualitatively, much larger sums of money were involved in each transaction; and commercial dealings were increasingly taking place between businessmen far apart from and unknown to each other. In the interests of uninhibited commercial activity, therefore, it became necessary to provide a firmer basis for a greater degree of mutual trust and for a stronger sense of reliability between

---

2. Not "and": either condition in and of itself was sufficient to give rise to a cause of action against the head of family.

3. Summaries of the metamorphosis that overtook Rome by this time may be found in Besnier, 5–17, and in Brunt, Soc., chs. 1 and 4.

4. Casson, Anc., 182–188.

contracting parties. Thus, it was necessary to assure a trader that he would not have to conduct arduous and practically impossible investigations of his customer's personal status and financial condition. It was also necessary to assure him that the obligation which his customer had assumed, whether in his own name or — as was increasingly becoming the usual practice — in the name of someone else, would be satisfactorily discharged.

It was undoubtedly with these economic circumstances and their concomitant demands upon the legal system in mind that Ulpian, centuries later, wrote the preamble to the Edict on the Exercitorian Action which embodies the juristic tradition as to its origins.

> People every now and then enter into contractual relations with masters of vessels to meet the necessities incurred on a voyage without knowing what is their class or character, and it was therefore right that the person who appointed the master for the ship should be bound by the contract just as is a person who has placed an *institor* (commercial agent) at the head of a shop or a business, it being in fact more necessary to make an agreement with the master of a ship than with a commercial agent; as the circumstances of the case make it easy for the party to form an opinion as to what the class of the persons is to which the *institor* belongs and make a contract accordingly, but with the master of a ship the case is different, since, not uncommonly, place and time do not admit of a fuller judgment being arrived at.[5]

The historical circumstances which we have described, compounded with the mighty victories and phenomenal conquests of the Roman armies *after* the Punic and Macedonian wars, are convincing data for the hypothesis that the provisions of the law which are embodied in the so-called Exercitorian and Institorian Actions — and which are the cornerstone of such authorized commercial agency as is to be found — were already available, at the latest, by the second century B.C.E.[6]

These provisions are described rather fully by Gaius. Because of its unequalled importance for our study of agency in the Roman

---

5   Ulpian, D. 14.1.1 pr. It is to Costa, Az., 34–35, that we are indebted for first placing this Ulpian passage in its proper historical perspective, Beseler's characterization of the passage as a paraphrase (hence, a post-classical reworking) notwithstanding; *cf.* Beit. IV, 209.

6   Arango-Ruiz, 7.

classical law through general authorization, albeit in restricted fields, we quote the Gaius passage in its entirety:

> The *formula exercitoria* applies when the father or master has put his son or slave in charge of a ship, and there has been some transaction with the son or slave arising out of the business over which he has been put. For, since in this case ... the transaction appears to be effected in accordance with the father's or master's desire, it has been considered entirely equitable that an action enforcing full liability should be allowed. Furthermore, this praetorian action is allowed against one who has put even a stranger, whether slave or free, in charge of his ship. It is called *exercitoria* because the person to whom the current earnings of a ship go is called the *exercitor*.
>
> The *formula institoria* applies when a man has put his son or slave, or a stranger whether slave or free, in charge of a shop or other business, and some transaction arising out of the business over which he has been put has been entered into with that person. It is called *institoria* because a person put in charge of a shop is called the *institor*. This *formula* too enforces full liability.[7]

We have here two cases of the general authorization of persons, akin to agents, to carry on the business enterprises of their respective

---

7 G. 4.71: *Tunc autem exercitoria locum habet, cum pater dominusve filium servumve magistrum navi praeposuerit, ed quid cum eo eius rei gratia cui praepositus fuerit negotium gestum erit, cum enim ea ... res ex voluntate patris dominive contrahi videatur, aequissimum esse visum est in solidum actionem dari, quin etiam, licet extraneum quisque magistrum navi proposuerit, sive servum sive liberum, tamen ea praetoria actio in eum redditur. ideo autem exercitoria actio appellatur, quia exercitor vocatur is ad quem cottidianus navis quaestus pervenit. institoria vero formula tum locum habet, cum quis tabernae aut cuilibet negotiationi filium servumve aut quemlibet extraneum sive servum sive liberum praeposuerit, et quid cum eo eius rei gratia cui praepositus est contractum fuerit. ideo autem institoria vocatur. quia qui tabernae praeponitur institor appellatur. quae et ipsa formula in solidium est.* The sources for the exercitorian and institorian actions together with this Gaius passage are Inst. 4.7.2., D. 14.1. and 14.3, and C. 4.25. The two actions are generally treated together, for they are governed by the same rules. The rare differences between them are mainly due to the differences in the two types of enterprise. The requirements for sustaining both actions and their functions in the realm of agency are identical. The sources which describe one illuminate and are valid for the other. See Costa, Az., 36. See further Longo, Act., 582–584, who argues for the Gaian origin of the entire passage we have quoted.

principals — one on sea, the other on land. The authorization was not described as formal. Rather, it appeared as a *de facto* enterprise setting up in business *(praepositio)* an agent *(praepositus)* by an owner *(praepositor)* of a ship or of any commercial establishment. In other words, it sufficed simply to install the agent in the enterprise and to permit him to discharge the duties which it involved.

In the former case, that of the exercitorian action, the *exercitor*, the owner of the ship, is described more accurately as "the person to whom the current earnings of a ship go." This definition has the advantage of including cases of leasing and hiring and agency as well as ownership. The situation envisaged, then, is that of a citizen who, on his own account, had or took over a ship for mercantile purposes over oceans, lakes or rivers. His agent was the shipmaster *(magister navis)* to whom he had entrusted the ship and its operation. Alternatively, a citizen shipowner could have appointed a professional shipper to manage the shipping operations, to hire ship captains and to enter into mercantile transactions. In this case, the term *exercitor* refers to the shipper, i.e., the agent of the shipowner. It was the duty of the shipmaster or, alternatively, the shipper to accomplish all those acts for which the operation of the ship was undertaken (such as transportation of cargo or carrying passengers) and to create, if necessary, all those obligations arising out of and connected with such operation (such as ship repair and maintenance). This agency status was reserved only for the shipmaster and the shipper; a contract with one of the seamen did not give rise to the action, for the seaman had never been so authorized.[8]

In the latter case, that of the institorian action, the *institor* was the person to whom an owner *(dominus)* had entrusted the management of a business; to run a shop of some kind, to rent houses, to superintend buildings, to buy and sell corn or other commodities, to lend money on interest, to run a clothing or weaving establishment, to peddle wares, etc., etc. It was not necessary, however, that the *institor* carry out his duties at a fixed place or in a designated shop. He could have performed his function as a travelling agent without any changes in the legal rules governing the institorian arrangement.[9]

8 Ulpian, D. 14.1.1.1, 6 and 15–23. *Cf.* Solazzi, Scritti, V, 71–83; Casson, Ships, 314–321, and 328, n. 24.
9 P.S. 2.8.2; Ulpian, D. 14.3.3–5.16.

In either arrangement, exercitorian or institorian, principal and agent could have been male or female;[10] the liability of the principal was for the whole loss sustained by third parties who dealt with his agent;[11] and the actions had no time limit: at the death of the principal, they were available against his heirs, and at the death or alienation of the slave-agent, they were neither extinguished nor lost.[12]

The usual case mentioned in the sources is that of a principal who was a citizen *sui iuris*, a head of family. Nevertheless, as already mentioned, it was possible, especially in the exercitorian arrangement, for the principal (i.e., the *exercitor*-shipper) himself to be a person in someone else's *potestas*. If so, the *paterfamilias* of the *exercitor* would be liable *in solidum* to these actions only if he had given his consent or authorized the establishment of the business with the agent. If he had not done so, he could be held liable only to the extent of the *peculium* of his subordinate.[13]

B. HISTORICAL ORIGINS

The military conquests and territorial expansion of Rome mentioned at the beginning of this section had a profound and lasting effect upon the Roman economy. The conquests brought masses of slaves to Rome, and, as the subjugated territories increased, these slaves became the instrumentalities whereby small farms were converted into massive plantations and local manufacture and peddling were transformed into large industries and far-flung commercial enterprises.

---

10 P.S. 2.8.1; Ulpian, D. 14.1.1,16 and 14.3.7.1.

11 G. 4.71; Inst. 4.7.2; P.S. 2.6.8.1; Ulpian, D. 14.1.1.20,23; unless, of course, the agent is a person in *potestas* conducting the business on the basis of a *peculium*. I am aware of the objections of Martino, Stud., 20–31. They have been effectively refuted both on textual and theoretic grounds by Pugliese, 303–326. *Cf.*, however, Martino's reply, Anc., 274–300.

12 Ulpian, D. 14.1.4.3–4 and 14.3.15.

13 P.S. 2.8.3; Ulpian, D. 14.1.1.16, 19–20; and Paul, *h.t.*, 6 pr. On the point of the principal's liability *in solidum*, I have followed Wunner, 125ff, and Longo, Act., 597–598; and not Beseler, Rom., 57ff, nor Martino, Anc., 291, 299.

As a result of these great economic transformations, Roman law underwent numerous changes, one of which was the creation of the exercitorian and institorian actions. These provisions fitted perfectly into the gap they were meant to fill. In an essentially agrarian society, these provisions were unnecessary for normal, simple acquisitions and too clumsy for the efficient transfer of those obligations characteristic of agricultural activities. For the requirements of maritime commerce and inland trade, however, they were ideally suited.[14]

Like the other *actiones adiecticiae qualitatis* which we have described earlier — the *actio de peculio et de in rem verso* — the *actio exercitoria* and the *actio institoria* were part and parcel of the *ius honorarium*, the creation of the Roman praetor.[15] All these actions were nothing less than procedural innovations calculated to facilitate the employment of slaves, sons and others as agents. They thus served as excellent illustrations of the judicial magistrate's method whereby he succeeded in accommodating the legal machinery to new situations and to the new needs they engendered.[16]

Our earliest textual evidence for these actions, dating from the first century B.C.E.,[17] presents them as already fully developed. The existence of the *actio exercitoria* at the time of the late Republic is attested to by an Ulpian passage which shows that it was already recognized and dealt with by Aulus Ofilius. This jurist, who was a friend of Caesar and survived into the time of the beginning of the Principate, laid down the rule that when a shipmaster borrows money, expressly stating that he is doing so for the operation of his ship, the shipowner or shipper is liable for the debt incurred even if the shipmaster has made fraudulent use of the money. Thus, commercial transactions with ship captains. although requiring some minimum precautions, could be entered into more readily, for confidence had been established that the judicial authorities were ready and able to expedite matters by making remedies available when foul play

14 Mitteis, 23–24.
15 In all likelihood, *not* the *praetor peregrinus* but rather the *praetor urbanus*; *cf.* Daube, Praet., 66–70.
16 *Cf.* Jolowicz, Hist. Introd., 46–38, 95–105, 366–369; Wesenberg, 1590–1602. See Balogh, 263–276, 295–307. Balogh, 307–312, correctly adds to the praetorian activity the contribution of the jurists' *interpretatio*.
17 Watson, Ob., 184.

resulted.[18] The existence of the *actio institoria* in the times of the Republic is attested to by another Ulpian passage, which shows that it was recognized by Servius Sulpicius Rufus, holding fully liable any principal who puts someone in control of any kind of business. Servius was a prominent jurist who flourished during the last half-century of the Republic. He was the teacher of the aforementioned Ofilius.[19] We have already indicated in a note that both actions are treated together because of the great similarity between them.[20] As to their *relative* age, however, there is no clear evidence. It is conjectured that the *actio exercitoria* is older than the *actio institoria*.[21]

Inasmuch, then, as these actions were regarded in the first century B.C.E. as well-established provisions of praetorian law, they are obviously antecedent to the first century jurists mentioned in the previous paragraph who discussed them. Thus, the textual evidence would tend to confirm the points alluded to above, namely that as a result of military and economic expansion the two institutions were developed in the second century B.C.E.[22]

18 Ulpian, D. 14.1.1.9; for a summary of critical questions of text and interpolation with regard to this passage, see Watson, ibid., 190–191, and Longo, Act., 591–592. With regard to Aulus Ofilius, see Münzer, 2040.

19 The Ulpian passage referred to is found in D. 14.3.5.1. It has never been held to be interpolated; Watson, ibid., 192. On Servius see Münzer-Kübler, 851–860.

20 See p. 92 above at end of note 7. It should be borne in mind, however, that the Ulpian passage cited on p. 91 gives an additional *ratio* for the exercitorian action, namely the needs and the peculiar circumstances of maritime commerce, a *ratio* which, of course, is inapplicable to the institorian action.

21 Costa, Az., 31–36; Mitteis, R.P., 25. n. 40; Fabricius, 25; Huvelin, 177ff; Solazzi, Scritti, IV, 243–264.

22 Economic expansion was, of course, a gradual process. In the early stages of this process, the vast majority of shipowners were Hellenistic, sometimes southern Italians, rarely Roman; indeed, most of the shippers and sea-captains who came in contact with the Romans were foreigners. This has led a number of scholars to attribute the institution of the exercitorian action to the *praetor peregrinus*; e.g., Frank, Ec. Survey, I, 200–205, 274–282; *idem*, Italy, 346–350; Pugliese, 290, n. 2. See, however, Daube, Praet., for a brief but convincing argument to the contrary.

C. A JURIDICAL ANALYSIS OF THE PRINCIPAL-AGENT RELATIONSHIP IN THE EXERCITORIAN AND INSTITORIAN ARRANGEMENTS

Acts and transactions involving general, authorized agency of a non-contractual nature in classical Rome were performed mainly by slaves and freedmen, to a lesser degree by sons, and on a day-to-day domestic basis by wives. The relationship between slaves and sons performing such acts and their respective masters and fathers was governed by *potestas*, not by contract. Wives in the classical period were no longer in the *manus* of their husbands. Nevertheless, they, too, were obviously not acting under contract when they occasionally represented their husbands.[23]

The activities of freedmen, however, present a rather complicated picture. Although it will be our purpose to glean from the sources those passages which show that freedmen were retained in the service of their former masters,[24] the blurred nature of the actual situation in Rome makes it inevitable that here and there we will be making statements that are equally true of freedmen who did in fact become totally independent of their former masters.[25] Indeed, just as Tiro[26] and Philotimus[27] remained in the service of their former masters, Cicero and Terentia respectively, for the remainder of their lives, Trimalchio[28] became wholly free in all his financial ventures, employing in turn numerous freedmen to serve *him*. Bearing in mind, then, the large group of freedmen who succeeded in achieving total economic independence from their patrons, we may conclude that there was also a large group of former slaves who performed a wide variety of services on behalf of their patrons and that among these services were an appreciable number that may be classified under the general heading of agency and representation.

23 See below pp. 124–127.
24 See below pp. 127–140.
25 See below pp. 148–160.
26 See below pp. 135–138.
27 See below pp. 138–139.
28 See above p. 36. On the independent freedman generally, see Veyne, 224–231.

Juridically viewed, this wide variety of services performed by freedmen as agents of their former masters implies a number of possible relationships obtaining between principal and agent. The most obvious one is that which went under the term *procuratio*. The closest approximation to a formal agent in the modern legal sense of the term,[29] the *procurator (omnium rerum)* is defined by Ulpian as "a man who manages another person's affairs under the authorization *(mandatu)* of his principal."[30] Thus, the relationship was generally governed by the contract of *mandatum*; under certain circumstances it was governed by the rules of *negotiorum gestio*, also essentially contractual. The *procurator* was a general, authorized agent. In the course of his everyday duties, he would supervise those slaves of his principal who were assigned to the particular undertaking or business operation which was entrusted to him. He also served as his principal's representative in court in cases which arose out of those commercial activities which he had been carrying on on behalf of said principal. Mentioned frequently in juristic and in non-juristic literature, epigraphy confirms the fact that the procurator was invariably a freedman.[31] Since he was, however, an agent who was tied to his principal by contract,[32, 33] he stands outside the scope of our study.

Also subsumed under contract were those services which freedmen rendered on behalf of their patrons as a result of the obligation to do so created by the oath they had taken at manumission *(iusiurando liberti gratia)*.

It has been one of the express hypotheses of this study, however,

---

29 See, for example, Neratius, D. 41.1.13; Ulpian, *h.t.*, 20.2; Ulpian, D. 41.2.1.20.

30 D. 3.3.1 pr.

31 See, for example, *C.I.L.*, VI, 9830–9838; Treggiari, 150–153.

32 It is very possible that, before the contract of *mandatum* came to govern the relationship of freedman-procurator with his former master, the principal, the *actio institoria utilis* was employed; see the analysis of Papinian, D. 14.3.19 pr., in Fabricius, 23.

33 On the *procurator* as agent, see bibliography in Kaser, I, 265, nn. 44–45. (Add: Angelini, Proc.; Behrends, 215–299; Quadrato, 210–224). On the relationships of *procuratio*, *mandatum* and *negotiorum gestio* to one another, see Kaden, 342–345 (for the main problems and early literature); Arangio-Ruiz, 3–78; Watson, Mand., 6–10, 36–60.

that the above-mentioned contractual categories did not and could not exhaust the multifarious acts of agency that freedmen performed for their patrons in classical Rome. The object lessons afforded by such individuals as Cicero's Tiro and Terentia's Philotimus, as well as the numerous corroborating instances alluded to above, serve as reasonable proof that there were an appreciable number of such economic services that went above and beyond anything that could be included in the formal contractual categories.

In the description of the exercitorian and institorian arrangements which follows, therefore, the relationship between principal and agent could be, in the case of master and slave or father and son, that of *potestas*; in the case of husband and wife — rare indeed, if at all — non-contractual; in the case of patron and freedman, non-contractual or contractual. Moreover, the relationship between principal and agent could also be between two citizens *sui iuris*. In such an event, unless the parties were relatives or close friends to each other, the relationship was undoubtedly governed by contract.

Regardless of the basis upon which the principal-agent relationship was built, the principal's obligation in the exercitorian and institorian enterprises was based upon his intention and consent *(voluntas)* to be involved in the business dealings of his agent; mere knowledge *(scientia)* without consent is insufficient.[34] But, on the other hand, whereas in the latter the principal's consent invariably manifested itself in an express authorization before the act or in an express ratification thereof after the fact, the principal's consent in the case of general authorization was implied, the implication being generally derived from the very act of the principal setting up his agent in the enterprise *(praepositio)* on land or on sea. And so, if the principal is a ward *(pupillus)*, whose intention and consent were regarded legally as incomplete, the complementary assent *(auctoritas)* of his guardian

---

34 Ulpian, D. 14.1.1.20, and Paul, *h.t.*, p 6r. The wording of the Ulpian passage is confusing. At first, mention is made that a difference exists in this matter between the exercitorian and institorian arrangements. The text, however, then proceeds to lay down the same rules for both. Moreover, the distinction between *voluntas* and *scientia* may very well be non-classical; see Beseler, Rom., 56–58. Nevertheless, I have accepted the conclusions of Longo, Act., 598–602.

was necessary.[35] If the guardian's assent had not been given, third parties could not invoke the *actio exercitoria* or *institoria* in the event of breach of contract. The only remedy available to them might be the *actio de in rem verso* if, that is, the profits of transaction of the ward's agent had been applied to the accounts of the ward.[36] Again, if the principal was a son or slave who had acted without the consent of the head of family, then the latter could be held liable to the exercitorian or institorian action only to the extent of the principal's *peculium*.[37] Thus, the basic principle is preserved throughout: Liability is based upon consent, express or implied.[38]

It follows, therefore, that the principal's liability was limited to those acts of his agent which were performed in the line of duty which devolved upon the latter and to those contracts which fell within the scope of the business which had been entrusted to him.[39] Here, too, it made no difference whether the principal-agent relationship was based upon *potestas* or contract.[40] In the case of shipping, for example, the action would not be available if the ship had taken on a type of merchandise for which the owner had never given the shipmaster any authorization, if the ship had sailed in unauthorized waters, or if the ship had been leased without authorization.[41] Similarly in the case of an enterprise conducted on land, if, for example, a shopkeeper *institor* had been appointed to sell certain merchandise and, instead, went out and made certain purchases, the *actio institoria* against the principal would not be available.[42]

The "scope of the business," however, must be construed sensibly

---

35 Ulpian, D. 14.3.9.
36 Gaius, D. 14.3.10.
37 Ulpian, D. 14.1.1.19–22. For valuable textual analysis *cf.* Martino, Stud., 20–31; Martino, Anc., 291–297, and Pugliese, 303–309; but also Longo,
38 See further Costa, Az., 57–61, and Buckland, Slavery, 169–170, 174–175.
39 Ulpian, D. 14.3.5.11; Lenel, E.P., 257–259.
40 Costa, ibid., 61–64, and Buckland, ibid., 170 and 174.
41 Ulpian, D. 14.1.1.12. For an enlightening comparison of the relative degree of discretion granted to the Roman *magister navis* and the modern sea-captain, see Martino, ibid., 14.
42 Ulpian, D. 14.3.5.12; also Papinian, D. 14.3.19.3. See the brief but illuminating survey of the gradation of liability among the various *actiones adiecticiae qualitatis* presented by Powell, 54–56.

and realistically. It included not only those acts which were literally part of the normal discharge of the commercial activity to which the agent had been assigned. It also included such transactions which were legitimately connected with that activity. And so, if the agent borrowed money to carry out his commissioned activity, it was — unless specifically prohibited — considered within the scope of the business and obligated the principal. In most cases, the situation was clear, and the creditor had no trouble in proving the liability of the principal — *res ipsa loquitur*. And even if the agent subsequently did *not* apply the money to the purpose for which he had borrowed it, the principal was still liable, the only condition being that the creditor had taken care to see that the alleged reason for the loan had been reasonably necessary and that the amount borrowed was appropriate to the needs.[43] It was not necessary, however, that the creditor see that the money was actually spent for the purpose for which it had been borrowed.[44]

Similar principles governed the employment of sub-agents.

Ulpian informs us that Julian was called upon to deal with shipmasters, themselves appointed by shipowners or shippers, who, in the course of operation and within the scope of their assignments, had appointed others as shipmasters.[45] In opening the discussion as to whether the principal, shipowner or shipper ought to be held liable for transactions entered into by the appointee of the ship-

43 Ulpian, D. 14.1.1.7–11 and 14.3.5.12–15. For a brief comparison with English Law, see Powell, 53–54.

44 African, D. 14.1.7 pr.–2. See Costa, ibid., 64–69, and Buckland, ibid., 173–174. For the problems involved in delineating the exact degree of the principal's liability, see Martino, Stud., 7–14, Martino, Anc., 283–288, and Pugliese, 298–303. Despite the differences between these two scholars, their analyses reveal that the classical law underwent a change. According to Ofilius, a jurist of the last century of the Republic, and Pedius, ca. 100 C.E., the loan would not obligate the principal unless the agent had entered into the contract of loan with the express intention of using the money to carry out his commissioned activity. This rigorous requirement was superseded by the more lenient one, cited in the text above, i.e., the mere requirement of proof of objective need, e.g., for repairs. This development was accomplished, apparently, by Julian, *fl. ca.* 130 C.E., and reported by African, ibid. See also Watson, Ob., 190–191, and Longo, Act., 543–595.

45 D. 14.1.1.5.

master, Ulpian first described a case where the decision was self-evident and legally sound, namely where the sub-appointment was made by the agent with the knowledge and consent of the principal. The sub-appointment under such circumstances was clearly valid; and the acts and transactions performed by the sub-agent rendered the principal liable, for "he [the principal] is regarded as having put the person there himself."[46]

Ulpian then proceeds to describe the case which came before Julian, namely where the sub-appointment was made by the agent without the knowledge of the principal. Julian's decision was that it, too, was valid. Ulpian expressed his approval of Julian's decision in the following manner:

> This appears to me to be a reasonable view; if I appointed a ship-master, I am bound to make good whatever he does, otherwise those who contract with him will be disappointed; and the rule ought to be applied in the case of a shipmaster still more readily than in the case of an *institor* on grounds of public utility.[47]

Now, the first case was a standard one. It conformed to the normal rules of agency and would have undoubtedly applied to a sub-shop-keeper as well. The second case, somewhat irregular in that the conditions of the agency and its limitations were not stated expressly, could still be understood in terms of a concept of agency — although Ulpian is cited as explaining it in terms of practical utility. This explanation was probably the product of post-classical thinking. But the rule itself allowing for the substitution of a sub-agent *exercitor ignorans* was in all likelihood of classical authenticity. Although, according to the classical law, the contractual liability of the *exercitor* was based upon and defined by the terms of the *praepositio* — and the *praepositio* under discussion did not provide explicitly for the employ-

---

46 *ipse eum imposuisse videtur.*

47 *quae sententia mihi videtur probabilis: omnia enim facta magistri debeo praestare qui eum praeposui, alioquin contrahentes decipientur: et facilius hoc in magistro quam [in] institore admittendum propter utilitatem.* The insertion is by the editor. The passage is poor syntactically. (Perhaps we are to take the words *ceterum . . . videtur* as a parenthetical remark of Ulpian creating the context in which Julian's decision must be understood and regard this *quae sententia* passage as referring to Julian's decision.)

ment of a sub-agent — the rule represented nothing more than the tendency of the later jurists to widen the limits of the transactions of the agent. As a result of this tendency, the use of a sub-agent was evidently regarded as implied in the original appointment.[48]

The Digest discussion then proceeds to cite a third case. On the basis of Julian's decision, Ulpian found grounds for regulation with regard to another possibility, namely, where the sub-appointment was made by the agent against the express instructions of the principal. Here, too, states the Digest, it must be held valid, for the interests of the promotion of marine commerce reign supreme. This decision was most certainly post-classical.[49]

Any condition imposed by the principal on the agent's power of contracting had to be observed. The agent could be barred from entering into contracts with a specific person or class; or, on the contrary, he could be limited to dealings with a specific person or class. Several agents could be appointed, each one with a specific task and with a specified authorization to act. The principal could

---

48 Pugliese, 294–298, and Wunner, 114–125. *Contra* Solazzi, Scritti, IV, 246–249, and Martino, Stud., 14–20 and *idem.*, Martino, Anc., 278–283, who allege that the substantive rule itself allowing the employment of sub-agents without an explicit authorization of the principal is post-classical. Viewing this second decision cited in the name of Ulpian as an unclassical reason for an unclassical decision, Martino emends the text to read: *magistrum autem accipimus* [non] *solum quem exercitor praeposuit* [sed et] *(non) eum quem magister.* His view that the classical law would not surrender its fundamental dogma that the principal's liability to the *actio exercitoria* is strictly limited to the terms of the *praepositio* to the interests of "public utility" is correct, but not necessarily so regarding a sub-appointment made without the knowledge of the principal. *Cf.* further on this passage Beseler, Beit., II, 70; Rabel, 9, n. 4; Wunner, 115ff; and the very interesting citation from papyrological literature in Wieacker, 137, n. 28.

49 This appears to be the unanimous opinion of the scholars cited in note 48 (*contra* Ankum, I, 20). Passages such as Ulpian, D. 14.1.1.7.14 make it clear that the terms of the *praepositio* are determinant as to the measure of the principal's liability. An appointment that was made *exercitor ignorans* may be construed as being implied in the *praepositio*; *exercitor prohibens* obviously cannot be so construed. See also Longo, Act., 588–590. For a careful study of the weight given to considerations of *utilitas* in classical and late classical law, see Ankum, 1–31, and Lepien, 51–72.

insist that his agents always act together, and that a contract entered into by an agent individually not be binding. Modification of the enterprise was also permitted, but notification thereof had to be made to the public in clear language and in a conspicuous place. In the case of an *institor*, the most common form would be a notice set up over the shop door.[50] "But if he has forbidden contract now with this man and now with that, with continual changes, all of them are entitled to the institorian action against him, for persons making contracts ought not to be misled."[51]

To summarize briefly, the basic principles of liability in the exercitorian and institorian arrangement were two: (1) the liability of the principal was based upon consent, express or implied,[52] and (2) it was limited to those transactions of his agent which were legitimately connected with the scope of the business, which he, the principal, had authorized. These principles were carefully explicated, and a close reading of the sources indicates that they were sufficient in themselves to serve as the basis of the principal's liability. Most scholars are of the opinion that references to general utility and the promotion of maritime interests[53] are superfluous; they were undoubtedly post-classical accretions.[54]

D. RELATIONS BETWEEN THE PRINCIPAL AND THIRD PARTIES

As indicated at the beginning of our treatment of general authorization, the purpose of the praetorian institution of the exercitorian and institorian actions was to promote commerce by assuring third parties of the availability of remedies in the event of breach of contract. Henceforth, if they did business with shippers or shopkeepers, then, in addition to the normal civil actions that could be brought against the latter, rights of action would be granted against their employers. This was especially important in the cases where the shippers and shopkeepers were subordinates in power. Since such persons could

---

50 Ulpian, D. 14.1.1.13–14; Ulpian, D. 14.3.11.2–3; Paul, D. 15.1.47 pr.
51 Ulpian, D. 14.3.11.5. See also Buckland, Slavery, 170–171.
52 See further Wieacker, 135–137 (*contra* Wunner, 105–133).
53 Ulpian, D. 14.1.1 pr.: *utilitatem huius edicti*; ibid., 5: *dicendum tamen erit eo usque producendam utilitem navigantium*. See Pugliese, 291–298.
54 Wiesmüller, 367.

not be sued either because of legal incapacity (slaves) or because of economic dependence (sons), the rights of action granted against their respective heads of family were the only legal remedies that were truly worthwhile. Then again, even if shippers and shop-keepers were not subordinates of a head of family, their economic resources were rather modest. Third parties who contracted with them ran the risk that, in the event of breach of contract or other irregularities, meagre reserves would prevent adequate compensation. Knowledge that the courts would obligate the principals of these agents to make good the losses incurred through the latter encouraged third parties to contract with them freely. Thus, the crucial impedi-ments to uninhibited trading, namely the uselessness of suits against shipmasters and shopkeepers who were in power and the unpredic-tability of the economic position of those who were *sui iuris*, were overcome by the availability of actions against their principals.[55]

As for the ability of the principal to sue third parties who had contracted with his agent, the praetorian provisions of exercitorian and institorian actions were *not* available, for they were unnecessary. If, as was usually the case, the agent was a slave of the principal or his son in his *potestas*, there was no problem, for all acquisitions and rights of action that the agent had obtained were automatically transferred to the principal.[56] If, as happened more frequently as time went on,[57] the agent was not a subordinate in the power of his principal, they could be assigned to the principal.[58] If the agent re-

---

55 The Praetorian Edict providing for the *actio exercitoria* has been re-constructed as follows: *Quod cum magistro navis gestum erit eius rei nomine, cui ibi praepositus fuerit, in eum, qui eam navem exercuerit, iudicium dabo.* If the exercitor was *alieni iuris*, the Edict probably read as follows: *Si is, qui navem exercuerit, in aliena potestate erit eiusque voluntate navem exercuerit, quod cum magistro eius erit, in eum, in cuius potestate is erit, qui navem exercuerit, iudicium datur.* The formula was probably *in ius concepta* and undoubtedly contained the fiction *si liber esset*; Lenel, E.P., 258ff. For a summary of contrary opinions, see Martino, Ex., 1092. Regarding the formula for the *actio institoria*, the principles are the same.

56 Ulpian, D. 14.3.1.

57 Buckland, ibid., 172, n. 2.

58 Assignation could be accomplished by *novatio* or by giving the principal a mandate to sue the *procurator in rem suam*.

fused to transfer them, the principal could recover any thing or any right of action rightfully his by proceeding against the agent himself or, if the agent were someone else's slave, against *his* master. If the principal had paid for his agent's services he could have proceeded with an *actio ex conducto*; if the services had been rendered gratuitously, he could have proceeded with an *actio mandati* or an *actio negotiorum gestorum*.[59]

Again as time went on, still in the classical period however,[60] the law did provide for direct suit of third parties by the principal. In the case of shipping, for example, officials in charge of the distribution of food (the *praefecti annonae*) were concerned lest the smooth flow of food supplies be hindered by irregular business practices. In transactions connected with these operations, therefore, direct suit of third parties by the *exercitor* of a shipmaster was allowed. Governors in the provinces also utilized their powers of extraordinary procedure *(extra ordinem)* in the interests of a more efficient method of coping with the legal problems involved in maritime transactions. They, therefore, also made direct suit of third parties available to principals in the areas under their jurisdiction. And, finally, the needs of business on land also motivated the praetor to grant an action to the principal of an *institor* against third parties when there was no other way of protecting his interests. Thus, for example, if the *institor*, not in his power, was insolvent, or if the *institor* was someone else's slave and had accepted an appointment as agent without his master's permission, the praetor allowed suit directly against the third parties involved. The reason for this concession is clear. In the former case, the bankruptcy of his agent rendered a suit against him futile. In the latter case, the slave himself was without any means unless he possessed a *peculium*, in which case any action brought against him was limited to the extent of the *peculium*. But whether the slave-*institor* possessed a *peculium* or not, his owner could never be sued because he, the owner, had not authorized the employment of his slave to serve as an agent of the principal.[61]

---

59 Ulpian, D. 14.1.1.18 and 14.3.1.
60 Buckland, ibid., 171.
61 Ulpian, D. 14.1.1.18; D. 14.3.1 at end, citing Marcellus; Gaius, D. 14.3.2; Paul, D. 46.5.5. See Costa, Az., 96; Mitteis, Trap., 200; Powell, 44–46; and, especially Watson, Man., 79–84.

The availability of an action on the part of the principal directly against third parties who had contracted with his agent, whether the agent was a shipper or a shopkeeper, was, however, exceptional. The praetorian institution of the exercitorian and institorian actions was essentially to protect the interests of third parties entering into transactions with these shipmaster and shopkeeper agents.

E. EXTINCTION OF THE AGENCY

Inasmuch as the principal-agent relationship in the exercitorian and institorian arrangements (the *praepositio*) depended for its existence primarily on the positive intent and consent (the *voluntas*) of the principal (the *exercitor* or the *dominus*), the relationship was extinguished when this consent expired, either explicitly or implicitly.[62] This was true where either the relationship was that of master to slave and father to son *(potestas)* or where the relationship was a contractual one.

Explicit cessation of consent was (1) an open act of revocation of the *praepositio*, (2) cancellation of the contract between principal and agent, or (2) removal of the business from the hands of the slave or son or removal of the slave or son from the business. Here, too, as in the case of the modification of the terms of the *praepositio*, the public had to be clearly apprised of the new situation and of the revised conditions.

Moreover, once the *institor* has been set up, the burden of a clear and public revocation, cancellation or removal of his power of agency rested upon the principal. For if the purpose of these praetorian actions was, in the language of Roscoe Pound,[63] "security of transactions," then it was only reasonable that

> the rule is not indeed that there may be dealing with an *institor* only
> if it is permitted, but that one who wishes to prevent contract with
> him must prohibit it.[64]

62 Costa, ibid., 45–46.
63 Pound, 17ff. Pound is speaking generally of legal values. He does not refer specifically to these praetorian actions.
64 Ulpian, D. 14.3.11.2–4, from which were taken the quotation as well as the idea contained in our words introducing it.

Manumission or alienation of a slave or emancipation of a son would naturally imply the cessation of the agency inasmuch as the *potestas* upon which it was based had been removed. Under such circumstances, were the agent to continue to do business in the name of his (former) master on his own initiative and without authorization, it would have constituted an act of theft *(furtum)*.[65] But, as already shown, it happened very often that the manumission was not meant to bring the enterprise and the principal-agent relationship upon which it was based to an end. If the (even tacit) intention was to continue the former business relationship, the courts construed the new relationship as contractual and the agency survived.[66] The same holds true if the principal died and the heir allowed the agent to continue management of the business.[67]

It was possible to maintain the principal-agent relationship on its former basis and yet to lose the right to an exercitorian or institorian action against the master. If, for example, the agent-shopkeeper or the third party made a stipulation (known as *novatio*) with the intention of superseding the existing institorian obligation, this act destroyed the right to an *actio institoria*, for the new obligation which was created was not that contemplated by the principal when he set up the business.[68]

Death undoubtedly extinguished the principal-agent relationship in both the exercitorian and institorian arrangements.[69]

It must be pointed out, however, that death did not automatically extinguish the rights and liabilities created by the transactions of the agent. The principal's liability to these actions was perpetual. If he died, his heirs were subject to the suit; if the third party died, *his* heirs inherited the right of action. If the agent died, or if the agent

---

65 Ulpian, D. 46.3.18, and Paul, D. 47.2.67.3. For a discussion of the Paul passage, see Jolowicz, Dig., XXVI–XXVIII and 102.

66 Papinian, D. 14.3.19.1.

67 *Arg.*, Ulpian, D. 14.3.9.11 pr. and 1; Paul, *h.t.*, 17.2.

68 Ulpian, D. 14.3.13.1.

69 Although the sources are not explicit in the matter, it is reasonable to assume that the same principle obtains in the exercitorian and institorian arrangements as in *mandatum* (G.3.160; Paul, D. 17.1.26 pr.; Gaius, D. 17.1.27.3) and in *locatio conductio* (at least till the time of Labeo, D. 19.2.60.1); Wiesmüller, 369.

was a slave who was alienated or manumitted, the principal remained liable. The basic principle was maintained throughout: The *voluntas*, the consent of the principal which constituted the basis of his liability, persisted in the face of the death of his agent or of the third party. In the case of the death of the principal himself, the liability already created by the consent he had given during his lifetime was now passed on to his heirs.[70] Certainly, the purpose for which these actions were created by the praetor, namely, "'security of transaction,'" required that this be so.

F. THE ABSENCE OF AN UNDERLYING THEORY OF AGENCY IN THE EXERCITORIAN AND INSTITORIAN ARRANGEMENTS

Nineteenth century continental students of jurisprudence were divided as to the correct interpretation of the source of the principal's liability to the exercitorian and institorian actions. One school of thought maintained that the liability of the principal had nothing to do with the idea of agency and representation but was rather based upon the will and intent *(voluntas)* of the principal. Whether the principal-agent relationship was governed by *potestas* or by contract, express or implied, this *voluntas* was implied in the very act of the principal setting up *(praepositio)* the maritime enterprise or the business establishment. In other words, according to this school, the principal's liability stemmed from the relationship between principal and agent and was independent of the intent and frame of reference of third parties entering into contracts with the agent. Thus, these actions were divorced from any notion of representation. Theoretically, the agent did not "represent" his principal as far as third parties were concerned; he rendered the principal liable to the actions because the latter set him up in business. Practically, this line of thinking allowed for the availability of these actions on the basis even of transactions with undisclosed principals. Third parties need not have had any knowledge of nor any reference to the principal at the time they entered into contracts with the shipper or shopkeeper agent.

The second school of thought asserted that the exercitorian and

---

70   Ulpian, D. 14.1.4.3–4, and 14.3.15; Costa, Az., 46ff.

institorian actions created a praetorian law of agency whereby third parties entering into contracts with a shipper or shopkeeper agent were actually relating themselves to the agent's principal and thereby rendering *him* liable on those contracts. Thus, an undisclosed principal could never be rendered liable on such contracts. Both schools, however, were agreed that the very need to create these actions on the part of the praetor was *ipso facto* proof positive that the formal *civil* law was lacking in a concept of agency. Otherwise, there would have been little point in these innovations.[71]

At the turn of the century, Romanists gave the discussion a new turn by approaching the problem with a greater sense of caution. Voicing methodological strictures against their nineteenth century predecessors, they rejected the idea that a modern notion of representation was the principle underlying these praetorian measures. These scholars roundly condemned the method of analysis which made use of the tools of a particular modern system of law — with principles, definitions, and lines of reasoning peculiar to itself — to study the classical law.

Thus, in his Appendix entitled, "The Relation of the Contractual Actions *Adiecticiae Qualitatis* to the Theory of Representation," W.W. Buckland expressed the following views:

> The Romans never reached any comprehensive principle which would cover all cases. It cannot even be said with certainty that any one principle underlies all these actions. It is not possible to be sure how the Praetor and his advisers looked at the matter, what need, exactly, he set himself to satisfy, what considerations would be most likely to define his rules, and what analogies would be likely to present themselves to his mind. For moderns, the matter is simple; the notion of representation can easily be made to cover the whole ground. But it is not easy to apply this to the classical law of Rome. As has been said by Mitteis, our law is so saturated by the conception of representation in contract that we find it difficult to admit a legal system which ignores it. Yet it is common knowledge that the classical law did not admit of representation to create liability in contract, at least (to beg no question), apart from these actions. Nevertheless, the opinions held by modern commentators on them make a constant appeal to this

---

71   Mitteis, 25–32. Representatives of the first school of thought were Mandry, Elsässer and Hellmann; of the second school — Gensler and Mitteis.

principle. No doubt all notion of representation is not to be summarily rejected. But in view of the intensely personal nature of obligation in Roman law, evidenced by a number of limitations which modern law rejects, it is difficult to believe that the Romans built up these actions on any theory of representation, and still more to suppose that that theory was the one held in any particular modern system.[72]

In accordance with these strictures, we must proceeded cautiously, studiously avoiding the danger of intruding or imposing our modern ideas upon the classical law. We must point out how the exercitorian and institorian arrangements accomplished those purposes and fulfilled those functions usually accomplished and fulfilled by the law of agency in modern legal systems. And, finally, we may then take upon ourselves the task which — following S. Perozzi's observation[73] — alone is proper under such circumstances, namely that of determining to what point a modern concept of agency and representation had indeed been achieved in the classical Roman world.

We begin, then, our examination of these arrangements by indicating the precise point where the praetor appears to have created a law of agency, namely the liability of citizens on the transactions of shipmasters, shippers and shopkeepers whom they had set up in business. These arrangements were already recognized by Labeo of the first century C.E. as representative in character. Labeo states:

> Where a provincial trader has a slave stationed at Rome as a factor (*institor*) to sell goods, any contract made with the slave is to be treated as if it were made with his owner; accordingly [the trader] must defend actions at Rome.[74]

---

72 Buckland, Slavery, 702–703. Perhaps the best illustration of the wisdom in these strictures against analyzing Roman institutions in the line of reasoning of any specific modern system may be found in the problem of the undisclosed principal with regard to the exercitorian and institorian actions. Karlowa, II., 1128–1129, in maintaining that the fact of the agent's appointment must be known to the third party in order that these actions be available to him, indicates that one of the reasons that impels him to so insist is that an unknown principal could have no juristic importance. Such a statement could not and would not be made by a lawyer familiar with the liabilities of an undisclosed principal in Anglo-American law; see Seavey, 4–5, 169–170, 186–187.

73 Perozzi, I., 141, n. 1.

74 Ulpian, D. 5.1.19.3: *Si homo provincialis servum institorem vendendarum*

Moreover, in so far as the liability could be created by agents who were outside the *familia* and hence not in the power of the principal, the agent could not have been dismissed as a mere "third arm" of the principal. At this point, therefore, the exercitorian and institorian arrangements bear a remarkable resemblance to the principal-agent relationship found in modern legal system.[75]

As indicated, however, the exercitorian and institorian agents did not create corresponding rights for their principal. Thus, the transactions of these agents did *not* create for their principal rights of action *against* the third party. The failure to create such rights, readily explained as unnecessary, is our first clear indication that a concept of agency is not at work here; the later classical legal development, creating such rights of action when the public welfare demanded them or where no other remedies were available, impresses us with the essential pragmatic approach the praetor took to these problems.

But the most convincing proof that an arrangement akin to our modern law of agency was far removed from the mind of the praetor lies in the following comment made by Paul:

> This edict [which provides for the exercitorian action] does not in fact bar any other person at all from proceeding against the shipmaster, for no transfer of any action is effected by this edict, but one is added.[76]

For essential to a concept of agency in legal theory is the requirement that the transaction of the agent, properly executed, *not* produce any effects, neither rights nor liabilities, on the representative.[77] In the exercitorian arrangement, however, the primary, i.e., civil law, results

---

mercium gratia Romae habeat: quod cum eo servo contractum est, ita habendum atque si cum domino contractum sit: quare ibi se debebit defendere.

75 Indeed, in these arrangements — as well as in cases of simple authorization *(quod iussu)* and of profits accruing directly to the principal *(de in rem verso)* — the later classical law saw the employment of the *condictio,* the regular remedy for unjustified enrichment, as an alternative for the relevant *actiones adiecticiae qualitatis; cf.,* Inst. 4.7.8.

76 Paul, D. 14.1.5.1.: *nam et cuivis alii non obstat hoc edictum, quo minus cum magistro agere possit: hoc enim edicto non transfertur actio, sed adicitur.*

77 Sohm, 247.

of the transaction, namely that the action be available against the agent as the one who contracted directly with the third party, were not extinguished by the creation of the praetorian actions. Rather they are "superadded" *(adiectus)* thereto. The agent still remained liable in full *(in solidum)* and forever *(in perpetuum)*; and third parties had the choice of suing either the principal or the agent. The same held true with regard to the institorian arrangement.[78]

For example, if someone had purchased an article from a shop-keeper-agent and wished to bring suit on the transaction, two paths were open to him. He could have sued the shopkeeper or his principal. The former suit would have been the standard one on purchases *(actio empti)*. The latter one would have been an institorian suit on the purchase *(actio empti institoria)*. The former suit would have been framed around a formula which made no mention of the principal. The institorian suit would be framed around a formula which contained the name of the shopkeeper in the introductory clause *(intentio)*, the relationship between the shopkeeper and his principal in the explanatory clause *(demonstratio)*, and the name of the principal in the condemnation clause *(condemnatio)*.[79]

Dogmatically we may look upon the principal[80] and his agent in relation to third parties as correal debtors, each one was liable in full: the agent by force of the contract into which he entered, the principal by force of his *voluntas* directed to the transaction.[81] Payment on the part of one of these correal defendants extinguished the right of action against the other.[82] Further evidence that the praetor, in making the relevant actions available against the principals of shipmasters and shopkeepers, was motivated essentially not by an underlying concept of agency, but by pragmatic considerations

---

78 Ulpian, D. 14.1.1.17, and Paul, D. 14.3.17.1. See Girard, Man., 715; Zulueta, Gaius II, 268; and Betti, Ist., 574.

79 Costa, Az., 87–91; Lenel, E.P., para. 102., esp. p. 263 (for the *actio exercitoria*, see Lenel, ibid., 258f).

80 Except where the principal himself was a subordinate in power, in which case the head of family could be held liable only to the extent of the subordinate's *peculium*.

81 Continental students of jurisprudence would call this "passive solidarity"; Schulz, para. 827.

82 Ulpian, D. 14.1.1.24 and 14.3.13.1.; see Costa, Az., 88–89.

113

of promoting commerce and by a sense of fairness and justice may be found in the rules of these actions where there was a plurality of principals and where the principal's estate was passed down in inheritance.

(1) A plurality of principals. Both on land and on sea, if an agent carried on the business of a partnership, each partner was formally liable to an action on the whole amount *(in solidum)* without any regard to his proportionate share in the business.[83] In actuality, however, he would suffer only a loss commensurate with his share in the business, for he had available to him the normal action between partners whereby he could recover the money he had paid on behalf of his partners.[84] Moreover, if, for any reason the normal action on the partnership was not available to him, then *ab initio* "it is clear law that each partner is liable to condemnation only for his part."[85]

Some have attempted to explain the legal basis of the formal liability of each partner for the whole amount *(in solidum)* as lying in the common, corporate will and intent of all the partners who were co-obligated to back up any act of their common agent.[86] Indeed, their common *voluntas* was made manifest in their joint appointment and in their undivided use of the agent. It would appear, however, that this reasoning which attempts to correlate liability with will and intent *(voluntas)* and, incidentally, to bring the rule in line with conventional principles of agency is fallacious. Since each partner's share of the profits and each principal's enjoyment of the fruits of the labor of the agent were obviously and clearly limited proportionately to his share in the business, why would his *voluntas* have extended beyond that proportionate share? Any attempt to distinguish between the partnership will to act — which addresses itself to the whole act — and a limitation on liability is fruitless, for obviously each partner's will to act was intimately related to his proportionate share of the proceeds that would result from said act.

---

83 Ulpian, D. 14.1.1.25 and 14.3.13.2. Ulpian's statements in D. 14.1.3.1. and 2 are logical extensions of this rule.

84 Paul, D. 14.1.3. and Ulpian, D. 14.3.13.2. The normal action on a partnership is known as *actio pro socio* and, sometimes, *iudicium societatis.*

85 Paul, D. 14.3.14: *pro parte sua condemnari oportere constat.*

86 Costa, Az., 92.

Why, then, we ask again, should the individual partner's will to act have extended beyond his share in the profits? One is impelled to conclude that the reason for this formal liability on the whole amount is to be found simply in commercial expedience. Gaius said so expressly, "in order that a person who contracted with one may not be compelled to split up his claim against several opponents."[87]

Ulpian's statement that if "several *exercitores* manage the ship themselves, they are to be sued each to the extent of his share in the business,"[88] should not be construed as contradicting Gaius' reasoning. For, as Ulpian himself stated, the reason for this was that "they are not to be considered as acting as shipmaster for each other." In other words, commercial convenience or not, the praetorian provisions were simply not applicable in this case, for in the eyes of the law there was no agent in such a situation.[89]

(2) Inheriting the principal's estate. The law stated that if the principal died and his heir allowed the shopkeeper-agent to continue in his functions, the heir was liable on the latter's transactions.[90] That this permission need not be formal is apparent from the fact that the law was formulated also with regard to an heir under the age of fourteen *(impubes).*[91]

Of greater significance, however, was the status of a contract entered into by said agent before the inheritance was formally accepted by the heir *(ante aditam hereditatem)*. It was valid and binding, rendering the subsequent heir liable to the exercitorian or institorian action. This held true where the third party was unaware of the principal's death on grounds of fairness and justice *(aequitas)*.[92] Paul, moreover, ruled that it also held true even where the third party knew of the principal's death "on the ground of advantage to the common course of trade."[93] This latter ruling by Paul, that an

---

87 D. 14.1.2: *ne in plures adversarios distringatur qui cum uno contraxerit,* contra Martino, Anc., 295, and Beseler, Beit., IV, 278.
88 D. 14.1.4 pr.
89 On the foregoing, cf. Wunner, 129, n. 79, with whom I cannot agree completely.
90 Ulpian, D. 14.3.5.17.
91 Paul, D. 14.3.17.2.
92 Ulpian, ibid.
93 Paul, D. 14.3.17.2. and 3., ending with the words *propter utilitatem*

heir was liable to the exercitorian and institorian actions on transactions entered into by the agent of the deceased after his death and before the heir formally accepted the inheritance, even where the third party was aware of the death of the original principal, is difficult to accept as authentic. It presents difficulties to every interpretation of the nature of the liability of the principal for the transactions of his agent. It contradicts, first of all, that school of thought which maintains that the principal's liability in the exercitorian and institorian arrangements was due to the fact that third parties dealing with the agent were actually relating themselves to the principal.[94] The contradiction is formulated as follows:

> If the right of the third party rests, in the *actio institoria*, on the knowledge of the authorization, it is difficult to see how the rule is arrived at that he has the action even though the principal was to the third party's knowledge dead when the contract was made.[95]

Paul's ruling also contradicts the school of thought which understands the liability of the principal as deriving from the principal-agent relationship itself without regard for the frame of reference of the third party. How, we may ask, would one explain the heir's liability under contract entered into after the death of the first principal and before his own acceptance of the inheritance *(aditio)*? At the time such contract was entered into there was no principal-agent relationship upon which the liability could base itself! Considerations of fairness and justice may not be invoked for the contracting party that knew that the principal had died and that no heir had accepted the inheritance. Nor may the heir's subsequent acceptance be construed as a ratification of all of the contracts made by the agent in the interim period, for Paul's ruling applied to the cases of an heir

promiscui usus. Although paragraph 3, citing Pomponius for the rule in reference to contracts entered into *vacante hereditate*, states merely, "for no blame attaches to one who, knowing that the *dominus* has died, contracts with the *institor* who is carrying on the business," it is clear that on the basis of this reading the pervading principle is "the advantage to the common course of trade" of the previous paragraph.

94 It will be recalled that this school of thought denied the availability of these actions to third parties contracting with an undisclosed principal.

95 Buckland, Slavery, 705.

who was mentally incompetent *(furiosus)* and of one who was a minor *(impubes).*

Moreover, even in the light of the interpretation we favour, namely that the praetorian establishment of the principal's liability was an eminently pragmatic measure, Paul's ruling strikes one as bad law; it was too extravagant. It comes as no surprise, therefore, that scholars[96] — not on dogmatic, but rather on independent textual grounds — have concluded that the text is the product of post-classical interpolations and that only third parties ignorant of the former principal's death were granted an institorian action under such circumstances.

The "superadded" nature of the principal's liability and the rules with regard to plurality of principals and the inheriting of the principal's estate, then, preclude a concept of true agency as the principle underlying these praetorian actions. With this impressive evidence in mind, we approach the tort liability of the principal in the exercitorian and institorian arrangements with no attempt to read into said liability any notions of agency and representation. Evidence of the tort liability of principals for the actions of their shipmasters and shopkeepers is readily available. The following are three examples:

(1) Conversion of monies. A shipmaster borrowed money with the declared intention of spending it in the promotion of the maritime enterprise which had been entrusted to him. He subsequently converted the money to his own use. The principal was nevertheless liable to suit on the loan.[97]

(2) Fraudulent withholding of vital information. If the shopkeeper wilfully concealed from third parties the terms of his appointment as agent and the scope of the business which was entrusted to him, the principal was still liable to an institorian action on the transaction. For, although the transaction itself was outside the scope of the agency, "the fraudulent act of the shopkeeper himself ought to affect the person who appointed him."[98]

---

96 Beseler, Beit., III, 116; Longo, Act., 609–610.

97 Ulpian, D. 14.1.1.9., see also Paul, D. 44.4.5.3. The name of the action is *actio certae pecuniae exercitoria.*

98 Ulpian, D. 14.3.11.4: *dolus ipsius praeponenti nocere debet*; cf., Paul, D. 44.4.5.3.

(3) Robbery and desecration. An undertaker slave *(pollinctor)*, employed by a funeral director *(libitinarius)* to prepare corpses for burial, despoiled a corpse. A number of actions were available against the principal, i.e., the funeral director who owned the slave: a quasi-institorian action, an action on the theft, and an action on the injurious desecration.[99]

The first observation to be made from the examples cited is that in order to render the principal liable for the delictual acts of his agents, it was sufficient that the deed be performed in the course of the duty to which the agent had been appointed. It was not necessary that the delictual act itself be commissioned by the principal (i.e., that it be a product of the *voluntas* of the *dominus*).

The second observation to be made is that it is both unwarranted and unnecessary to explain the principal's liability for the torts of his shipmaster, shipper or shopkeeper on the basis of a concept of representation: unwarranted — for such liability applied to the seamen aboard as well as to the shipmaster or shipper despite the fact that any contract entered into by these same seamen with third parties would be null and void as totally unauthorized;[100] unnecessary — for such liability appears to be nothing more than a Roman version of a principle analogous to *respondeat superior* obtaining between master and servant. This last statement demands explanation.

The tort liability of an employer is usually looked upon as one of the hallmarks of the principal-agent relationship in general and of the master-servant relationship in particular. Thus, to make the statement that we are dealing with an ancient version of *respondeat superior* and at the same time to assert that it is unnecessary to predicate a concept of agency would, at first glance, appear to be an inner contradiction. We venture to suggest, however, that although the liability of a principal for the torts of his agent is the product of both the historical development and logical extension of the liability of a master for the torts of his servant,[101] one need not

---

99 Ulpian, D. 14.3.5.9, citing Labeo. The *actio institoria* is *quasi* because, strictly speaking, it is not based upon a transaction involving a commercial establishment. The other two actions are known in Latin as *actio furti* and *actio iniuriarum*.

100 Ulpian, D. 14.1.1.2.

101 Seavey, 6–7.

assume that the latter is based upon a concept of agency. On the contrary, such an assumption could easily be anachronistic.

Theoretically, we could formulate the tort liability of masters, whether it be the pre-modern forerunner of the Anglo-American principle of *respondeat superior* or its operation in the classical Roman law, in non-agency terms: It is the law's answer to the question, "What risks should a master, who provides his servant with the means of trading and gives him authority to trade, be reasonably expected to undertake?"[102] Viewed this way, the similarity between Anglo-American and Roman pronouncements, that the tort liability of employers arises out of their responsibility to hire dependable employees, comes as no surprise. Thus, placing the following statements — the first from Anglo-American law, the second from Roman law — in juxtaposition,

Employing him as agent, or as his agent to do that thing, he became responsible for the methods which his agent adopted in doing that thing.[103]	The *exercitor* was bound to answer for the behaviour of all his seamen; and it is quite reasonable that he should be so, as he himself employed them at his own risk.[104]

we find both legal systems attributing the tort liability of principals to the responsibility they must bear for their choice and authorization of their employees. But, as indicated, this similarity does not warrant the conclusion that Roman law was operating with the principles of agency and representation as understood in modern jurisprudence.[105]

---

102 Formulation by Buckland, Slavery, 706.

103 Supreme Judicial Court of Massachusetts, 1890, in the case of Haskell v. Starbird; cited by Seavey, 235.

104 Ulpian, D. 4.9.7 pr.

105 It is relevant to point out that our attempt to interpret the Roman equivalent to *respondeat superior* in non-agency terms may be unnecessary. According to some scholars, those passages which attribute the liability of principals for the torts of their agents to the responsibility of the former for their appointments are the product of post-classical interpolations. For example, when Ulpian (D. 14.1.1.9.) gives the reason of the responsibility of an *exercitor* for the act of delict of his shipmaster whereby the latter converted monies borrowed for the operation of the

Having shown that the exercitorian and institorian arrangements were not based upon a theoretic concept of true agency, we come to the inevitable conclusion that although certain features of the arrangements strike one as bearing resemblances to some of the rules of agency in modern legal systems these similarities are superficial. The praetor was not operating with an underlying and pervading principle of representation when he made these actions available to third parties. Rather, there appeared on the economic scene certain problems and certain needs for which the law had to find a solution so that business could be carried on smoothly. It must be borne in mind that not only were the interests of third parties dealing with shopkeepers and shipmasters who were employees of others being protected by granting them the right of action against the employers. It was equally vital to the capitalist-employers themselves that such remedies be available to third parties. Otherwise no one would be willing to do business with the agents they were employing to conduct their affairs. These actions represent products of the practical approach of the Roman praetor to economic and legal problems which came before him and were *ad hoc* palliatives which he provided precisely in those areas where the need for them was felt. These areas were principally maritime commerce and inland retail trade. The praetor did not bother himself with the theoretical implications of these remedies which he made available nor did he find it necessary to create systematic and general legal doctrines based upon them. Therefore, in measuring these arrangements in the light of modern jurisprudence, it does not suffice to say that, in retrospect, they represent primitive and undeveloped manifestations of the institutions of contractual agency.[106] This narrow view over-

ship to his own personal use, he cites Ofilius as stating, "the *exercitor* had himself to blame [*imputaturum sibi*] for appointing such a man shipmaster." Again, in another passage, Ulpian is quoted as saying, "in respect of his own fault [*culpae . . . suae*] for employing such men" (D. 4.9.7.4.). The "blame" aspect *(imputare, culpa)* has given rise to the suspicion that we have here *emblamata Triboniani*, i.e., Justinian-inspired interpolations that are *not* representative of the classical law. See Eisele; also Beseler, Beit., II, 85, 125; III, 1166.

106 *Cf.*, Poste, 519; Buckland, Slavery, 702–706; Biondi, 76–77; Zulueta, Gaius, II, 268.

looks the great practical value and economic usefulness of the praetorian institution of agency that they contained within themselves. A deeper awareness of the function of law in society leads us to the conclusion that these arrangements and the praetorian law built around them are a magnificent illustration of how the classical Roman law coped with the needs of society as they arose. Rather than employ an indeterminate general conception, the Roman legal genius addressed itself with dynamic and uncircumscribed efforts to meet such new situations directly and effectively.[107]

107 *Cf.* Pugliese, 291, n. 7. On much of the foregoing, see further Powell, 41–49.

CHAPTER IV

NON-POTESTAS RELATIONSHIPS AND AGENCY

A. ON THE PERIPHERY OF THE *FAMILIA*

1. *Extra*-potestas *Relationships*

a. *Introduction*

In Chapters I and II, we saw how children and slaves were legally regarded as instrumentalities capable of acquiring property for the head of family in every branch of economic activity.

In Chapter III, we examined the role of children and slaves as agents in authorized commercial transactions. In the exercitorian arrangement, for example, we showed that agency was possible in two forms. The shipowner himself could conduct the business operations and hire a ship captain to act as his agent at sea and abroad, or the shipowner could hire a professional shipper as his agent to conduct the business operations of the ship and the shipper in turn could hire a ship captain to act as his sub-agent at sea and abroad. In either case, the ship captain as agent or the shipper as agent and the ship captain as sub-agent are often referred to as persons in *potestas*. Similarly in the institorian arrangement, the shopkeeper as agent of the capitalist who set him up in business was also often referred to as a person in *potestas*.[1] Roman law recognized that the

---

1 Ulpian, D. 14.1.1.4 and 16. In the Digest title devoted to the exercitorian

familia, including slaves as well as children, was not merely a social unit but an economic one as well, with the family's wealth vested in the head of the household, the *paterfamilias*. Industrial enterprises and commercial ventures in classical Rome were often an integral part of the *familia*-organization. It comes, therefore, as no surprise that the shopkeepers running the large number of business establishments and the shippers and shipmasters conducting the innumerable maritime activities were in so many cases slaves and sons; the basis of the relationship between the principal (the *praepositor*) and his agent (the *praepositus*) was *potestas*, that power in which the Roman head of the family characteristically held his children, slaves, and, in earlier times, his wife.[2]

But although the exercitorian and institorian arrangements were the main forms whereby agency under the general authorization of the principal was accomplished, they were not the only ones. Numerous acts of agency under general authorization were performed outside of these arrangements. Moreover, both within the exercitorian and institorian framework and beyond it, *potestas* was not the exclusive relationship that governed non-contractual agency in Rome. The wife, for example, who contracted a "free" marriage was not in the *manus* of her husband, yet she could serve her husband occasionally in the capacity of his agent. Freedmen, too, were socially and psychologically often members of the *familia* of their

action, the subordinate in power serving as an agent is invariably a slave. However, the juxtaposition of a person in power with a slave in 16 obviously implies a son. Gaius, 4.71 mentions sons explicitly. On the other hand, in the Digest title devoted to the institorian action, the subordinate in power serving as agent is often, in addition to the slave, the son of the principal. The subordinate in power could also be someone else's slave *(servus alienus)* hired or lent by his owner to the principal who then proceeded to employ him as a shipmaster, shipper or shopkeeper with the powers of agency implicit in these types of employment. See, for example, Ulpian, D. 14.1.1.4; Paul, *h.t.*, 5 pr.; Ulpian, D. 14.3.1; and Paul, *h.t.*, 14; further Fabricius, 7–8.

2 Fabricius, 15–17. The key role of *potestas* as governing the relationship between principal and agent is illustrated by the fact that there is no requirement that the subordinate have specific legal capacity before an action could be brought against the head of family. Minors, women and slaves may act as "agents"; Ulpian, D. 14.1.1.4 and 14.3.7.1.

former masters, yet the ties of *potestas* had been severed by manumission. Indeed, freedmen were the major source of non-contractual agency among the Romans of the late Republic and especially of the Empire. We therefore turn now to a broad examination of these two members of the Roman *familia*, the wife and the freedman, who were no longer bound to the *familia* by the traditional ties of *manus* and *potestas* but who nevertheless could, and indeed did, serve as agents of the head of the family. Strictly speaking, once the ties of *manus* and *potestas* had been dissolved, the relationship should have been governed by contract. We propose to show, however, that this was only partially true. The principal-agent relationship where wives acted as the agents of their husbands and freedmen served as agents of their patrons was often non-contractual or, at most, quasi-contractual.

b. Husband-Wife

As attention is turned to non-*potestas* bases of principal-agent relationships, it is pertinent to examine in detail the role of the wife as agent. Although in earlier times an occasional act of agency on behalf of her husband performed by the wife in *manus* was subsumed under the rules pertaining to *potestas*, in classical times such acts of agency were based neither upon *potestas* nor upon contract. Thus, the natural matter-of-fact nature of the services of one's wife as the economic manager of the household generally and as shopkeeper in her husband's store specifically[3] must not be overlooked as a modest, albeit ever-present, source of non-contractual agency.

Among the lower classes, women were often found alongside their husbands running shops and carrying on petty business transactions. It is beyond any doubt that these duties occasionally included services that the modern lawyer would consider as constituting acts of agency. Among the upper classes, the well known social and economic independence of the Roman woman[4] did not mean, of course, that common bonds of affection and mutual concern, normally associated with marriage, did not exist. On the contrary, her com-

---

3 See Ulpian, D. 14.3.7.1.
4 See, for example, Friedländer, 236–240; and Frank, Aspects, 15, 21–23.

mercial abilities and business experience, added to the normal responsibility of running the household,[5] made it all the more likely that she would on frequent occasions perform functions analogous to those of agency and representation — undoubtedly on a non-formal basis. The husband of a Roman matron would frequently be absent on campaigns, on state commissions or in court. Thus, important decisions as well as unimportant ones regarding the estate and the household often rested upon her shoulders.[6]

This aspect of Roman economic life is so prosaic, so taken for granted, and the agency aspect so far from the realm of legal obligation and contract, that it is to the non-juristic sources that we must turn to recreate a meaningful picture of the everyday situation. We are fortunate that the wealth of Cicero's correspondence has survived, for from many of the incidental details contained therein we can reconstruct vivid evidence of how a Roman wife could act as her husband's general agent. The relationship between Cicero and his wife, Terentia,[7] is a most instructive example of the kind of non-formal, non-contractual agency of a wife that was imbedded in the very fabric of Roman domestic life.

Terentia was an intelligent and forceful woman who had vast properties in her own right.[8] Her influence over the everyday business affairs of her husband was very great. And, as his correspondence reveals, he left her for a long time absolute mistress of the household. He was very glad to shift onto somebody else those everyday occupations and the manifold petty and prosaic transactions that, necessary as they were, did not suit him: sales and purchases, collections and payments, repairs and accommodations.

Indeed, she, with her freedman, succeeded in entangling him in

---

5 *domus administranda, familia regenda, claves custodiendae, victus procurandus*; Tertullian, *Exhort. castit* 12, cited in Schroff, *R.E.*, XIV, 2302.
6 See Balsdon, Rom., 205–206, 270–277.
7 The following description is based in the main upon Boissier, 91–99; and Carcopino, Cic., 141–147. We are not concerned with Carcopino's main thesis; see the reviews thereon: J.P.V.D. Balsdon, *Classical Review*, N.S. II (1952), 178–181, and *Journal of Roman Studies*, XL (1950), 134–135. See further Balsdon, Cic., 171–214.
8 E.g., Cicero, *Epistulae ad Atticum*, 2.4.5; *Ad familiares*, 14.1.5; 14.2.3. On Cicero's letters, *cf.* Bailey, Letters, and Bailey, Ep. *passim*.

some financial affairs that Atticus himself, who was not overly scrupulous, did not think very honourable.[9] Cicero distrusted Philotimus,[10] and, when he was named heir to a legacy, warned both Atticus and Terentia not to allow the freedman to mix himself up in the matter.[11]

He then gradually grew to distrust Terentia herself, that is, in the very management of his estate and its assets. His suspicions appear to have been well-founded. Although the details do not concern us,[12] one fact emerges as most significant for our study. When his wife's financial treachery was substantiated, no legal action was taken against her. She held a fortune of her own independently of her husband and therefore could have legally been compelled to make good the losses her husband had incurred through her. Nevertheless, the misappropriation of his funds on her part did not result in litigation and suit, but rather in divorce. The violation of non-contractual agency inexorably leads to the dissolution of the relationship of good faith that was its essential creator. Indeed, in the ensuing settlement, when Terentia was making difficulties with regard to the details of Tullia's dowry and with regard to a will to be made in favour of the young Marcus, their son, Cicero was willing to give her all that she claimed in order to bring the painful matter to a respectable close.[13]

As indicated above, it is from the incidentals that we cull our information about women as instruments of non-contractual agency. "Literature," observed Ludwig Friedländer, "prefers dwelling on the frailties and vices of women, as being better copy, than on the inconspicuous virtues; and most of this description is thereby limited to the evil side."[14] The virtuous, self-sacrificing woman, who ran the overwhelming majority of Roman households of all classes — with their myriads of menial chores and mundane responsibilities, of

9 For details see Carcopino, Cic., 111–115.
10 *Ad Att.* 6.4 at end; 7.1.3.
11 *Ad Att.* 6.9.2; 7.1.9; *Ad fam.* 14.5.2.
12 The distrust of his wife's financial management may be traced in his letters *Ad Att.*, especially 11.1.2; 11.2.2; and 11.24.3.
13 *Ad Att.* 12.19.4; 2.21.3.
14 Friedländer, 261.

which commercial transactions, petty and repetitious make up only one part — remain the unsung heroines.[15]

The wife, then, was the source of agency which included the performance of institorian services on behalf of her husband but which also went far beyond the institorian arrangement to encompass innumerable other types of transactions. Not based upon *potestas*, the principal-agent relationship of husband and wife was nevertheless not governed by contract either.[16]

c. *Patron-Freedman*

Another source of non-contractual agency, indeed, a major source, was the patron-freedman relationship.[17] Similar to the wife in classical times, the manumitted slave was no longer tied to the *paterfamilias* by the bonds of *potestas*. In contrast to the wife, however, the freedman's closeness to the *familia* from which he was legally detached[18] was subject to major variations. There were, for example, many freedmen who were totally independent of their former masters. When such freedmen were hired by their former masters as exercitorian or institorian agents, the agency relationship between them was governed by the same two or three formal contracts that governed free born agents who were *sui iuris*: If the agent was construed as a hired employee, the contract which governed his relationship with his principal was that of leasing and hiring *(locatio conductio)*. If he was construed as a mandatary, his relationship with his principal was governed by the contract of the mandate *(mandatum)*. And if, because of the circumstances involved, he was construed as an unauthorized manager, then the relationship was governed by the rules of *negotiorum gestio*.[19]

---

15 Friedländer, 261–267. But not always; *cf.* the commentary on Catullus 61.149–156 in Pearce, 16–33.

16 See Schulz, Princ., 147, n. 5.

17 See Schiller, 623–639, who points to the patron-freedman relationship as a rich source of information concerning the commercial law of Rome. Concerning this relationship, *cf.*, Lambert; Cosentini, Studi; and Pescani; in addition to the standard textbooks. (Pescani's work, however, should be consulted critically and with caution.)

18 The detachment, however, by law, could not be complete; see below.

19 Ulpian, D. 14.1.1.18 and 14.3.1; Paul, D. 14.1.5 pr.

On the other hand, many slaves continued after manumission to live in the (former) master's house and to perform the same tasks in the household as before. These freedmen, who maintained close, quasi-familial relations with their patrons, are of the greatest significance for our study. By examining the activities of numerous former slaves of this type, it can be shown that the legal rules, social habits and customary practices rooted in the former master-slave relationship, constituted the fabric of the present ties between patron and freedman. These quasi-familial relations, even more than formal contract, governed the behaviour of patron and freedman as principal and agent.[20]

Our thesis, then, is that the conglomeration of rules, habits and practices that constituted the way of life of a former slave in his relations with his former master created a non-contractual agency relationship between many patrons and freedmen whose basis the student of law and sociology would regard as somewhat midway between *potestas* status and formal contract.[21] It is, therefore, necessary to survey briefly the legal relations between patrons and freedmen in classical Rome.[22]

Ulpian declared:

> The person of a father and of a patron should always be held honourable and sacred in the eyes of a freedman and a son.[23]

This statement of Ulpian implies that the freedman and his patron were the subject of correlative rights and duties with regard to each

---

20 *Cf.* Veyne, 221–223.
21 The question whether the rules and practices governing the relations between freedmen and their former masters are the product of pre-classical and early classical legal attempts to whittle down the full freedom which the original law of manumission created — as propounded by Cosentini, Studi, I, 69–91 — or, rather, the product of pre-classical and early classical legal attempts to whittle down the former master's strong hold on his liberated slave — as maintained by Lavaggi, II, 75–91 — does not concern us; *cf.* Pescani, 15.
22 The following presentation is based upon Lemonnier, 106–126; Duff, A.M., 36–49, 93–98; Michel, 146, 157–167; Buckland, Text., 87–90; Watson, Per., 226–236; Staerman, 146–170; Treggiari, 68–81; and Arms, chs. 2 and 6.
23 D. 37.15.9: *Liberto et filio semper honesta et sancta persona patris ac patroni videri debet.*

other that were similar to those obtaining between son and father. The duties which were incumbent upon the patron and which he was duty-bound to perform on behalf of his freedman were essentially three. The first was guardianship *(tutela)*. The patron was expected to protect the interests of all his freedmen under twenty years of age and of all his freedwomen at any age, to give them legal advice and to guide them in the administration of their property. The responsibility of guardianship was converted into a privilege, for it conferred on the guardian some control in the succession to the property of the freedman upon the latter's death. Another duty was that of support and sustenance *(alimenta)*. The patron, on pain of losing his right to the services and succession of his freedman, had to furnish him with food in times of need. A third duty of the patron, also on pain of losing his share in the succession if he neglected to do so, was the avenging of the freedman's death *(vindicatio necis)*, such as bringing the latter's assassin to justice.

It is, however, the corresponding duties of the freedman to his patron that are of particular interest to us. The filial respect and homage which the freedman was obligated to pay his patron are summarized in two somewhat vaguely-defined terms, *obsequium* and *officium*. The actual duties subsumed under these words were never formulated specifically, but everyone in Rome knew what they signified. *Obsequium*, for example, prohibited the freedman from bringing a civil lawsuit against his patron[24] and severely limited his right to bring criminal charges against him. In contrast with the negative *obsequium*, *officium* was the sum total of positive duties a freedman had to perform for his patron: the care and protection of the patron's children, the ceremonial duties of a client, support and sustenance *(alimenta)*, and gifts *(munera)* which the freedman was expected to present to his patron on special occasions.[25] *Officium*

---

24 Similarly, a son, even possessing a *peculium castrense*, could not proceed against his *paterfamilias* — at least in classical times; see Daube, Act., 433–474.

25 Except for the *munera* which were more or less standardized, the substance and extent of all these services were defined by the needs and demands of the patron. The latter, however, was forbidden by law to exact money from his freedman which would result in making his life of freedom unbearable or impossible *(onerandae libertatis causa)*; Modestinus, D. 28.1.32.

may also have included the duty to accept the domestic position of managing the master's storerooms *(dispensator)* or of purchasing the needs of the patron's household *(procurator).*

In addition, it was the prerogative of the former master, if he so found it to his interests, to contract with his freedman that the latter should undertake the systematic rendering of services known as *operae.*[26] The contract was formed by administering an oath to the freedman at manumission, and the duties incurred supplemented those ill-defined ones subsumed under *obsequium* and *officium.* "The oath of a freedman" *(iusiurandum liberti),* as it was known, was then enforceable by a civil law action. Gaius pointed out that this was the only case in Roman law of a binding contract arising out of an oath.[27] The duties *(operae)* that constituted the substance of this contract were in the form of a given number of days of service per week or per month. Performed either in the former master's house or factory, they were either domestic or skilled. The skilled services could be that of a physician, an artist or an architect, of a craftsman or a tradesman.[28]

Since the *operae* serve as the framework within which we would expect to find, among others, those tasks and services that may be characterized as agency, their rules of operation deserve special attention. The basic unit of work was a day's labour. The day could not be subdivided; and so, even if he might have completed his assignment before the day was done, the freedman had not discharged his obligation and could not consider himself dismissed.[29] Although the *officia* duties were regarded as non-transferable obligations of the freedman to the person of his patron, the *operae* services were viewed as economic assets which could be passed on to others. Thus, they could be inherited by the heirs of the patron. Indeed,

26 See Schiller, 627–630.

27 G. 3.96; see Zulueta, Gaius II, and Buckland, Text., 458–459. The civil law action enforcing the oath was known as *iudicium operarum* and was along the lines of a *condictio certae rei*; see Lenel, E.P., para. 140. For a detailed study of the oath, see Tomulescu, 461–471.

28 On the duties of freedmen to their former masters, see Mitteis, Op., 143–158; Lambert, *passim*; Cosentini, Stud., I, 125ff; Robertis, 201–222; Lavaggi, 91–105 (whose views are to be preferred to those of Cosentini); Pescani, 70–96; and Watson, Per., 226–231.

29 Paul, D. 38.1.1, and Pomponius, *h.t.*, 3.1. *cf.* Pescani, 14, 99, 140.

says Julian, "if a freedman exercises the calling of a comic actor, it is evident that he should employ his services not only for the benefit of his patron himself, but also gratuitously for the entertainment of [the patron's] friends; just as a freedman who practices medicine should, at the desire of his patron, treat the friends of the latter without compensation."[30] Similarly, these *operae* could be hired out to a third party.[31]

The problem of abuses in the relationships between patron and freedman recurred sporadically during the Principate. On the one hand, there were ungrateful freedmen who did not treat their former masters with the obeisance due them or who did not perform the *operae* properly.[32] On the other hand, there were patrons who took undue advantage of their superior position and mistreated their former slaves.[33] The irksome nature of the *operae* led to the practice on the part of freedmen of undertaking to pay their former masters a lump sum of money in exchange for immunity from these burdens.[34]

The services performed by freedmen *(operae liberti)*, then, were technically contractual, and, by performing them, the freedman was, again technically speaking, discharging his contractual obligations. The contract was unique in that the source of its binding quality was the freedman's oath. But did Roman legal theory really regard these *operae* as gratuitous services?[35] Or were they viewed as payment for manumission?[36]

30 Ulpian, *h.t.*, 6, and Julian, *h.t.*, 27. On the transmission of the *obligatio operarum* of freedmen to the heirs of their respective patrons, see Robertis, 97–98; Cosentini, ibid., II, 39–111; and Lavaggi, 105–111.
31 C. 6.3.4. Michel, 158 and 161, gives the opposite impression. I believe he is mistaken in citing C. 6.3.7 to the effect that *operae* could not be hired to third parties. The passage merely states that the patron may not receive money in *lieu* of the *operae*.
32 E.g., Suetonius, *Claudius* 25; Tacitus *Annales* 13.26–27.
33 See the legal countermeasures enumerated in D. 38.1; see further Lenel, E.P., 338–341.
34 Here, too, there were a number of legal provisions to guard against abuses. For example, so that the freedman should not be rendered a debtor for life, the lump sum he paid his patron was limited by law. For details, see Duff, A. M., 45–47, and Michel, 158–159.
35 As indicated by the language of Julian, D. 38.1.27.
36 As indicated by Ulpian, D. 38.1.7 pr. and Paul, D. 39.5.8.

There is no doubt that the contract binding the freedman to perform the prescribed services for his former master was gratuitous in form. Neither its origin nor its fulfilment was conditioned upon the discharge of any obligation, any service, or any payment on the part of the patron. But the facts that the basic unit of labour was measured in terms of one indivisible day and that the labourer could be hired to third parties would indicate that the *operae* had an affinity to the general rules of hired labour *(locatio operarum)* and hence were not gratuitous.[37]

However, the expenses incurred by the freedman in the course of performing his *operae* were charged to the patron[38] in the same manner that all beneficiaries under gratuitous contracts were liable for the expenses incurred by their benefactors. In this respect, the similarity between the freedman's *operae* and gratuitous contracts is remarkable.[39] Moreover, the very fact that the burdens imposed upon the freedman were not the automatic result of manumission, but were contingent upon the oath,[40] meant that from the vantage point of the formal law the *operae* were more the result of the unilateral will *(voluntas)* of the promissor than of the inexorable requirements *(necessitas)* of the law.[41] It would appear, then, that the burdens performed by freedmen for their patrons belong to that genre of services that are generally associated with gratuitous contracts. A major school of anthropologists teaches us that a gratuitous gift or a gratuitous service is grounded not in altruism but rather in reci-

---

37 The fact that, even on the days on which he had to work for his former master, the freedman could take time off for food and for his other needs (Paul, D. 38.1.18; Gaius, *h.t.*, 19 and 22; Alfenus, *h.t.*, 26; and Iavolenus, *h.t.*, 33) indicates nothing; for this rule held true for anyone rendering any service, gratuitous or paid for (Neratius, D. 38.1.50, following the reading of Haloander alluded to in the Mommsen-Krueger edition of the Digest).

38 Iavolenus, D. 38.1.21, accepting the Mommsen-Krueger deletion or at least giving the passage some reading which approximates the meaning achieved by said deletion.

39 See Michel, 364–370.

40 Ulpian, D. 38.1.7 pr., 2 and 3.

41 In this respect, the manumitted slave's obligation is similar to that found in gratuitous contracts as expressed in Paul's exposition of *commodatum*, D. 13.6.17.3.

procity.[42] Therefore, in the light of the facts we have presented, the most reasonable conclusion would be that these *operae* were formally gratuitous, but in theory they were rendered as payment for manumission.[43]

But overshadowing the legal provisions governing the relationship between patron and freedman were social forces derived from ancient customs and psychological habits. Thus, the origins of *obsequium et officium* are undoubtedly rooted in the early days of Roman history. The number of slaves and freedmen was small, and the slave was usually an Italian captive whose intelligence and talents were not superior to those of his master. When the slave was freed, inasmuch as his labour experience was limited to agricultural or domestic work, he normally remained dependent upon his former *dominus* for food and shelter and perforce continued to reside in his master's house — no longer a legal, but rather a social member of the *familia*.[44] The social bond between patrons and freedmen could be, and often was, a very close one, even to the point where the former would occasionally institute the latter as heirs.[45] The habit of obedience which he had acquired through years of slavery strongly influenced the manumitted slave for the rest of his life, and it was this habit and mentality — and not the formal provisions of the law — which assured his *obsequium* and *officium*.[46]

In later times, what was originally a custom that had been produced out of circumstances was gradually transformed into a tradition which was legally binding on all freedmen — whatever their means of livelihood, whatever their national origin, and whatever their habits of behaviour and thinking may have been. Even in these later times, when the economic and social life of the Romans had undergone profound changes, the slave upon manumission would, more often than not, continue in the same employment he had had before his freedom. If he had been active in trade and commerce,

---

42 The development and documentation of this teaching will be presented below.

43 The foregoing three paragraphs are based in the main upon Michel, 160–161.

44 For example, see Ulpian, D. 9.3.5.1.

45 For example, Paul, D. 17.2.71.1.

46 Schulz, Princ., 20, 24.

he would pursue the same economic activities on such terms as his former master imposed upon him in the form of *operae*. We have already seen how slaveowners frequently set their slaves up in business, lent them capital (sometimes in the form of a *peculium)*, and the slave paid them a share of the profits,[47] or how masters made their slaves their agents, took the profits for themselves, and encouraged the slaves with wages or presents.[48] In either case, many a slave might receive his freedom by free gift or by payment from his *peculium* but would continue in the same occupation after as before manumission.[49] Alternatively, however, it could have been not a slave but a freedman that was set up. Having earned his freedom in the house of his master, he then, entered into his master's commercial service.[50]

But, as already indicated, it would be a distortion of history to assume that the actions and transactions performed by a slave-turned-freedman in behalf of or in the service of his master-turned-patron are comprehended exhaustively by the law of *(dominica) potestas* transformed into a *ius patronatus*. They were not exclusively contractual services arising out of the formal oath taken at manumission *(iusiurandum liberti)*. Rather, side by side with the formal elements which made up the *ius patronatus*, there existed an extra-legal supplementary principle, *fides*, which also served as the basis of the right relationship between freedman and patron.[51] Although the legal classifications of master and slave, patron and freedman would appear to reveal a formal process leading from servile status to contractual *operae*, the transition is neither consistently as rigid nor the results as departmentalized as would appear. There were numerous instances of freedmen performing a large variety of services on behalf of their former masters that were of a non-contractual character

---

47 Such an arrangement was the basis of the praetorian action *de peculio et de in rem verso*; Ulpian, D. 15.3.1 pr.

48 The slave-agent in the exercitorian and institorian arrangements was undoubtedly granted gratuities as an incentive for devoted and efficient services. These gratuities formed part of the slave's *peculium*, *cf.* Paul, D. 15.1.8, and Florentinus, *h.t.*, 39.

49 E.g., Papinian, D. 14.3.19.1.

50 Much of the foregoing is based upon Duff, A.M., 36–37, 89–92, 98–104.

51 Schulz, Princ., 231f; Treggiari. 80–81. See further: Imbert, 407–415.

and that were totally independent of any oath that they may have been required to take at the moment of manumission.

The thesis, then, is that many freedmen, motivated by feelings of gratitude and affection and habituated to obey and serve by years of servitude, ministered as agents of their former masters upon a basis above and beyond contractual obligations. The very nature of this non-contractual agency, with its social and psychological — as opposed to legal — underpinnings, forces us to leave our legal literature and to turn to the non-juristic classical sources for documentation. It is in the correspondence of some of the leading Roman personalities, as well as in occasional references in other literary creations, that we find the illuminating material which substantiates this point of view.

An excellent illustration is the relationship between Cicero and Tiro, his freedman and secretary. The affection between them is most inspiring: "Cicero's solicitous and generous letters to Tiro, which if unaddressed might be taken for missives to some highly favoured young relative, show how unrestrained the friendship might grow between master and freedman in the daily intercourse over books and business."[52]

Inasmuch as his name is a Latin one, one is led to believe that Tiro was one of those slaves who were born in the master's house *(vernae)*, in contrast to those bought in the market-place. Such slaves were generally looked upon as belonging to the *familia* with a greater degree of intimacy and affection than the latter. As a result, Cicero became attached to him early and had him carefully educated. Tiro played an important role in Cicero's domestic affairs, and his powers were varied, wide and great. In Cicero's house, it was Tiro who

52 Frank, Ec. Hist., 333; *cf.*, Book XVI of Cicero's *Epistulae ad familiares*. McDermott, 259–286, admittedly speculative on a number of points, is valuable for obtaining a full picture of the relationship between them. Although this relationship is exceptional (McDermott speculates that Tiro may have been Cicero's illegitimate son), Frank's remarks are well taken. Nor is Pliny the Younger any different in his relations to his slaves and freeedmen; see his *Epistulae*, 5.19., 6.3 and 8.1. In *Epistulae* 8.16, for example, Pliny encourages his slaves to make wills and then subsequently proceeds to honour the provisions therein, although by the law of the *peculium* all the slave's property should have passed to Pliny himself at the death of the slave (*Arg.*, D. 15.3.8; 15.2.1.3–4; 15.2.3.).

represented order and economy. All financial matters passed through his hands, and he dealt with them efficiently and with discretion: He scolded debtors who were in arrears in their payments of the debts they owed Cicero; on the other hand, he regularly appeased Cicero's creditors who were impatiently pressing for payment. He used to revise the accounts of Cicero's steward, Eros, when mistakes crept into them, and, in moments of difficulty, he would obtain credit for Cicero from bankers. Confidential and delicate negotiations were entrusted to him, as, for example, when it was necessary to elicit some money from Cicero's son-in-law, Dolabella, without arousing his wrath or displeasure. He was sent to supervise the gardens, spur the workmen on, superintend building operations. It was his tact, diplomacy and good sense that were exploited to solve delicate social problems such as invitations to dinner for guests who were hostile to each other.[53] In addition, he was secretary, confidant, and even literary collaborator.[54]

Tiro was manumitted in the year 53,[55] but the letters written about that time and thereafter indicate no perceptible change in the relationship between him and Cicero: He continued to serve the latter with the same devotion, intelligence and honesty as he had done before; and he continued to fulfil *the same role* in Cicero's life as he had before. Note the data which follows:

(1) Writing from Leucas three years after having manumitted him, Cicero declares to Tiro:

> Your services to me are past all reckoning — at home, in the forum, in the City, in my province; in private as in public affairs, in my literary pursuits and performances. You will surpass them all, if only I see you, as I hope to do, in good health.[56]

Obviously, no formal *obsequium et officium* could motivate an ex-slave to such multifarious activities, nor could any legal oath bind

---

53 Boissier, 109–110.
54 Cicero *Ad fam.* 16.10.2. (*cf.* Bailey, Ep., I, 346); Aulus Gellius *Noctes atticae* 7.3.
55 Boissier, p. 110; Carcopino, Cic., 67, n. 3.
56 *Ad fam.* 16.4.3; *Innumerabilia tua sunt in me officia domestica, forensia, urbana, provincialia; in re privata, in publica, in studiis, in litteris nostris. Omnia viceris, si, ut spero, te validum videro.*

him to such varied services;[57] the intangible faithfulness and the unusual constancy implied in them are beyond the reach of contract.

(2) A vivid illustration of the "services past all reckoning" performed by Tiro "in private as in public affairs" is found in Cicero's letter to him in November, 44, when Antony and Octavian were vying for the hegemony of Rome. Having left Rome more than a month earlier, when the breach between him and Antony had become irreparable, Cicero wrote the following letter — brought in its entirety — to Tiro from his native Arpinum:

> Although I had sent Harpalus earlier in the day, still, finding that I had a trustworthy letter-carrier, although there is nothing new, I wanted to write to you again and again on the same subjects — not that I have lost confidence in your application *(diligentiae tuae)*, but the importance of the matter makes me restless.
>
> The "stem and stern"[58] (as the Greek proverb goes) of my sending you away from me was that you might straighten out my financial affairs *(ut rationes nostras explicares)*.
>
> It is imperative that Ofillius[59] and Aurelius[60] should have their claims satisfied *(satisfiat)*. I should like you to wring out *(extorqueas)* of Flamma, if not all the debt, at least some portion of it; and especially to see that the instalment[61] is cleared off on January 1st. As to the assignment of debts, make some settlement *(de attributione conficies)*; and please see to their paying ready money *(de repraesentatione videbis)*.
>
> So much for my private affairs *(de domesticis rebus)*.
>
> On public affairs *(de publicis)* let me have every possible information

57 See further *Ad fam.* 16.1.3. and 16.15.1.
58 There are differences of opinion as to the exact connotation of this expression. Some take it to mean "the sum total" and render it in translation "the Alpha and the Omega"; Tyrrell-Purser. Others understand it as "the law of the prophet" and understand it as Cicero's characterization of Tiro as his confidential man of business who was relied upon to reduce chaos to order; Carcopino, Cic., 68.
59 (The Jurist) A co-heir with Cicero to the estate of Cluvius of Puteoli. This and the following explanatory notes are by W. Glynn Williams, the translator of Cicero *Letters to his Friends*, Loeb Classical Library. Explanatory notes in parentheses are based upon Bailey, Ep. II, 491–492.
60 An agent of one Montanus who had become surety to Plancus for Flaminius Flamma and was now obliged to meet Flamma's obligations (*cf.* Bailey, ibid., for additional details).
61 I.e., of Tullia's dowry by Dolabella.

that can be trusted — what Octavianus and what Antony are up to,
what is generally thought, and what you suppose is going to happen.
I can hardly keep myself from coming to you hot-foot. But I stand
still;[62] I patiently await a letter from you; and let me tell you that
Balbus was at Aquinum on the day you were told, and Hirtius on the
next day. I imagine both of them were going there for the waters; but
it is no business of mine![63]

See that Dolabella's agents have their memories jogged.[64] Send a
reminder to Papia[65] also. Goodbye.[66]

This letter, of course, was not unique. Book XVI of the *Epistulae
ad familiares* is replete with all sorts of requests and mandates for
Tiro to perform on behalf of Cicero and his family, to act as their
agent and representative in various matters — without the remotest
thought that such agency had any contractual element in it and without the slightest suggestion that the idea of possible recourse to legal
action was being entertained should there be any irregularity in the
actions of the freedman.

(3) That same summer, Cicero asked Tiro to collect a debt for
him. "In the matter of Aufidius' debt, I put no pressure upon you
(nihil te hortor). I know it is an anxiety to you *(scio tibi curae esse)*.
But settle the business *(sed confice)*." Cicero obviously wanted to
see the job done; but the request was made politely and delicately
with the liberty of initiative left to Tiro.[67]

The extent of the services rendered by freedmen on behalf of
their patrons and incontrovertible evidence of the non-contractual
nature of the relationship that existed between them are afforded us
also by the case of Terentia's *libertus*, Philotimus. A careful reading
of Cicero's correspondence reveals the following:[68] When, in 59,
Cicero was away at Antium, Philotimus was in charge of the upkeep

---

62 Following the reading and interpretation of Williams.
63 Bailey interpretates the phrase as connoting, "What are the odds?"
64 About the repayment of Tullia's dowry. (Dolabella was still in Italy at
   the end of October, but now had apparently left for the East.)
65 Nothing more is known about Papia. (Probably no lady, but a slave or
   freedman of Dolabella).
66 *Ad fam.* 16.24.
67 *Ad fam.* 16.19; Summer, 45. Bailey, Ep., II, 322). See further on Tiro:
   Treggiari, 218–219, 259–263.
68 See Park, 63–64.

of his Roman house.[69] In 55–54, he directed the rebuilding of the houses of both Cicero and Quintus.[70] In 51, he acted for Cicero in money payments[71] and as *socius* in the purchase of Milo's property by his friends.[72] When Cicero was absent in Cilicia, Philotimus went to him to report his private transactions in connection with Milo's property.[73] In 49, we find him again in charge of Cicero's household at Rome[74] and of Cicero's finances.[75] It is upon him that Cicero depends as the means of information from and communication with Rome[76] and with various friends.[77] A sure indication of his capability and discretion is his assignment to see Caesar in 47 in the interest of Cicero's family.[78] When relations between Cicero and Terentia deteriorated, Philotimus' usefulness to him ceased. Indeed, so closely identified was Philotimus with Terentia's interests that Cicero's distrust of the former was the actual prelude to his breakup with the latter.[79] The reading of the source material relating to all these matters leaves one with the undisputable impression that wherever questions of business were concerned, Philotimus' services to Cicero and to Terentia as their agent were totally devoid of any contractual basis. *Sui iuris* though he was, the freedman's loyalty and sense of responsibility in themselves served as the basis of the relationship between patron and freedman.[80]

Nor was Cicero unique in his relations with his freedmen. When the freedman of Pliny the Younger exceeded his patron's instructions and engaged him in a sale to Corellia (to whose family Pliny had close ties of friendship) of an estate to which he was co-heir, Pliny stood by his freedman's action at the expense of his promise to the co-heirs. A careful reading of the case reveals Pliny's total

---

69 *Epistulae ad Atticum* 2.4.7.
70 *Ad Att.* 4.10.2. *Ad Quintum fratrem* 3.1.6; 3.9.7.
71 *Ad Att.* 5.4.3; 5.19.1; 8.7.3; 10.5.3.
72 *Ad Att.* 5.8.2–3; *Ad fam.* 8.3.2.
73 *Ad Att.* 6.1.19; 6.3.1: etc.
74 *Ad fam.* 14.18.2.
75 *Ad Att.* 8.7.3; 10.5.3; 10.7.3.
76 *Ad Att.* 8.1.1; 8.16.1; 9.7.6; 9.9.3.
77 Atticus: *Ad Att.* 7.22.2. Servius Sulpicius: *Ad fam.* 4.2.1.
78 *Ad Att.* 11.23.2; 11.24.4; *Ad fam.* 14.24.
79 See Boissier, 96–98, and Carcopino, Cic., 102–103, 111–114.
80 See further on Philotimus: Treggiani, 253, 263–264.

disregard of the *legal* relationship between himself and his freed-man. He defended his action not on legal but on moral grounds.[81]

The picture of freedmen as a significant source of non-contractual agency emerges with crystal clarity. Many of their actions and transactions were obviously performed above and beyond those required within the framework of the *operae liberti* and rendered obligatory by the freedman's oath. The line of demarcation between formal *operae* and informal ones, however, was never clearly delineated. In the light of the psychological and social factors which we have described as part of the process of manumission, this lack of clear line of demarcation comes as no surprise. Indeed, it is part and parcel of the very nature of the patron-freedman relationship.[82]

d. *From Status to Contract*

In sum, then, agency in commercial transactions that were entered into under the general authorization of the principal is the major feature of the exercitorian and institorian arrangements, the former at sea and the latter on land. In these arrangements, those who acted as agents were slaves on behalf of their owners, sons on behalf of their fathers, wives on behalf of their husbands, and freedmen on behalf of their patrons. In the case of slaves and sons who acted as agents of their masters and fathers, the principal-agent relationship was defined by the agent's status as a subordinate in the power of his principal. Wives, who — in the classical period — were generally without *manus*, were a constant, albeit modest, source of non-contractual agency. In the case of freedmen, however, the principal-agent relationship cannot be defined so simply. Being *sui iuris*, they were, like wives, free of the status of *potestas*. On the other hand, their services as agents of their patrons could very well be governed by the terms of contract which governed the agency of freemen who were shippers, ship captains and shopkeepers,[83] namely *locatio con-*

---

81 Pliny the Younger, *Epistulae* 7.11 and 14; see Heitland, 318 and Sherwin-White, 414.

82 *Cf.* the illuminating interpretation of Paul, D. 34.2.4, by Watson, Prop., 79–80. On all the foregoing, see further Treggiari, 215–228.

83 Ulpian, D. 14.1.1.4 and 14.3.1.

ductio, mandatum and *negotiorum gestio*. Nevertheless, many freed-men acted as the agents of their patrons in a fashion that cannot be explained in terms of contract. Although subjected at manumission to an oath of service which gave rise to contractual obligations, there was often a supplementary moral tie that bound the freedman to his patron. The many years of servitude, as well as the present duties subsumed under *obsequium, officium* and *operae*, engendered in numerous former slaves habits of obedience and service that were totally devoid of contractual considerations. Thus freedmen often served their former masters as agents in the exercitorian and insti-torian arrangements and outside these arrangements[84] in a manner above and beyond the requirements of contract.

The exercitorian and institorian arrangements, then, provided for the employment of agents who were well within the family structure, i.e., slaves and sons in power and wives; agents who were on the periphery of the *familia* circle, i.e., freedmen who maintained quasi-familial ties with their former masters; and agents who were totally divorced from the *familia* of the principal, i.e., freedmen who had achieved total independence from their patrons and from other freemen. Thus, the employment of the exercitorian and institorian agents who were totally outside the familial structure indicates the replacement of *potestas* by contract. The information necessary to establish with any degree of certainty when the transition took place whereby persons *sui iuris* began to be employed as exercitorian and institorian agents does not exist. Such employment is certainly much older than the texts that attest it. Indeed, in the two passages of

---

84 The shipper's liability for his officer's undertaking in a *receptum nautae* agreement (Ulpian, D. 4.9.1.3; the same principle applies to innkeepers, D. 4.9. *passim*) was still within the exercitorian-institorian arrangement. The rights and obligations which a principal acquired through his *procurator's* acts may, however, have been outside of this arrangement, e.g., the rights in an object borrowed for gratuitous use (*precarium*; Ulpian, D. 43.26.6.1); and the rights acquired for the collection of a reconstituted debt (*constitutum debiti*; Ulpian, D. 13.5.5.6, citing Julian and Pomponius). Certain rights and liabilities may have been acquired through a *non-procurator*, e.g., those that inhered in the quasi-heir (the *bonorum possessor*; Ulpian, D. 37.1.3.7). In many, many instances, un-doubtedly, it was the freedman who served as the agent of his former master and performed these and similar acts.

Ulpian which contain the earliest references to these actions,[85] there is nothing to indicate that the agent who had been appointed was a subordinate in the power of another at all. It may well be that an agent *sui iuris* was intended. The feverish economic growth during the last century of the Republic as well as the breakdown of the *familia* make that time the most likely one for the development of exercitorian and institorian agency outside the familial power concept.[86]

But although the "when" of this transition is shrouded in mystery, the "how" of it is not. It is to be found in the patron-freedman relationship. It was this relationship which preserved the acts, dealings and arrangements which obtained between citizens and their former slaves. The slave-shopkeeper and the slave-shipmaster upon manumission would often remain in the same position of general agent for his principal as he had been before manumission. Since manumission took place frequently and in large numbers,[87] the Roman business world was often faced with the *de facto* situation of a manumitted slave, now a freedman, acting as an agent in a maritime or commercial establishment with ties to his principal which, originally based on *potestas*, were now replaced by an implied contract. The contract between them was taken as "implied" because it was entered into unwittingly by both principal and agent; it was the jurist who inferred that the general terms of this "contract" were to be defined by the tacit agreement of the parties involved to continue the same arrangement that existed prior to the manumission. Once this contract which arose *de facto* was recognized and categorized — and the agent was construed as a hired employee, as a

85 It is, of course, possible that in the time of Ulpian it was an *actio utilis* (D. 14.3.12) which omitted the requirement that the institor be in *potestate*; Fabricius, 17–18. But see also ibid., 20–22, where it is maintained (*contra* Lenel) that the *actio utilis* was granted for the case where the institor was a *servus alienus*.

86 The account contained in this and the following paragraph is based in the main on Costa, Az., 39–44. See also Poste, 519. I have followed Solazzi, Scritti, "L'eta dell'*actio exercitoria*," *passim*, and Watson, Ob., Ch. 11, and have rejected Fabricius' position, ibid., 24–32, that the *actio institoria* was not granted where the institor was a free man until the time of the Empire.

87 For a variety of reasons; see Duff, A.M., 12–21.

mandatary, or as an authorized manager — the relations between principal and agent were redefined while the services of the agent on behalf of the principal with regard to third parties continued uninterrupted and unabated.[88] Once the transition from *potestas* to implied contract and then to defined contract had been accomplished, the results could be applied directly to govern the relationship of two persons *sui iuris* who wished to establish between themselves an exercitorian and institorian agency arrangement *ab initio*.[89]

The bridge, then, between generally authorized agency based upon *potestas* and that based upon contract was the manumitted slave who became the freedman of his former master. Recalling the famous theory of Sir Henry Maine that "the movement of progressive societies has hitherto been a movement from *Status to Contract*,"[90] the non-contractual services of the freedman on behalf of his patron may be regarded as the transitional midpoint in this movement.

The Roman legal development of agency was, however, not limited to the transition from status to contract *within* the exercitorian and institorian arrangements themselves. Already in classical times, we have clear evidence of the granting of the right of suit along the lines of the *actio institoria* against business owners when an employee — who was *not* an *institor* — had, in the course of discharging his duties, incurred obligations. The scope within which non-slaves could obligate others directly vis-à-vis third parties by means of transactions which the former had concluded on their behalf was thereby widened.[91]

---

88 Illustrations of freedmen carrying on activities and concluding transactions on behalf of their patrons in the same manner as they had done before manumission may be found in Scaevola, D. 27.7.58 and 14.3.20; and Papinian, D. 14.3.19.1. See next sub-section.

89 These observations are in no way contradicted by de Martino's insistence that the exercitorian action is independent of the Roman family structure. De Martino's analysis of the classical law regarding the exercitor is essentially correct. Our observations here are concerned with the *historical* development which led to the emergency of the classical law. Cf. Martino, Stud., 17–20. Our position is thus in conflict with that taken by Wunner, 108–114, and in agreement with Wieacker, 135, n. 26.

90 Maine, 100. Italics by Author.

91 The exposition of the *actio quasi institoria*, also called the *actio utilis*

The early classical jurist, Labeo (d. *ca.* 20 C.E.), mentions a slave corpse-washer who, by his misdeeds, rendered his undertaker master liable to an *actio quasi institoria*.[92] This liability was established apparently on an *ad hoc* basis, for the slave appears certainly not to have been an *institor* and not to have had the power to make a contract obligating his master.[93]

Some two hundred years later, Papinian (d. 212 C.E.) spoke of an *actio utilis quasi institoria* against someone employing a *procurator* in terms indicating a more regular basis.[94] Now, *institores* were employees who had been assigned on a permanent basis to run a specified business, and *procuratores* were trusted agents of whom men of means availed themselves for the administration of their affairs. Both were in an extensive dependency relationship with their principals.[95]

Despite their affinity, however, there were marked differences between *procuratores* and *institores*. *Institores* were usually of a lower social and economic class. Thus, for example, writes Livy regarding one C. Terentius Varro:

> ... whose antecedents were not merely base but even sordid. It is said that his father had been a butcher, himself the pedlar *(institor)* of his wares, and that he had employed this very son in the menial tasks associated with that calling.[96]

Procuratores were generally freedmen; rarely slaves. *Institores* were often slaves; seldom freedmen. In contrast to the *institor*, who as

ad exemplum institoriae, which follows is based mainly upon Rabel, 1–26. For the textual analysis of the passages cited and the problems of interpolations, Rabel's article should be consulted directly. The most important passages are: Papinian, D. 3.5.30 pr.; Ulpian, D. 14.3.5.8. 10; 13 pr.; Paul, D. 14.3.16; Papinian, D. 14.3.19 pr.; D. 17.1.10.5; Ulpian, D. 19.1.13.25. Also of significance are the following passages regarding the *procurator*; P.S.5.8; Paul, D. 12.6.6 pr.; and Julian, D. 46.3.34.3.

92 Ulpian, D. 14.3.5.8.
93 Rabel, 5.
94 Papinian, D. 17.1.10.5.
95 Rabel, 7.
96 Livy, 22.25.18–19: *loco non humili solum sed etiam sordido ortus. patrem lanium fuisse ferunt, ipsum institorem mercis, filioque hoc ipso in servilia eius artis ministeria usum.* See also Livy, 26.16.8; Martial, 7.61.

a rule was a factor in small trade and a petty agent in money changing, the *procurator*, as a man of trust with composite duties acting according to his own discretion, could be found managing the affairs of rich women, high officials, distinguished citizens, and, later, of the Emperor himself and of the imperial family.[97] *Institorium* invariably involved a more limited authorization, a more individual enterprise; the authorization engendered through *procuratio* was less limited, the enterprise more general.[98] Thus, for example, if one paid one's debt to an *institor* against the express instructions of the creditor, the obligation was not discharged; if one did so to the *procurator* of the creditor against his express instructions, the obligation was discharged.[99] Why? Because the *procuratio*, addressed to third parties as well as to the agent himself, created a liability which was based upon the publication of the authorization which had originated from the appointment and could be affected negatively only by a similarly publicized cancellation.[100]

The contrast was indeed great; and presumably it would have normally never occurred to a Roman jurist to grant an institorial suit against a personage of importance whose freedman was managing his estate on the basis of a *praepositio agris colendis* when that activity was in the tradition of the Roman aristocracy, whereas an institorial suit would be granted against him were the *praepositio* made with a slave or some freedman of inferior quality for the purpose of commercial pursuits, e.g., the management of a bank for loans and money-changing, which were not in consonance with the aristocratic spirit.[101]

Thus, Papinian's contribution was the application of the *actio (quasi) institoria* on a *regular* basis to the transactions of the *procurator* — i.e., doing precisely that which would have not occurred to the jurist to do. He was able to do so by examining the charac-

---

97 Rabel, 7–8.
98 *Procuratio* was associated with an appointment that gave rise to a number of powers of representation variously phrased as *"paene dominus,"* *"omnium bonorum,"* *"libera administratio."*
99 Julian, D. 43.3.34.3. *Cf.* the parallel (in the opposite direction) passage, Paul, D. 12.6.6 pr. citing Celsus.
100 Rabel, 9–13.
101 Rabel, 9.

teristics of the institorian arrangement. He thereby discovered that the elements comprising the institorian appointment *(praepositio)* were as follows:

(1) The appointment implied a stable relationship of subordination between employer *(dominus negotii)* and agent *(praepositus)*.

(2) The appointment was related to a business enterprise, not an industrial one; the main occupation of the subordinate was the conduct of commercial transactions, not labour production.

(3) The appointment was for activity in a sphere of business objectively delimited.

(4) Although practically based upon economic and social relations, the liability of the employer — upon which third persons placed their reliance — was theoretically based upon the appointment.

The analysis of the elements of the typical *praepositio institoria* served Papinian as the basis upon which institorian-type liability could be applied to non-institorian, yet analogous arrangements. The application was juridically arrived at by viewing the liability of the employer-*dominus* for all the transactions of the representative-*praepositus*, within the scope of the authorization, of course, as being based upon the appointment-*praepositio* itself.[102]

The extension of the employer's liability *ad exemplum institoriae* was not limited to the transactions of the trusted agent who was in his steady employ *(procurator praepositus)*. It was also extended to cases (1) where one's freedman apparently *(not a procurator)* or one's friend was mandated to borrow money — the terms *libertus* and *amicus* being mentioned in all probability not to indicate a social standing that precludes the granting of the normal *actio institoria* but rather to indicate the stable relationship between employer and employee which was a characteristic element implied in the normal institorian appointment. This stable relationship served as the basis of the reliance third parties placed on the added responsibility of the *dominus negotii* and therefore justified the juristic extension; and (2) where the agent had been mandated only for an isolated transaction — the *mandatum* being apparently regarded as sufficiently equivalent to the stable relationship between employer and employee which was the characteristic element implied in the

102 Rabel, 6 and 13; Burdese, 199–201.

institorian appointment, or the circumstances being such that the need for said relationship was dispensed with.[103]

In these extensions, the type of relationship obtaining between employer and employee determined the type of knowledge thereof that third parties had to have in order to avail themselves of the *actio utilis ad exemplum institoriae*. If the relationship was indeed a most stable one, e.g., that of a *procurator omnium bonorum* with his superior, general awareness thereof on the part of the third party sufficed to render the superior liable. On the other hand, if the transaction was conducted on the basis of an isolated *mandatum*, specific knowledge thereof on the part of the third party would be necessary to render the employer liable. For certain purposes, however, if there existed a rather fixed relationship, such as that of patron-freedman or that of friends, between employer and employee, then again, general knowledge of that relationship — and not necessarily specific awareness of the individual *mandatum* — would suffice. It should be pointed out, moreover, that the significance of the words "knowledge" and "awareness" lies in their serving as the basis of the *reliance* by third parties on the backing of the *dominus* of his subordinate.[104]

The Papinian innovation was a highly practical one. But, although the exercise of commercial representation was thereby advanced, the idea of true agency was not. The employee-agent continued to be liable to the third party. Like the *actio institoria* itself, it represented one-way representation; the employer-principal could not make use of it to sue the third party. Moreover, we find no concomitant change in the writings of the post-Papinian jurists, no hint of direct, true agency. On the contrary, the *actio quasi institoria* formed for the later classical and the post-classical business practice a highly necessary device to overcome the inadequacy of the classical Roman theory of representation.[105]

As indicated earlier, however, the line separating the contractual services of freedmen from the non-contractual ones was blurred.

---

103 D. 3.5.30 pr.; D. 14.3.19 pr.; D. 17.1.10.5; and D. 19.1.13.25. Watson, Mand., 81; Angelini, Osserv., 245–248; Burdese, 192, 202–209. We have omitted reference to the *vilicus*; cf. Burdese's treatment, 197–206.
104 Burdese, 206–209.
105 Rabel, 23–25. See further the brief remarks of Powell, 47–48.

Similarly, the demarcation between the innumerable business and commercial activities of these persons *before* manumission and those performed *after* manumission was also hazy. In the latter case, however, the line was not blurred in the eyes of the law but rather in the economic market. When Cicero, for example, entreats Cornificius, the Governor of Africa, to protect the business interests of his good friend, Lamia,[106] he identified these interests as being represented by Lamia's "[contractual] agents, freedmen and slaves."[107] Thus, in the survey below of the role of agents functioning under a general authorization of their principals in the everyday life of Roman agriculture, business and trade, there were numerous instances where slaves, freedmen under contract, and freedmen operating on a non-contractual basis were indistinguishable.[108]

2. Non-Contractual Agents in the Economic Life of Rome

We have, then, four classes of persons who, in varying degrees, served as non-contractual agents in the market-place with the general authorization of their principals either implied or expressed: slaves, sons, freedmen and wives. In view of the overwhelming economic significance of slaves and freedmen in the Rome of the late Republic and the Principate, however, we must isolate among *their* multifarious activities their particular role as agents and describe this role in some detail.[109]

The main reasons for the dominant role of slaves and freedmen generally in Roman economic life also account specifically for their

---

106 L. Aelius Lama had defended Cicero vigorously in 58 and was made to suffer banishment for doing so. In 48, he acted as mediator between Cicero and Antony; Cicero *Letters to his Friends*, Loeb Classical Library, II, 470, note a. See further Bailey, Letters, III, 203.

107 Cicero *Ad fam.* 12.29.2: *procuratores, libertos, familiam.*

108 Park, 60–67.

109 A selected bibliography with regard to the role of slaves in the life of classical Rome has been given in the opening of Chapter II, above. In addition to those books, the following works with regard to freedmen were also used in the preparation of this section — Duff, A.M.; Dill, Bk. I, chap. III; Frank, Ec. Hist., 321–337; Loane; Frank, Ec. Surv., I, 274–277; Park; Fabricius, 26–30; Treggiari, 87–110, 142–153.

ubiquitousness as agents. Ancient legal restrictions prevented Romans of noble birth from engaging in business activities.[110] The traditional social averseness to trade felt by the Romans bolstered this legal prohibition.[111] Moreover, the superior *savoir-faire* as well as the unscrupulous character of many hellenized Orientals that had been brought as slaves to Rome were the concomitant personal and psychological qualities that account for their generally uninhibited dynamic activity in the field of commerce and for their specific usefulness as agents.[112]

In rural areas,[112a] for example, slaves and freedmen functioned in the dual roles of managerial employees and business agents. The everyday operation of large plantations involved the employment of these persons to act on behalf of absentee landlords in the supervision of the farmhands and the labour force, the acquisition of food and farming implements, the sale of produce, the collection of rents, and the like. In this agricultural setting, slaves and freedmen served as agents in basically two forms. The first was a *procurator*, the landlord's "attorney" or full legal representative — in most cases a freedman. The agency relationship between a *procurator* freedman and his principal was usually formal and governed by the contract of *mandatum* and the rules of *procuratio*.[113] To the extent that this relationship was contractual, it is beyond the scope of our study. Of greater relevance for our purposes was the *vilicus-actor*. The term *vilicus* refers to the administrator of a country estate *(villa)* who supervised the slave-farmhands, a farm-bailiff who directed the operations on the farm in *lieu* of the farm- or plantation owner. The term *actor* refers to the manager of the business aspects of the farm. The *vilicus-actor* was, especially on smaller farms, one person. Invariably beginning as a slave farm-labourer, he worked himself up into a managerial position by virtue of his diligence, initiative,

---

110 See, for example, Dio Cassius *Roman History* 69.16 and C.Th. 13.1.21.
111 See, for example, Cicero *De officiis* 1.150–151.
112 See, for example, Petronius *Satyricon* 75–76. On the entire paragraph, see our remarks at the beginning of Chapter II.
112a For a summary of the pre-classical development of Roman agriculture, see Besnier, 17–23.
113 Cicero *Pro Caecina* 57.G.2.64.95; 3.155–162; 4.84. Inst. 2.1.42–43; 2.9.5; 3.26; 4.10. D. 3.3; 17.1; 41.1.9.4.13, 20.2; 41.2.1.20, 34.1, 42.1. C. 2.12; 4.35.

dependability and administrative skill. Whether he remained in his servile state or was rewarded with manumission,[114] his managerial duties invariably brought him into circumstances in which we find him in a position of agent for his master: buying food or tools for his worker-slaves, occasionally collecting rents from the free tenants of his master, sometimes selling the produce of the plantation-farm. The situation necessitating his conduct as an agent was fluid: the absence of the master, the smallness of the enterprise which made the employment of a full-time *procurator* uneconomical, his own business acumen and skill. If these factors were lacking, it could very well be that a *vilicus* never, or most rarely, acted in the capacity of an agent for his master.[115]

In industry and manufacture, we also find capable slaves achieving managerial status in a manner similar to that which we described regarding the *vilicus-actor* in agriculture. Although management and administration were their central tasks, nevertheless such persons, in the course of their duties, were occasionally called upon to act as agents and business representatives of their masters — again, with little practical difference whether they had been manumitted or not.[116] Thus, in brickmaking, the many brick stamps that are available for scrutiny usually indicate the names of both the Roman noble owner and the superintending manager of the brickyard. The latter, invariably a slave or freedman, corresponds in every way to the *vilicus* of the plantation.[117]

114 Examples of slave *vilici: I.L.S.*, 3521, 3523, 3604, 7367, 7368; free *vilici* in *I.L.S.* are much rarer.

115 See, for example, Ulpian, D. 14.3.5.2, citing Labeo; Paul, D. 14.3.16.17. Heitland, 124–126, 137, 140, 149, 153, 158, 182, 194–196, 216–219, 224, 258–259, 263–265, 300. Heitland's documentation may be supplemented by the following Ciceronian passages: *De oratione* 1.249; *Pro Tullio* 17; *Pro Caecina* 57–58; *De republica* 5.5; *Pro Plancio* 62; *Epistulae ad Quintum fratrem* 3.15; see also Park, 72, and Treggiari, 106–110, and White, 332–357, 379–381.

116 Historians tend to assume, although accurate statistics are necessarily lacking, that in fact the *vilicus-actor* usually retained his slave status whereas the departmental director of a factory and the *institor* of an industrial or commercial establishment generally had obtained their freedom; contrast the remarks in Heitland, with those of Duff, A.M., 93.

117 Frank, Ec. Hist., 230–231; Loane, 38–39, 101–105; Duff, A.M., 92. See *C.I.L.* XV, part I.

Even more enlightening is the inscriptional evidence regarding the manufacture of jewellery and gold ornaments. In addition to private jewellers and individual free goldsmiths, wealthy patrons often equipped an artisan's shop for a skilled slave or freedman as a profitable way of investing capital. Frequently, a *dominus* would manumit a skilled goldsmith or jeweller, set him up in business, and have him work with the profits being shared. The freedman would continue to serve his (former) master with the same devotion, diligence and honesty as before — as is evidenced by the following inscription:

> To M. Canuleius Zosimus — The patron to his freedman. He did nothing contrary to the wishes of his patron. Though he always had much gold and silver in his possession he coveted none of it. He excelled in carving Clodian ware.[118]

The exact legal relationship between the slave or freedman artisan *(praepositus)* and his (former) master *(praepositor)* may be defined as *potestas* or contract, as already mentioned. But, as the inscription would seem to indicate, the informal feelings of affection and gratitude as well as the formal duties of *officium* and *obsequium* may have been the true governing factors in the relationship.

Other tombstone inscriptions[119] indicate the existence of a kind of jewellers' street, a row of shops where gem-engravers took orders and worked. Their names seem to indicate that they were freedmen. Having been trained as slave apprentices, they, too, may have been set up in business on an institorian basis, or alternatively, they may have saved enough by extra labour to accumulate a *peculium* from which they could purchase their freedom and set up shops of their own.[120]

In pottery manufacture, also, there is both literary and inscriptional evidence which indicates that factories were owned or operated by freedmen. For example, some of the owners of red-glazed pottery factories appear to be the very persons who designed the patterns of an earlier style — an indication that slave artists sometimes secured

---

118 *C.I.L.*, VI, 9222; see also *I.L.S.*, 7695.
119 *C.I.L.*, VI, 9433–9436, 9545–9549, 33872.
120 Frank, Ec. Hist., 242–243; *idem.*, Ec. Surv., I, 379; Loane, 86–90, 133–135; Duff, A.M., 113.

their freedom and became either directors of branch factories of their former masters or owners of their own establishments. In the event of the former, their managerial roles inevitably led them to act as agents of their patrons and the contractual terms were undoubtedly subsumed under the rules associated with the *actio institoria*.

Judging from the frequency of Greek *cognomina* inscribed on numerous clay lamps,[121] the manufacture of these cheap wares also was in the hands of freedmen, at least in the Early Empire — in all probability with the same relationship to their patrons as that which existed in the red-glazed pottery industry.[122]

In agriculture, industry and manufacture, then, the role of slaves and freedmen as the general agents of their present or former masters was in the main incidental to their role as managers and administrators of the latter's plantation or factory. As supervisors of slave farmhands and as foremen of factory workers, they would contract sales, purchases, loans, rentals, etc., creating thereby rights and obligations in their superiors. Such agency functions were, however, not the prime purpose of their employment; hence, they took place occasionally, haphazardly and unsystematically.[123]

It was in commerce and trade, however, that we find the employment of subordinates in and out of power as general agents a well-established practice. In overseas commerce and inland trade, freedmen, slaves and, to a lesser degree, sons acted as agents of their patrons, masters and fathers, respectively, in a fashion rather well-defined by law. By virtue of the exercitorian and institorian arrangements instituted by praetorian law, principals and third parties were quite clear as to the contractual rights and liabilities created by transactions entered into with these subordinates as general agents.

---

121 On the various problems involved in identifying Greek *cognomina*, see Solin.

122 Frank, Ec. Hist., 222, 225, 230–231; *idem.*, Ec. Surv., I, 378–379; Loane, 106–109, 111–112; Park, 79–84; Duff, ibid., 93, 108–113; Treggiari, 91–94; Prachner, *passim*. Because of their inferior status, slaves tend to be less represented in the inscriptions than freedmen and citizens. In any event, the skill, initiation and trustworthiness of a slave which earned him his freedom undoubtedly also made him the inevitable choice of his patron to act for him as his agent wherever it was necessary and feasible.

123 On the relationship of *officina*, the place of production, to *taberna*, the place of sale, see Bonetti, 13, 14–16.

Here there was nothing incidental, indirect, or haphazard in the utilization of these persons as agents.

Closely allied to industry and manufacture was the distribution of the wares produced. Hence we often find craftsmen and artisans not only manufacturing their products, but selling them as well. Thus, slave or freedmen clothiers *(vestiarii)* and linen weavers *(lintearii)* sometimes manufactured their products and had them peddled by other slaves or freedmen in the employ of their (former) masters and sometimes filled the role of pedlar *(circitores)* themselves.[124] The same is true of the baking industry:[125] Slave and freedmen bakers *(pistores)* were set up in business by their masters, and they peddled or delivered their bread to various customers; loaves bearing the *signacula* of these freedmen have been found — they are on display in the Naples Museum.[126] One such freedman specialized in the baking and distribution of bread made of fine wheat flour *(similaginarius)*.[127] In many of these activities, ownership of the factory and of its product was vested in the head of family, if the agent was a slave or son, or in the patron, if the agent was a freedman. Any breach of contract on the part of the agent-employee, sale of faulty merchandise, failure to deliver, and the like, laid the principal open to suit. Payments and profits made to and by the agent accrued to the accounts of the principal. In cases of non-payment to the agent, the principal had the right to sue the third party in the first instance if the agent was his son or slave, and, as a last resort to protect his interests, if the agent was a freedman.[128] It was this ability to create rights and liabilities on behalf of his principal, especially evident at the time of suit, as well as the large measure of discretion granted to him in his employment, that distinguished the agent-*institor* from an ordinary employee.

Another area where prominent use was made of the institorian agency relationship was banking. Romans, wealthy and aristocratic,

---

124 E.g., Ulpian, D. 14.3.5.4.6; *C.I.L.*, III, 5683; VI, 9964, 9969–9973. See Loane, 33–37, 69–73, 128–133, 149.
125 For slaves in the baking industry, see Moritz, 67–73, 97–102.
126 E.g., Ulpian, D. 14.3.5.9; *C.I.L.*, VI, 9803–9805. See Loane, 65–69; Frank, Ec. Hist., 269–270.
127 *C.I.L.*, VI, 9812.
128 Ulpian and Gaius, D. 14.3.1 and 2.

would not openly engage in investment business and in the placing of loans. Instead, they employed clever and trusted stewards, invariably slaves and freedmen. These latter were employed as money-changers, lenders of money on interest, and dealers in foreign exchange. Their functions, variously subsumed under the terms *argentarius, nummularius, mensarius* and *faenerator*, are well-represented in the Digest title describing the details of the institorian arrangement.[129] These banking operations through the agency of slaves and freedmen sometimes reached gigantic proportions. They may help us explain, for example, the rather startling statement of Plutarch that the elder Cato, the conservative statesman fiercely loyal to Roman traditions, lent money in marine insurance partnerships.[130] We have already made mention of the stigma attached to monetary investments in Roman aristocratic circles. Plutarch probably means that Cato, among the other wealthy Roman aristocrats of Campania, was financing Italiote-Greek slaves, freedmen and freemen in their mercantile pursuits. These financial investments were effective enough to have wrested much of the Delian trade from the veteran and practiced Syrians, Egyptians and Islanders. And so, at the time of Mithradates' raids in Asia and at Delos, although few Romans appear to have been slain, the great financial loss was sustained by the Roman capitalists.[131] The relationship, economic and legal, between these capitalists and their agents was probably that of *potestas*, in the case of slaves, and contract, in the case of the freedmen and freemen *sui iuris*. The arrangement with regard to third parties was undoubtedly exercitorian.

A fascinating example of the institorian set-up in banking and of the functioning of slaves and freedmen as business agents for wealthy Romans may be found in the use to which the *tesserae consulares* were put.[132]

---

129 E.g., D. 14.3.5.2.3; 19.3.20. Inscriptional evidence of freedmen and, to a lesser degree, slaves as bank employees and agents may be found in *C.I.L.*, III, 5094, 6424; VI, 9155–9185 (esp. 9172), 9683, and 9713.

130 Plutarch *Lives*: "Cato Major" 21; *cf.* Mitteis, Trap., 201, n. 2.

131 Frank, Ec. Hist., 292–293, 296.

132 The account herein given is based mainly upon Herzog; Cary, 110–113; and Frank, Ec. Surv., I, 272–273, 350.

Tesserae are small bone tags, square tablets which give an appearance similar to tickets in modern times. A rather large number of these tags were found, mostly at Rome. They all have legends bearing the following elements: (1) a name in the nominative, (2) a name in the genitive, (3) *sp.*, *spectavit*, or *spectat num.*, (4) a date specifying day and month, and (5) the names of the Consuls of that year (the earliest 96 B.C.E., the latest 88 C.E.).[133]

> *Philargyrus*
> *Epilli*
> *Sp[ectavit] Kal. Jan[uariis]*
> *M Tul[lio] C Ant[onio consulibus]*[134]

Of great significance is the fact that the names in the nominative are those of slaves and freedmen. Very rarely is the name of a Roman citizen to be found, and then only in the *tesserae* bearing the latest dates. It is therefore clear that the names in the genitive are those of their respective masters, present in the case of slaves, past in the case of freedmen.

For many years it was thought that these discs were worn by gladiators just as identification tags are worn by soldiers today. There were, however, two great difficulties to this theory: One, there was no adequate explanation of the need gladiators would have for such tags; and, two, most of the names in the nominative are Greek, and we know that there was an extremely small number of Greek gladiators.

Rudolf Herzog has apparently succeeded in explaining that these tickets were not *gladiatoriae* but rather *nummulariae*, i.e., related to banking. These tags were tied to bags of money certifying that the bags contained a fixed, standard amount and that the coins were of good quality. The *nummularii* were money-changers who, among other things, specialized in changing foreign coins for Roman ones, charging a percentage (*collybus* or *agio*) for the service. Wherever there were problems of alloyed coins, they also charged a percentage for testing: *spectatio.*[135] *Sp.*, *spectavit*, etc., indicate that the coins had been inspected. The lack of any number on the tickets leads one

---

133 *C.I.L.*, I², 889–951; see also nos. 2517, 2663 a–c.
134 Ibid., 907.
135 Cicero *In Verrem* 3.181.

to the assumption that the bags contained a uniform and standard amount of money. In this way, the coins were easily and conveniently available to provide for the needs of bank customers.

A careful study of the names found on these *tesserae* and also found in a wide area of literary sources has established that most of the names that are in the genitive, though not all, are those of *negotiatores*, tradesmen and bankers, money lenders and financial magnates — in a word, banking firms. Tenney Frank, however, emphasizes that there is firm evidence that at least some of these *tesserae* were not used by bankers and concludes:

> Perhaps the best hypothesis at present is that during a time when much foreign and some plated money circulated at Rome, business firms, merchants, bankers, knights and landlords who had dealings in sums of a thousand sesterces (presumably), adopted the custom of testing and conveying in sealed bags the larger amounts. The seals then bore the name of the owner and his "financial secretary," with the date of sealing. If this should prove to be correct, only a fraction, though perhaps a considerable fraction, of the seals belonged to bankers.

Thus, the inscription presented *supra*, on page 92, means as follows: "Philargyrus [the slave and agent] of Epillius, inspected [and sealed this] on the first of January in the consulship of Cicero and Antonius [i.e., 63 B.C.E.]."

How shall we understand the role of the above-mentioned "financial secretary"? What, in other words, is the exact relationship between the name found in the nominative, which bears the unmistakable mark of that of a slave or freedman, and that following it in the genitive, which represents (generally) a banking establishment of some sort?[136]

Citing Ulpian who states, "So also if a man has put a slave in charge of a money changer's table, he will be held liable on his account,"[137] Professor Herzog maintains that the institution of the *institor* as described in the legal sources was the faithful juridic

---

136 Names in a similar construction are also found in the literary sources; see, for example, Cicero *Ad fam.* 13.45.

137 Ulpian, D. 14.3.5.3: *Sed et si in mensa habuit quis servum praepositum, nomine eius tenebitur.*

formulation of the relationship of the slave or freedman to the *negotiator*; hence the nominative followed by the genitive.[138]

Engaged in this business in the capacity of an *institor*, an alert, efficient and enterprising slave could work himself up from a *nummularius* at a *mensa argentaria*, merely engaged as a clerk exchanging money, to that of the manager of a bank, engaged in large transactions of money-changing and commercial loans. His success could eventually enable him to buy his freedom. Then, as a freedman, he could continue to manage the same business of his former master. Thus we find this process reflected in the following Digest passage:

> If a master, who had a slave *institor* at a table for receiving deposits of money, also, after he has freed the slave, carries on the same business through the freedman, the conditions of the liability will not be affected by the change of status.[139]

Alternatively, the various coins with which the slave operated the business of money-changing and commercial loans, the standard sized money-bags to which these *tesserae* were attached, and the *vicarii*, sub-slaves, who served as clerks under his supervision, could all be converted to a *peculium* for the slave. This could be accomplished by removing these assets from the books of the *dominus*, entering them into a separate account, and turning them over to the slave with a general authorization, explicit or implied, to run the enterprise as he sees fit. This alternative arrangement had the added convenience of limiting the liability of the master for any of his slave's banking transactions only to the extent of the *peculium* — a liability which could be exceeded only when the master made the transaction or transactions his own by converting the proceeds thereof to his own account.

It is obvious that it was to this live situation that the classical jurist was alluding in the following passage:

> If, on the other hand, the business is carried on by a slave — which

---

138 The banking firms could, of course, be partnerships; Ulpian, D. 14.3.13.2; 17.2.24 and 52.5; Paul, D. 2.14.9 pr. and 25 pr.

139 Papinian, D. 14.3.19.1; *Si dominus, qui servum institorem apud mensam pecuniis accipiendis habuit, post libertatem quoque datum idem per libertum negotium exercuit, varietate status non mutabitur periculi causa.* Similarly Scaevola, D. *h.t.*, 20. *Cf.*, Mitteis, Trap., 211.

157

it may be — then if the slave carries it on with his owner's consent, the owner can be compelled to produce accounts, and an action is allowed against him, just as much as if he carried on the business himself. But if the slave acted without his master's knowledge, it is enough for the owner to swear that he has not got the accounts asked for: if the slave carries on the business with his *peculium*, the owner is liable *de peculio* or *de in rem verso*; but if the owner has got the accounts and declines to produce it, he is liable for the whole.[140]

Inasmuch as the *peculium* consisted of the master's property held in an account separate from that of the master, the slave conducted the business *servi nomine*, i.e., in his own name.[141] With this datum, Professor Herzog explains the hitherto problematic initials occasionally found on some *tesserae*. For example:

Protemus. Faleri
spectavit
N. S.
. . . .

N. S. meaning *nomine suo*. The ticket indicates, therefore, that the bag of money belonged to one Protemus; that this Protemus was a slave belonging to Falerius; and that the *mensa argentaria* that was being operated by Protemus was part of a *peculium*. Hence Falerius would not be liable *in solidum* for any transaction entered into or carried out by Protemus but only *de peculio*. The existence of an institorian relationship between Falerius and Protemus or its abrogation or its conversion to a peculiary one was usually indicated by a sign in front of the shop or table.[142] The *N. S.* indicates that although Protemus is a slave, he is not acting as an *institor* of his master but on his own account — i.e., on the basis of a separate *peculium*.

---

140 Ulpian, D. 2.13.4.3; *Sed si servus argentariam faciat (potest enim), si quidem voluntate domini fecerit, compellendum dominum edere ac perinde in eum dandum est iudicium, ac si ipse fecisset. sed si inscio domino fecit, satis esse dominum iurare eas se rationes non habere: si servus peculiarem faciat argentarium, dominus de peculio vel de in rem verso tenetur: sed si dominus habet rationes nec edit, in solidum tenetur.*
141 Ulpian, D. 15.1.9.8 at end; *cf.* G. 4.69–74.
142 Ulpian, D. 14.3.11.2ff, and Paul, D. 15.1.4.7.

Writes Professor Herzog:

> The painstaking precision with which Roman jurisprudence deals with
> all these questions of liability indicates how easily and how often
> swindles and resultant trials of all sorts took place in connection with
> these transactions entered into by slaves and freedmen.

We may also add that "the painstaking precision" of the jurists
faithfully reflects actual conditions which existed in Roman economic
life.

In addition to the distribution of manufactured goods and to
banking operations, trade in its various forms also was a prominent
field of activity to which the institorian and exercitorian arrangements pertained. Indeed, the *major* application of these arrangements
was to imports and exports, wholesale and retail sales and purchases,
petty shopkeeping and merchandising. It was in this field of trade
that the agency services of slaves and freedmen was at its maximum.
Variously referred to in inscriptions and in juristic sources as *negotiatores, mercatores, magistri navis* and *institores*, a remarkable
number of these merchants and dealers bear Greek *cognomina*.
Many of these Greeks were originally slaves who acquired their
liberty through diligent and industrious application of their business
capabilities. Applying the skill they had shown as slaves in managing
some rich man's firm and investing the money their former master
— with the prospect of good returns — had willingly provided them,
they pushed boldly into commercial ventures that senatorial Romans
traditionally shunned.[143]

Thus, we find slaves and, especially, freedmen acting as commercial agents in the distribution and sale of copper and bronze
imports, marble imports, wine and related products; in the purchase
and sale of oil; in the import and distribution of grain and vege-
tables.[144] This has led one student of industry and commerce in
ancient Rome to write:

> The craftsmen who sold directly from their combined artisan-shops
> and the freedmen of Greek or Oriental origin who distributed pro-

---

143 Frank, Ec. Hist., 321–323; Treggiari, 102–106.
144 See, for example, D. 14.3.5.1.14; 13 pr. *C.I.L.*, III, 5087; VI, 9664, 9671,
   9683, 33886; X, 545. Lemonnier, 273–275; Loane, 16–20, 39–62, 92–95,
   121–126.

vincial imports from small sales booths supplied most of the needs of this simple economic system.

and to conclude that "they are the true middlemen of the city."[145]

With regard to the exercitorian arrangement, it was after the Gracchan period that Roman capitalists entered the area of maritime trade. This field, especially in eastern waters, had long been dominated by Greeks and Orientals.[146] When wealthy Romans undertook the role of promoters and managers of mercantile projects, the actual operations were carried on by slaves and, even more, by freedmen. Indeed, an entire title in the Digest (14.1) assumes that the owners of vessels *(exercitores)* employed shipmasters *(magistri navis; navicularii)* to transport goods for businessmen in the importation and exportation involved in a variety of commercial enterprises.[147]

Rather than cite the myriad cases in which shopkeepers, wholesalers, shipmasters and commercial importers acted as agents of the principals who had set them up in business, we refer the reader to our exposition of the various legal aspects of these services involving agency and representation. In the course of that exposition, we cited a number of cases which illustrated the legal rules presented.

B. OUTSIDE THE CIRCLE OF THE *FAMILIA*

In combating the idea that the law is nothing but a body of legal propositions, Eugen Ehrlich set forth the primacy of the norm for a proper understanding of society in general and law in particular. "The inner order of the associations of human beings," he wrote, "is not only the original, but also, down to the present time, the basic form of law. The legal proposition [i.e., the precise, universally binding formulation of the legal precept in a book of statutes or in a law book] not only comes into being at a much later time, but is largely derived from the inner order of the associations." The group of

---

145 Loane, 147–153.

146 Casson, Anc., 173–188, 206–239.

147 See also D. 4.9.7.2; Petronius *Satyricon* 76; and Cicero *Ad Att.* 2.16.4. Loane, 13–16, 20–24, 44–47, 55–57; Brewster, 35; Frank, Ec. Hist., 300–303. See further Frank, Rom., 286, 289; and Frank, Aspects, 141, n. 6.

human beings who, in effect, ascribe to a specific inner order of association, recognize, in their relations with one another, certain rules of conduct as binding and actually regulate their behaviour in accordance with these rules — be they of law, morals, religion, ethical custom, honour, decorum, tact, etiquette, or of fashion.[147a]

Ehrlich's approach is to minimize the differences between law and other norms of social compulsion inasmuch as social compulsion, and not the authority of the law, the sovereign, and the state, is of prime essence. Whether one subscribes to this approach or not, it is undisputed that tribal allegiance, family, religion, among other bases of association, provide potent motives of obedience to social norms including legal norms. Indeed, many legal norms never find expression in formal legal provisions even in developed systems. In other words, the law is something much wider than formal legal formulation and formal legal regulation.[148]

A telling illustration of the aptness of these remarks is the law of agency in modern society. In its opening page of introductory definitions, the *Restatement of the Law of Agency* declares that

> Agency is the relationship which results from the manifestation of consent by one person to another that the other shall act on his behalf and subject to his control, and consent by the other so to act.

It then proceeds, in the more than one thousand pages that follow, to formulate and to expound the many laws and rules that govern this "manifestation of consent" and that control the results thereof. But it comes nowhere near exhausting the myriad instances of agency that never enter within the purview of the law and that never reach the courts — the non-contractual forms of agency, the informal and casual deeds by which people in all walks of life accomplish tasks for their dear ones, their intimates, their friends, relatives, and neighbours.

147a Ehrlich, 37–39. The consequences of this distinction between legal propositions and norms and the primacy ascribed to the latter are summarized by Ehrlich himself:

At the present time as well as at any other time, the centre of gravity of legal development lies not in legislation, nor in juristic sciences, nor in judicial decisions, but in society itself.

148 See Friedmann, *Legal Theory*, 247–249.

In Rome, too, the formal legal system covered only a very small portion of those acts which we have described previously as related to agency and representation, especially of the non-contractual kind. Taking for granted the relative stability of human nature, we may safely assume that the staples of interpersonal relationships were the same in Roman society as they are in ours and that untold acts which could be subsumed under the Restatement's definition of agency were in fact performed in an infinite variety of ways by friends, guests and neighbours, relatives, slaves and freedmen[149] casually and informally — although never or rarely mentioned by the jurists *(iurisprudentes)* and never or rarely brought to the attention of the judges *(iudices)*.

This phenomenon of the inadequacy of the legal literature in exhausting all acts of agency and representation in society is even more marked in the Roman *Corpus Iuris Civile* than in modern legal *corpora* for two reasons:

(1) The slowness and lateness with which Roman law recognized the idea of agency. The sphere within which formal agency was applied remained restricted and not fully developed. The rights and duties arising out of juristic acts in the classical *ius civile* accrued to the person who carried out the form, and to no one else. The mere intention of that person that the form should operate in behalf of or to the liability of another person — the projected "principal" — had, as we have already indicated, no effect whatever.

(2) The Romans' fine sense of the limitations of the law. The Romans' highly developed sense of dignity and decency prevented them from discussing many (to them) intimate matters in Court and motivated them to exclude such matters from legal regulation. The Romans were enmeshed in a web of inner associations, such as *familia, amicitia,* and *patronatus,* which were the sources of numerous and powerful extra-legal restrictions and duties. The intimacy and strength of these associations can hardly be appreciated by modern man in his atomized existence. The Romans "were largely dependent on their own and their wives' relatives, on friends and patrons, on the public generally, and often more strictly confined by the opinion of such persons than by a judicial ruling." Moreover,

149 *Cf. Ad Att.* 1.20.7.

beyond the private law, "quite apart from the restrictions of public law, those imposed by *pietas, fides, humanitas* (in short, by the *officium*) were exceedingly real and powerful." Hence, we find the relative reticence of the jurists with regard to many acts performed in the day-to-day lives of the Romans, among them acts that we would construe as fulfilling the function of agency.[150]

An exhaustive catalogue of such acts and services would be futile. They are too numerous, too petty and too much taken for granted to have been recorded in any but an incidental and haphazard fashion. Moreover, such a catalogue would contain many acts that are familiar to us from our own experiences. The main purpose of the exposition which follows, therefore, is to place in bold relief those sociological aspects of Roman life which, on the one hand, have a direct bearing on agency and representation while, on the other hand, differ sufficiently from the sociological aspects of agency in our society as to warrant discussion, analysis and interpretation.

1. *Friends and Neighbours*

a. *Introduction: The Roman Theory of Friendship*

In order to describe with full understanding the role of friends and neighbours in the area of agency, viewed juridically or non-juridically, we must first address ourselves to the phenomenon of the gratuity in Roman law.

A gratuity, whether it be a gratuitous gift or a gratuitous service, is characterized by the absence of any obligatory counterpart, whether in money or in kind, to a legal act which, by reason of its economic function, normally requires one.[151]

Of the greatest significance to the history of law is the thesis[152] that "trade and contract are built upon the forms of gifts which, although theoretically voluntary, are in reality made or rendered to

---

150 Schulz, Princ., 21–22, 158.
151 Michel, 235. The following discussion is drawn mainly from Michel's excellent study.
152 Originally formulated by Mauss, Gift.

fulfil some obligation." A thorough examination of this thesis is outside the scope of our study; but the operative concept upon which it is based, namely, that a gratuitous gift or a gratuitous service is grounded not in altruism but rather in reciprocity, is central to the proper understanding of friendship in its role of agency in Roman society.[153]

A linguistic analysis of Indo-European roots related to concepts of giving and receiving in general as well as of the Latin terms, *mutuum* (originally and essentially, "an object of exchange"; in usage, "a loan for consumption"), *donum* ("a gift"), and *munus* ("a customary gift given on a specified occasion" or "a voluntary compensation for services rendered") reveals the following:

> The Indo-European languages have preserved unmistakable traces of an ancient system of reciprocal gratuities analogous to that which some anthropologists have described as typical of primitive societies.
> This terminology of reciprocal gifts and services serves as the basis of the terminology of contracts.
> The word *munus, munera* underwent an interesting evolution whereby the connotation developed not into the obligatory character of gifts and services but rather into the sanctions for such obligations.[154]

153 Indeed, anthropological observations of primitive behaviour, in the many societies studied, have shown that the exchange of gifts often follows, with few exceptions, certain universally accepted rules of behaviour and attitudes of mind. These rules may be summarized as follows:

It is improper to solicit a gift or a gratuitous service. The initiative ought to reside in the donor or the one rendering the service although certain conditions may suggest to the donor the necessity of said gift.

A gift symbolizes friendship. Acceptance implies not only an (economic) obligation to reciprocate but also a (socio-psychological) relationship between donor and donee. This relationship is made manifest in an infinite variety of ways, one striking example of which is the psychological understanding that to have received a service, gift or favour from someone entitles the recipient to expect or receive them again.

To accept a gratuity is to place oneself under some obligation to render one in reciprocation. Conversely, to refuse to accept a gratuity implies either an affront to the intended donor or as a source of reproach to the intended recipient; the latter's refusal is tantamount to a confession that he is either unwilling or unable to reciprocate, i.e., to undertake the obligations such acceptance would create. See Mauss, Soc.; Herskovits: Hoebel; Levi-Strauss; and Hogbin.

154 Michel, 469–501.

With these observations, we are furnished with sufficient background material for a proper understanding of the Roman concept of friendship. This concept, inherited in seminal form from the Greek philosophical tradition, was fully developed by the Latin moralists.

The philosophical heritage of the Greeks with regard to the conception of friendship may be summarized as consisting broadly of two opposing, although sometimes overlapping, tendencies. The first tendency received its inspiration from a close observation of social practices. It saw in the relationship obtaining between friends an exchange of beneficial acts: a series of services rendered mutually, profiting both, and tending to persist and endure with the tacit understanding that such acts (and the feelings they imply and engender) are to the respective advantages and interests of the parties involved. This sociological view of friendship is normally to be found in those schools of thought which were based upon the doctrine of pleasure, i.e., the Cyrenaics and the Epicureans.[155] It immediately and inevitably brings to mind the primitive system of reciprocal gratuities and results, of course, in a utilitarian theory of friendship.

The second tendency, on the other hand, views friendship, not as the confluence of two enlightened, self-interested parties, but, rather, as the harmonious accord obtaining between two souls guided by a concept of the good held in common and provided with an appreciable amount of similar qualities of character. This spiritual or psychological conception of friendship is to be found naturally among those philosophers preoccupied with metaphysics and carried away by abstract thinking, i.e., Aristotle and the Stoics.[156]

Reflecting upon these two tendencies, we see clearly that the first one, the utilitarian theory of friendship, is descriptive; its point of departure is the every day manifestations of the exchange of mutual services. On the other hand, the psychological theory is less interested in the outward signs of friendship and is more concerned with the feelings and sentiments which inspire these outward signs; it addresses itself to a delineation of the conditions to which an ideal friendship

155 *Cf.* Dugas, 28–33, 127.
156 Aristotle *Nicomachean Ethics* 8.2 (§1155b); Vogel, II, 174; Dugas, 191–202.

ought to correspond — a friendship purified of considerations of self-interest and conceived of as a tie, no longer social, but exclusively spiritual.

Cicero was the direct heir of the Greek heritage.[157] In the treatises in which he wrote about friendship at length, *De amicitia* and *De officiis*, the two theories developed by the Greeks served as the basis of his discussions. In the *De amicitia*, for example, Cicero attacked the problem of friendship at its very base: Is friendship founded on self-interest or not?

> The oftener, therefore, I reflect on friendship the more it seems to me that consideration should be given to the question, whether the longing for friendship is felt on account of weakness and want, so that, by giving and receiving favours, one may get from another and in turn repay what he is unable to procure of himself; or, although this mutual interchange is really inseparable from friendship, whether there is not another cause, older, more beautiful, and emanating more directly from Nature herself.[158]

Note how Cicero tied the utilitarian conception of friendship to the practice of reciprocal gifts and mutual services and how he expressed this tie in terms reminiscent of trade and exchange.[159] As for this conception of friendship with which the Romans were acquainted, to the extent to which one can detect therein the influence of Epicureanism, one must insist upon two points: (a) Regard for reputation and social prestige, so prevalent among the Romans, were completely foreign to the Epicurean philosophy;[160] and (b) Epicureanism was regarded, at least by Cicero, as incompatible with the study of the *ius civile*.[161]

When Cicero came, however, to formulating that conception of friendship acceptable to himself, he repudiated the utilitarian theory and found true friendship in the communion of hearts, not in an

---

157 Cf. Douglas, 135–170.

158 8.26. The translation is from the Loeb Classical Library edition of Cicero *De senectute, de amicitia, de divinatione*.

159 *De amicitia* 14.49; 16.56, 58. The Epicurean doctrine of friendship is illustrated in a striking manner by the life of Atticus, analyzed at length in Carcopino, Cic. II, 432–467.

160 Cicero *Tusculanarum disputationum* 2.12.28; Carcopino, ibid., 440, n. 7.

161 *Ad familiares* 7.12.2. But this may have been a jest on the part of Cicero; *cf.* Michel, 509, n. 23, and Bailey, Ep. I, 339.

identity of interests. It was neither born in nor sustained by self-interest; if it were indeed true, it was self-sufficient. *Amicitia* was derived from *amor*.[162]

In his opposition to the utilitarian theory of friendship, Cicero chose to ignore not only the ideas and attitudes generally prevalent among his contemporaries, but even the manner in which they actually carried on their friendships. The Romans were quite cognizant of the omnipotence of friendships, we would say relationships, based upon self-interest: They did not hesitate to demand of their friends the most onerous services, indeed most questionable ones — services which would never occur to us to expect of our friends and which we would not hesitate for a moment to refuse to render if anyone would have had the audacity to demand them of us.

The second treatise in which Cicero discussed friendship from a philosophical point of view is *De officiis*. The term *officium*, as well as the term *beneficium* which formed the basis of Seneca's moral essay (to be considered next), connotes a service voluntarily and beneficently rendered; the former term was used from the vantage point of the benefactor, the latter from the point of view of the beneficiary. A *beneficium* received was the source of an obligation to reciprocate with a new *officium*. Strictly speaking, an *officium* ought to apply to the first benefaction — gift or service — rendered by one partner or friend to his colleague, but, in practice, friendships generally did not have an exact point at which they were initiated and, most often, one could not point to the first benefaction on the basis of which the relationship had been launched.

In *De amicitia*, Cicero described the ties which create a mutual affection among friends. It is understandable that he placed the main emphasis upon the psychological aspect of this attachment and upon the moral duties that flow out of it. On the other hand, in his *De officiis* we find an analysis of the virtuous (Bk. I), of the useful (Bk. II), and of the conflicts which arise between them (Bk. III). It is a veritable manual of the virtuous and proper Roman. The posture

---

162 *De amicitia* 9.31; 8.26. Compare Cicero's expression *beneficium faeneramur*, to practice usury with benefits, to put one's favours on interest, with Terence *Phormio* 493.

that befits the citizen of a great community is given due weight, and the sentiments which ought to be proclaimed concerning consideration for one's fellow or which ought to be, conversely, aroused in the hearts of one's peers towards oneself are delineated precisely.

The aims set before him in composing his *De officiis* naturally led Cicero to expand beyond the narrow framework of the individual conscience and to concern himself with the social realities that faced any observer of the Rome of the last century of the Republic. It comes therefore as no surprise that his *De officiis*, even more than his *De amicitia*, contains numerous examples of the types of services rendered, the gifts exchanged, and the ceremonial reciprocities conducted between Roman friends. Thus, on reciprocal gifts and services, Cicero writes as follows:

> But since, as Plato has admirably expressed it,[163] we are not born for ourselves alone, but our country claims a share of our being, and our friends a share; and since, as the Stoics hold, everything that the earth produces is created for man's use; and as men, too, are born for the sake of men that they may be able mutually to help one another; in this direction we ought to follow Nature as our guide to contribute to the general good by an interchange of acts of kindness, by giving and receiving, and thus by our skill, our industry and our talents to cement human society more closely together, man to man.[164]

In another, extended passage,[165] Cicero points out, however, that *true* benefactions have their rules and limits:

> They must conform to the true interests of the receiver: Thus, personal service is often more beneficial — hence, more obligatory to be rendered — than gifts of money; for the latter tends to engender in the recipient a dependence upon and expectation of monetary support which may prove to be his eventual undoing.
>
> They must not exceed the means and resources of the benefactor,[166] for many have squandered their patrimony by indiscriminate giving.[167] Such extravagance, obviously, is motivated not by true friendship but

163 See *Epistles* 9.358a.
164 *De officiis* 1.7.22; see also 1.17.56. The translation is from the Loeb Classical Library edition.
165 Ibid., 2.15.52–55.
166 *Cf.* Seneca *De beneficiis* 2.15.3.
167 A common enough occurrence; *cf.* Martial 4.67; Pomponius, D. 42.1.30; Tryphoninus, D. 42.1.50.

by considerations of political expediency,[168] municipal prestige,[169] and/or patriotic duty.[170]

The gift must be in a measure proportionate to the deserts of the recipient.[171] Thus, repaying a kindness already received takes priority over granting favours with the hope of future kindness;[172] and requiting a favour *(reddere)* takes precedence over initiating one *(beneficium dare)*.[173]

Cicero's enunciation of this last principle, by its tacit assumption, corroborates principles of friendship already mentioned, namely, that to receive obligates one to repay and that, to be done properly, repayment must either be larger than or as large as that which was received — not less.[174, 175]

Another important source of the idea of friendship in Roman moral philosophy is Seneca's *De beneficiis*, which means, literally, "Concerning beneficences" or ". . . benefactions." The term "beneficence" connotes an act of kindness performed by the rich on behalf of the poor, by the powerful for the weak, by a superior person to an inferior. In contrast to this essentially Christian connotation, the term *beneficium* in classical Latin, i.e., "performing a good deed," connotes that type of service one performs in behalf of a colleague, one's equal, a friend. Thus, the major portion of Seneca's tract is

168 Julius Caesar comes immediately to mind.

169 *Cf.* Pliny *Epistulae* 10.110.1.

170 *Cf.* Hermogenianus, D. 50.2.2, and Ulpian, D. 50.4.6 pr.

171 *Cf.* Seneca *De beneficiis* 2.17.1.

172 *De officiis* 1.15.48: *Etenim si in eos, quos speramus nobis profuturos, non dubitamus officia conferre, quales in eos esse debemus, qui iam proferunt?* The first class is a striking example of *donatio principaliter facta*, a gift made or a service rendered with a view toward creating new ties of friendship by obligating the recipient to reciprocate. *Cf.* Michel, 282–284, for the relevant exegesis of Ulpian, D. 17.1.10.13 and 12 pr.

173 *De officiis* 1.15.47–48.

174 A most striking example of ceremonial reciprocity is the arranging of a funeral at one's own expense without being obligated to do so. The praetor enforced a form of reciprocity by granting an *actio funeraria* against the heir of the deceased who had not fulfilled his duty of piety and had not arranged the funeral himself; D. 11.7; C. 3.44. A thorough examination of ceremonial reciprocity would take us into the realm of public law (e.g., *munera municipalia, cursus honorum, opera publica, ludi, frumentum, alimenta, etc.*).

175 Much of the foregoing is based on Michel, 511ff.

devoted to the reciprocal services which friends render each other and to the rules which govern these courtesies. A survey of these services and their rules reveals the following:

It is improper to solicit a gift or a service. True friendship, therefore, obliges one to make such solicitation unnecessary: The initiative ought to reside in the donor. Once asked, one's response must be wholehearted and with discernment.[176]

A gift symbolizes friendship; and, by virtue of this principle, a gift will sometimes symbolize a friendship restored.[177] Moreover, having received entitles one to receive again. There is a bond created by a gratuity; and when a new situation arises that calls for another gratuity, abstaining from offering and extending assistance anew would constitute an open declaration that the relationship has been terminated.[178]

To accept a gratuity is to place oneself under an obligation to render one in reciprocation. "What difference does it make whether my benefits are returned? Even after they have been returned, they must be given again." Thus, a benefaction once made is never lost.[179] However, it is unseemly to pay back too hastily, for such payment indicates an uneasiness felt by the recipient friend. One must know how to reciprocate gracefully: in time (not too soon and not too late), in manner (not to press acceptance unduly and not to hope that one's benefactor will fall into dire straits so that one may repay him in turn), and in substance (not less than that which was received).[180]

A gratuity ought to evoke the acknowledgement and gratitude of the recipient but not the duty to pay back as a debt, for monetary payment and friendly benefaction are mutually exclusive. Similarly, the grandeur and mobility of gratuities vanish when the obligations they engender are no longer moral but have become actionable.[181] Although to expect reciprocal payment when granting the gratuity ill benefits a true friend, it is permitted to remind one's beneficiary of his duties. This must be done, however, tactfully, better, by renewed benefaction.[182]

The above summary of Seneca's observations concerning friendship reveals that the key to the performance of services among friends is

---

176 Seneca *De beneficiis* 1.2.1; 2.1.2.4; 2.2.1–2. See also Martial 11.8.3 and Pliny *Epistulae* 4.17.1.

177 *De ben.* 2.18.5; 3.27.1–3.

178 *De ben.* 4.13.3; 4.15.3. And one who has received a favour need not feel discomfited to receive another one; ibid., 4.40.2, and Cicero *Ad fam.* 2.6.2.

179 *De ben.* 4.13.3; 6.3.1.3. Also Plautus *Persa* 762 and Martial 5.42.7–8.

180 *De ben.* 4.40.4.5; 5.2.1; 5.4.1; 6.39.1. *Cf.* Martial 7.42.3; 10.17.2.

181 *De ben.* 2.17.7; 3.6.2; 3.13.2; 4.13.3; 4.21.1–3; 6.14.4.

182 Ibid., 1.1.9; 1.2.3.4; 2.11.1; 3.15.4; 5.23.2.

that they are based upon the exchange of gratuities. What constitutes the gratuitous element in these reciprocal donations? The positive facts that they are free and voluntary and the negative ones that they are neither legally binding nor subject to demand or coercion. Each partner or colleague may rely solely upon the courtesy and upon the sense of duty of the other. Each friend is bound to the other solely by his sense of honour or by his fear of dishonour.[183]

b. Friendship in the Life and Law of Classical Rome[184]

Paul's definition of friends, although written within the specific context of the law of guardianship, holds true for other areas of Roman law as well. Friends, he stated, are not those who are tied to each other by mere acquaintance, but rather those among whom there obtain special ties along the lines of a respectable familial relationship *(honestis familiaritatis rationibus)*.[185]

The last phrase, alluding to the quasi-familial character of the bond of friendship among the Romans, is a particularly felicitous one. *Amicitia* was rather frequently hereditary, transmitted from father to son.[186] It united not only two individuals, but two families as well. Between two people of similar age and background, it was sealed from adolescence[187] by an education received from the same teachers, by shared tastes and similar spirits, by military service performed together, and, later, by parallel careers pursued at the same time. Mutual service and reciprocal obligingness eventually ratified this relationship established during the early years of public life;[188] and the occasions for their usefulness presented themselves continually.

Having outlined the major themes found in the moralistic tracts re-

---

183 On the foregoing, see further Hands, ch. III.
184 Especially helpful in the preparation of this section were Friedländer, I, 207–227, and Michel, 520, 530–577.
185 Paul, D. 50.16.223.
186 Plautus *Trinummus* 737; Caesar *Bellum civile* 2.25.4; Cicero *Ad fam.* 6.16.
187 Terence *Adelphi* 440.
188 Cicero *Ad fam.* 6.11.1; Pliny *Epistulae* 1.19.1. For a balanced view of friendship in politics, see Brunt, Am., 1–20.

lated to friendship, we have been made aware that "side by side with the legal system is the system of custom and morals, that group of extra-legal restrictions which form the main content of the conception 'officium' and which is so particularly important for the legal life of the Romans."[189] A word of caution, however, is in place. Although the moralists were rooted in the life of Roman society, i.e., in the prevalent norms and mores, their writings contained much that partakes of projected ideals — ideals, incidentally, which themselves influenced Roman behaviour and attitudes, albeit to a limited extent. In the presentation of friendship in the life and law of classical Rome which follows, therefore, the material is drawn from juristic,[190] moralistic, and literary (epistolary and belleletristic) sources. The documentation is given in this way in order to emphasize the interplay of the moral ideal and the everyday reality of interpersonal relationships as well as the reflection of this interplay in the law.

Seneca divided benefactions into three general categories:

> [1] The necessary ones ... without which we are unable to live [e.g., rescue from death], [2] the useful ones ... without which we ought not to live [e.g., money, honour], and [3] the pleasurables ones ... without which we are not willing to live [e.g., pleasures, gifts].[191]

For our purposes, however, these categories are too broad. Hence we present a picture of the services and benefactions *(officia et beneficia)* which friends[192] rendered to each other by describing and sum-

---

189 Schulz, Princ., 20.

190 In the citations from juristic sources, preference will be given to those passages which employ words explicitly related to friendship, i.e., *amicus, amicitia, amicalis* and *amicabilis*.

191 *De ben.* 1.11.1–5: *necessaria ... sine quibus non possumus vivere, utilia ... sine quibus non debemus [vivere], iucunda ... sine quibus nolumus [vivere].* Cf. Paul, D. 5.3.38; Gaius, D. 5.3.39; Ulpian, D. 25.1.1ff; and Paul, D. 50.16.79.

192 Although the sources generally describe the behaviour of the upper classes, the conclusions drawn from them are applicable to friendship in Roman life generally; Schulz, Princ., 233. It must also be borne in mind that there were various levels of friendship. Not all friendships were "along the lines of a respectable familial relationship"; see Pliny *Epistulae* 4.17.2. With the steady increase in clients, it became necessary to make a practical distinction between *amici primi* and *secundi, amicitiae*

marizing the six main ways in which they were performed.[193]

(1) Duties *(officia)*. In contradistinction to the generalized mean-- ing of *officia* as services voluntarily and beneficently rendered, the term used narrowly refers to those specific moral duties that arose out of the relationship of family or friendship and that were incumbent upon a kinsman or friend in carefully and precisely defined situations.[193a]

---

superiores and *minores*; *De ben.* 6.33.4–34.5 and Pliny *Epistulae* 7.3.2. These distinctions, however, are of no great significance for our study.

193 Seneca *De ben.* 1.24 (moralistic); Cicero *Ad Att.* 3.11.2 (epistolary); Berger, Enc., *s.v. officium, res, fides, gratia, consilium propinquorum* and *operae* (juristic).

193a With due regard for the varying degrees of intimacy between friends and the resultant variety of levels of obligation to render certain *officia*, the following list represents their main manifestations:

Salutatio, the morning greeting which Romans of rank were in the habit of receiving from clients, friends and admirers in the *atrium* during the first two hours of the day; for this purpose the callers gathered in the vestibule even before sunrise waiting for the appearance of the honoured one. (Seneca *De ben.* 6.33.4; Cicero *Ad Att.* 14.1.2 and 2.3; Pliny *Ep.* 3.12; Martial 4.8.)

Deductio, ad forum deducere, domo deducere, escorting a distinguished Roman in public as part of his entourage. (Cicero *Ad Att.* 1.18.1; 4.1.4–5; *idem., Ad fam.* 10.12.2; *idem., De senectute* 18.63; Ulpian, D. 47.10.15, 22–23.)

Family events, such as the coming of age ceremonies of a fifteen year-old boy *(officium togae irrilis)*, a betrothal *(sponsalia)*, a wedding *(nuptiae)*, banquets, manumissions of slave, grave illness and death. (Pliny *Ep.* 1.9.2; Publilius Syrus 670; Gaius, D. 13.6.18 pr.; Ulpian 33.9.3.6.) The manumission of a slave in the presence of friends was a frequent and well-known ceremony among the Romans. This ceremony was variously referred to as *manumissio inter amicos, manumissio per mensam* (q.v. Kaser, *I*, 254, n. 22) and *manumissio in convivio*; G. 1.41 and parallels, P.S. 4.12.2, Ulpian 1.10 and 18, V.F. 261, Inst. 1.5.1 and parallels, Lex Romana Burg. 445, Gaius *Epit.* 1.12).

Testis ad testamenti factionem, to act as a witness at the drawing up of a will. (Cicero *Ad Att.* 14.3.2; 14.14.5; Ulpian, D. 28.1.20.10 and 21.2.)

Recitationibus adesse, to attend the public readings of one's friend's literary creations. (Pliny *Epistulae* 1.135.)

Epistulae, correspondence. Although not usually construed as an *officium*, correspondence among friends when one of them was not at Rome was a necessary service: to transmit national and political news,

Romans had the greatest regard and concern for prestige and, especially, for the outward signs thereof. One's friends were simultaneously both a source and a sign of power. Romans endeavoured, affected and pretended to have as many of them as possible and multiplied the occasions at which they could display evidence of such prestigious power. Concomitantly, it was the duty of one's friends to participate in such occasions, though such duty might become onerous and irksome because of the frequency and duration of these occasions.[194]

In addition to the aforementioned *officia*, which were more or less formally prescribed, there were a number of ways in which friends (and relatives) performed benefactions *(beneficia)* for one another.

(2) The simplest and most direct manner of performing a *beneficium* was with something substantial, some material contribution *(re)*. A gift *(donatio)*, for example, was a gratuity only in the technical sense; sooner or later it cost the recipient as much or even more than it was worth.[195] Other material benefactions were a loan of money *(mutuum)*,[196] a gratuitous loan for use, eventually to be returned *(commodatum)*,[197] hospitality *(hospitium)* and lodging *(deversorium)*.[198] A legacy *(legatum)* was the ultimate, and hence the most eloquent, testimony to one's feeling of affection for one's friends.[199]

(3) Making one's credit work for a friend *(fide)* was a common *beneficium* as, for example, by acting as a guarantor, collateral or security.[200]

---

to give particulars of one's own activities and private affairs, and to express sentiments of concern for one another. (Cicero *Ad fam.* 2.4.1; see Friedländer, III, 38ff.)

194 Pliny *Epistulae* 1.9.
195 Cicero *Ad Att.* 2.4.1; Pliny *Epistulae* 5.2.1–2; Martial 9.44.3–4; Ulpian, D. 39.5.5.
196 "If our friends remain loyal, money will be forthcoming," writes Cicero to Terentia; *Ad fam.* 14.1.5. See also *idem. Ad Att.* 1.13.6; Pliny *Epistulae* 3.11.2; Tryphoninus, D. 3.5.37.
197 G. 3.196; D. 44.7.1.4; Ulpian, D. 13.6.5.14; *idem.* D. 48.5.9 pr.
198 Cicero *Ad fam.* 7.23.3; *Ad Att.* 16.6.1; Pliny *Ep.*, 1.4.
199 Scaevola, D. 33.1.19.1; 33.2.32 pr.; Papinian, D. 33.1.10 pr.
200 Cicero *Ad Att.* 12.14.2; 15.16.2; G. 3.115; D. 47.10.19; Ulpian, D. 22.1.21; African, D. 28.5.47.

(4) To place one's influence, prestige and connections *(gratiā)* at the service of one's friends was a common *beneficium*. In effect, it was a declaration saying, "He who treats my friend favourably is acting kindly to me."[201] The letter of recommendation *(litterae commendaticiae)*, for example, was essentially an open manifestation, a public declaration of friendship between the writer and the recommendee.[202, 203] Similarly, for friends to be present at a trial, lending moral or legal support for one of their colleagues, was also a *beneficium gratiā*. This was especially important if the friend was abroad and could not protect his interests in court or before the praetor.[204]

(5) Another benefaction one bestowed upon a friend was to give him the benefit of one's insight, wisdom and experience *(praeceptis consiliōque)*[205] either in individual consultation or in the deliberations

---

201 E.g., see Pliny *Ep.* 1.24.
202 Cicero *Ad fam.* 5.5.1. Indeed, the entire Book XIII of Cicero's *Epistulae ad familiares*, seventy-nine all told, consists of such letters. Many others are to be found in other parts of his collected letters as well as in the correspondence of Pliny the Younger, Symmachus and Sidonius Apollinaris. Since the writing of this type of letter was incumbent upon friends, the recipient of such a letter was to understand it for what it was, a recommendation and not a mandate. Hence, should anything have gone wrong as a result of the recommendation, the author of the letter was not liable to an *actio mandati* (Ulpian, D. 17.1.12.12).
203 *Gratia* was a significant item. One could be chosen as a partner because of his financial resources; the second partner could be chosen because of his craftsmanship and skill; and a third because of his influence and connections; see Proculus, D. 17.2.80. Moreover, it was important in judging the reliability of a witness, for if the witness was a friend of the litigating party, considerations of *gratia* may have tainted his testimony; Callistratus, D. 22.5.3 pr.
204 See, for example, Cicero *Pro Publio Quinctio* 8.30. The praetor had decided that Publius and Naevius his opponent should enter into a kind of legal wager *(sponsio)* whereby the latter should pay a mere nominal sum if he had been found guilty of some irregularity. The friends and supporters of Publius objected. They maintained that a judicial verdict ought to be given on the matter, that either both or neither of the parties should be required to provide security, and that there was no need to imperil the good name of Publius. On the influence of *gratia* on litigation, see Kelly, 42.
205 Pliny, *Ep.*, 2.18.1: "What can be more agreeable to me than the duty you have enjoined upon me of finding a tutor for your nephews?... I

175

of the council of friends *(consilium amicorum)*.[206] The advocate in his role on behalf of a defendant and the jurist in his role as legal adviser to a litigant, magistrate or judge may be regarded as variations of friends granting *beneficia consilio*.[207]

Before proceeding to the sixth way in which *beneficia* were performed, we pause to summarize the data presented and to describe its significance for the conception of friendship that was peculiarly Roman. The serious implications that this data holds for our study may be gathered from the following observations made by Professor Fritz Schulz:[208]

> The Roman *amicitia*, the foundation and dissolution of which was not unattended by forms, gave rise to a number of serious and very real duties. Roman friends made mutual claims on each other which would in many cases cause a modern "friend" to break off the friendship without delay. In Rome there was no hesitation about asking a friend for help — either active or advisory — in any situation; a friend could be asked for hospitality, to execute commissions, to give recommendations to others, he might even be asked for money. Cicero, writing to his wife from his place of banishment, advised her to raise money in a crisis, not, as she had intended, by the sale of lands, but rather by applying to friends: "If they do their duty, there will be no lack of money."[209] The friends seem to have fulfilled his expectations, for in the next letter Cicero informs his wife that he has written to thank the friends whose names she has given him.[210] In the great mass of Cicero's letters almost every one contains some kind of request to the addressee or else expressions of gratitude for some service or kindness rendered by his correspondent. The Roman considered himself bound to help his friend by no matter what sacrifice. It is significant that

purpose to hear all the several professors; and when I have done so, I shall write you such an account of them as will make you imagine you have heard them yourself." See also ibid., 1.21.

206 Cicero *Ad fam.* 4.9.2; Pliny *Ep.* 1.21. Note the problem of drawing the fine line of distinction between *consilium* and *mandatum* underlying G. 3.156. On the role of the *consilium propinquorum et amicorum* in dispensing criminal justice within the framework of the *familia*, see Kunkel, 219–251.

207 Pomponius, D. 1.2.2.43; Paul, D. 50.7.9.2.

208 Schulz, *Princ.*, 233–234; see also Guillemin, I, 25.

209 *Ad fam.* 14.1.5; see also 14.2.3. The documentation in this and the following two notes is that of Schulz.

210 Ibid., 14.3.3.

Cicero in all seriousness discusses the lengths [unwise, immoral, and illegal] to which a man might and should go in his fidelity to a friend . . .[211]

In the totality of legal norms and social mores, friendship was regarded by the Roman citizen as well as by the moral philosopher as a permanent relationship based upon fidelity *(fides)*. "It may be possible to live as an isolated being in a modern metropolis but not in the Roman world; 'Roman individualism' is nothing but a legend."[212] Friendship was thus a necessity of life. No one, no matter how wealthy or independent, could dispense with it. In a sense, *necessarius* and *amicus* were synonymous.[213]

The conclusion emerges with crystal clarity. *Amicitia* among the Romans was a binding relationship;[214] it was not a matter of sentiment and feelings. The idealized view of friendship embodied in the expression "a communion of hearts," the psychological view promulgated by the moralists — desirable as it may have been — tends to camouflage the very practical and utilitarian character of this real, everpresent and dependable phenomenon which fostered and catered to the community of interest among people. The doctrines of the moralists were unable to liberate friendship from its utilitarian character, for it was the warp and woof of the Roman social and economic world, deeply imbedded in the Roman mentality — a world and a mentality that were the products of generations of tradition and that are amply attested to by the juristic and non-juristic literature of the end of the Republic and the Early Empire.[215]

(6) We have reserved for last that type of benefaction and service performed by one's activity, one's energy and personal exertion *(operā)*. Inasmuch as it was within the framework of this type of *beneficium* that friendship served as a source of non-contractual agency, it must be discussed at length.

---

211 *De amicitia* 10.35; 11.36–37; 12.40; 17.61.
212 Schulz, ibid. 233, 237–238.
213 Cicero *Ad fam.* 11.28.2.
214 Michel, 574ff.
215 For a thoroughgoing study of the Roman concept of friendship as a key to Roman international relations in pre-classical times, see Dahlheim, 111–274.

c. *Roman Friendship and Agency*[216]

Although, as indicated previously, many a Roman would entrust the discharge of his everyday business transactions to slaves, freedmen and freemen agents who were generally of an inferior economic and social status, nevertheless, in those matters of the greatest importance, the Roman aristocrat or big businessman reserved their execution for himself, or, in his absence, for his friends. The particular circumstances of Roman life rendered the occasions when one had to resort to the good offices of one's friends rather numerous.

These circumstances may be summarized as follows: The business concerns and proprietary interests of a rich Roman were not at all concentrated in the City. His *latifundia*, those great private estates and plantations that were the characteristic feature of the agricultural economy in the last two centuries of the Republic and that persisted well beyond the Republic, were spread along the length of Italy as well as in the provinces. These latter were an endless source for all sorts of financial enterprises. Moreover, public duties forced many aristocratic Romans to remain at Rome or in the particular province they were assigned to rule. On the other hand, the political upheavals toward the end of the Republic forced certain figures to flee or brought about their banishment — also preventing them from personally attending to their affairs.

As a result of such circumstances, many a Roman had to resort to the practice of enlisting the assistance of his trusted friends to conduct those transactions that he himself could not attend to. The correspondence of Cicero and, to a lesser extent, Pliny the Younger serve as particularly rich sources for such conduct and will be drawn upon to illustrate the points we wish to make. An especially rich source is the correspondence between Cicero and Atticus. Atticus (110–32 B.C.E., his real name was T. Pomponius), and Cicero were lifelong friends. During Cicero's absence from Rome, it was upon Atticus, more than any other individual, that he relied for news

---

216 The English renderings of the passages cited in this section from the correspondence of Cicero and Pliny the Younger have been taken from the Loeb Classical Library editions. In addition, the following works have been consulted regularly: Tyrrell-Purser; Bailey, Cic., Ep., and Letters; Carcopino, Cic.; Sherwin-White; and Michel, 544–546, 566–569.

and political analysis. Moreover, it was chiefly Atticus who took care of Cicero's manifold personal and financial affairs.

"Friendships," says Cicero, "are made with the object of furthering the joint interests of the parties by services rendered to one another."[217] Thus, although as indicated previously,[218] Cicero held an idealized, spiritual view of friendship, he was nevertheless very much aware of the practical uses to which friendship could be and was put. Indeed, his friendship with Atticus was a source of untold *beneficia* to him. Atticus constantly encouraged him to literary creativity and served as his literary critic;[219] he employed his large staff of literary slaves to copy Cicero's works and thus made many copies of them available for general circulation.[220] His extensive library was at Cicero's disposal on request;[221] and, as we shall see, he often bought books (among many other items) for Cicero. After the Civil War, Atticus undertook the general supervision of Cicero's affairs (details to follow); in certain delicate, private negotiations, as with C. Antonius in 61,[222] Atticus made a willing and suitable intermediary; and, throughout, he was for Cicero an inexhaustable source of political, financial and cultural counsel.[223]

> He [Atticus] was also so careful in endeavouring to carry through what he had once consented to undertake, that he seemed to be attending, not to another's commission, but to an affair of his own. He never wearied of an enterprise which he had once undertaken; for he thought that his own reputation was involved, and there was nothing that he held dearer. Hence it was that he managed all the business affairs (*omnia . . . negotia procuraret*) of the Ciceros, of Marcus Cato, of Quintus Hortensius, of Aulus Torquatus, and of many Roman knights besides.[224]

It is clear, therefore, that the offices and amenities exchanged between Cicero and Atticus, the reciprocal *officia* and *beneficia*, are not

217 *Pro Roscio Amerino* 3.
218 In the exposition of Cicero's moralistic writings, above.
219 E.g., *Ad Att.* 1.13.5 and 1.14.3.
221 E.g., 4.14.1.
222 See ibid., 1.12.1.
223 Boissier, *passim*; Carcopino, Cic., 412–481; Bailey, Letters I, 3–5.
224 Cornelius Nepos *De Latinis Historicis: Atticus* 15, transl., Loeb Classical Library, 681–682.

limited to them. They hold true with regard to Atticus and other great Roman figures, to Cicero and other benefactors and beneficiaries, indeed, to other Roman citizens and their respective friends, clients, guests and, of course, relatives.[225] Thus, the letters of Cicero to his friends and relatives, as well as those of Pliny the Younger, are an excellent source of agency services of a non-contractual type. These were relations that never reached the inside of a courtroom. Their entire tone precludes contract and suit, action and liability; yet they were most effective in fulfilling the roles and needs lawyers associate with agency. Our extended treatment of the Roman friendship heretofore is the explanation, above and beyond what the modern reader himself knows of friendship, of why any idea of legal action was most remote from the principals who were, in effect, engaging in agency — either as agents or as principals.

We turn now to a detailed examination of this non-contractual agency among Roman friends. Beginning our discussion with transactions involving property, we take as our object lesson two major projects undertaken by Cicero: the furnishing of his *villa* near the ancient city of Tusculum and the erection of a temple *(fanum)* in memory of his deceased daughter Tullia. The former project was carried out successfully; the latter, although important to us, was never brought to fruition. Since these undertakings have never been analyzed systematically for the purpose of shedding light on non-contractual agency among the Romans, we find it imperative to quote the relevant passages extensively.

At the end of 68, when Cicero had reached the Aedileship, he asked Atticus, who was then in Athens, to help him furnish his place at Tusculum.

> [1] Please carry out my commissions *(quae tibi mandavi)*, and, as you suggest, buy *(cures)* anything else you think suitable for my Tusculan villa, if it is not trouble to you. It is the only place I find restful after a hard day's work.[226]

225 "In Roman society a man's neighbours occupied a place analogous to that of his *amici, hospites,* and clients, with whom they are often mentioned"; Wiseman, 48.
226 *Ad Att.* 1.5.7.

In the next letter to Atticus, he wrote:

> [2] If you can come across any articles of *vertu* fit for my Gymnasium, please don't let them slip. You know the place [i.e., the *Tusculanum*] and what suits it. I am so pleased with my house at Tusculum that I am never really happy except when I am there.[227]

When, a month later, Atticus reported that he had been successful in fulfilling Cicero's request, Cicero immediately informed him that he would hand over to L. Cincius, Atticus' confidential business agent, the sum of 20,400 sesterces to cover the cost of the purchases.[228] In the next letter, he sent a supplementary order.

> [3] I have raised the 20,400 sesterces for L. Cincius for those statues of Megaric marble of which you wrote me. Those figures of Hermes in Pentelic marble with bronze heads about which you told me, I have already fallen in love with: so please send them and anything else that you think suits the place, and my enthusiasm for such things, and your own taste — the more the merrier, and the sooner the better — especially those you intend for the Gymnasium and the colonnade. For my appreciation of art treasures is so great that I am afraid most people will laugh at me, though I expect encouragement from you. If none of Lentulus' boats are coming, put them on any ship you like.[229]

After some weeks passed and the eagerly awaited works of art did not arrive, Cicero wrote again, including a supplementary, albeit rather vague, order.

> [4] I am awaiting impatiently the statues of Megaric marble and those of Hermes, which you mentioned in your letter. Don't hesitate to send anything else of the same kind that you have, if it is fit for my Academy. My purse is long enough. This is my little weakness; and what I want especially are those that are fit for a Gymnasium. Lentulus promises his ships. Please bestir yourself about it *(ut haec diligenter cures)*. Thyillus [a writer friend] asks you, or rather has got me to ask you, for some books on the ritual of the Eumolpidae [connected with the Eleusinian Mysteries].[230]

227 Ibid., 1.6.2.
228 Ibid., 1.7.1; see Bailey, Letters.
229 Ibid., 1.8.2.
230 Ibid., 1.9.2.

The next letter, very soon thereafter:

> [5] Please do as you say about the statues and the Hermeraclae: and have them shipped as soon as you can conveniently, and any other things you come across that are suitable for the place — you know what it is like — especially for the Palaestra and Gymnasium ... I give you a commission too *(tibi mando)* for bas-reliefs for insertion in the stucco walls of the hall, and for two well-covers in carved relief. Be sure you don't promise your library to anyone, however ardent a suitor you may find for it. I am saving up all my little gleanings to buy it as a prop for my old age.[231]

When, at the beginning of 66, the cargo finally arrived, Cicero, overcome with joy, wrote a series of letters expressing his profound gratitude and pleasure.[232]

This episode is most instructive for our purposes. The following should be noted:

Atticus was chosen by Cicero to make these purchases of art work because 1, Atticus lived in Athens, the art centre; 2, Atticus was his friend; and 3, Atticus was a connoisseur of art.[233] Since, as the letters clearly indicate, Cicero left all the important details to Atticus' discretion and good taste, such matters could not easily be placed in the hands of slaves.

Also to be noted is how remote the legal aspect of the affair was from the minds of the principals. The authorization of Atticus to make the purchases was not only general; it was positively vague as to how many pieces were to be bought, what the pieces were, what the maximum expenditure should be. In passage [4], for example, Cicero assured Atticus that he could afford anything the latter would see fit to buy for him. Moreover, at the end of that same passage, it is not clear whether Cicero was taking the responsibility for the purchase of the books on the Eleusinian rituals or not. It is clear that the parties involved never thought of the possibility that legal action would ever be resorted to. The library mentioned at the end of passage [5] was apparently acquired in Greece, perhaps in re-

231 Ibid., 1.10.3.
232 Ibid., 1.3.2; 1.4.3; 1.1.5. I have followed the chronology of Tyrell-Purser and Bailey, Letters.
233 In passage [3] above, Cicero contrasts his enthusiasm *(studium)* with Atticus' discriminating taste *(elegentia)*.

sponse to Cicero's request.[234] But the books were bought on Atticus' own account; not as a direct commission.[235] This explains Cicero's bid for priority of right of purchase. Where Cicero does use the verb *mandare*, to commission, e.g., in passages [1] and [5], it is clear that it was meant in its non-technical sense of carrying out a request, much as the verb *curare*, variously employed to mean "to care for," "to buy," "to be concerned over," was used non-technically. The familiar tone of the letters — sometimes jocular, often emotional[236] — confirms the non-contractual nature of the correspondence.

The second episode, the proposed erection of a memorial for his daughter Tullia,[237] is also valuable to us for the light it casts upon agency among friends. Tullia, Cicero's favourite daughter, died in mid-February, 45, shortly after child-bearing. Her father's plan to deify her with a temple[238] was first mentioned in a letter of March 11;[239] and from then on until early June,[240] it was a recurrent theme in this correspondence with Atticus: the site to be chosen, the columns to be acquired, the encouragement of the architect, negotiations with sellers unwilling to sell or unreasonable in their prices, the relative merits of gardens *(horti)* and groves or woods *(luci)*.

Note the following passages:

[6] You say my private affairs are being properly managed *(administrari)*. Write and tell me what they are; for there are some things I am expecting to hear about. See that Cocceius [perhaps an agent or surety of Dolabella, Tullia's husband] does not disappoint me; for I count the promise of Libo [who apparently owes Cicero money], of which Eros [Atticus' accountant] writes, as trustworthy. My capital of course I leave in Sulpicius' and Egnatius' [perhaps Cicero's sureties] hands.[241]

---

234 See *Ad Att.* 1.7.
235 See ibid. 1.4.3; Bailey, ibid., on 1.10.3.
236 Not included in the passages cited but emerging most clearly from their context.
237 This project and the activities around it are summarized in Carcopino, Cic., 169–177. Many technical textual details are discussed by Bailey, ibid., V, 404–413.
238 *Fanum*; as to what put the idea in Cicero's head, see Carcopino, ibid., 170, n. 3, and Bailey, ibid., 404, n. 1.
239 *Ad Att.* 12.18.
240 Ibid., 12.52.
241 Ibid., 12.18.3.

[7] I think at times of buying some gardens *(hortos aliquos parare)* across the Tiber [for the shrine in memory of Tullia], especially for this reason: I don't see any other place that can be so much frequented. But what gardens, we will consider together *(coram videmus)*; provided only that the shrine be completed this summer. However settle *(confice)* with Apella of Chios [the vendor, otherwise unknown] about the columns.[242]

A week after passage [7], Cicero was planning how to raise the cash necessary to make the purchase from Silius. Cicero preferred to pay cash rather than to make over property to Silius at a valuation because, on the one hand, Silius would not want luxury estates that did not yield an income while, on the other Cicero did not wish to reduce his own income by surrendering profitable properties. Thus,

[8] Silius will not want show places; and I can make myself contented on the income I have, though hardly on less. So where can I get ready money. You can extort *(exprimes)* 600,000 sesterces from Hermogenes [who apparently owed Cicero the money], especially as it will be necessary; and I see I have another 600,000 sesterces in hand. For the rest of the money I will either pay interest to Silius, until I get it from Faberius [the secretary of Caesar to whom Cicero had lent money], or get the money to pay with at once from some debtor of Faberius. There will be some coming in too from other quarters. But you can take charge of the whole matter *(Sed totam rem tu gubernabis)*.[243]

The deal with Silius fell through, at least for the time being.

[9] As I said in my letter yesterday, if Silius is the sort of man you think him and Drusus [another prospective vendor] is hard to deal with, I should like you to approach Damasippus [a third owner of *horti*]. He, I think, has divided up his property on the banks of the Tiber into lots of so and so many acres with fixed prices, which I don't know. So write and tell me whatever you do *(quicquid egeris)*.[244]

The next letter, from which the following passage is taken, is an excellent illustration of agency among friends in the context of the attitudes and services generally associated with Roman friendship.

---

242 Ibid., 12.19.1.
243 Ibid., 12.25.1.
244 Ibid., 12.33.1.

[10] The matters you have mentioned we will investigate together *(coram videbimus)*, as I am coming. Your kindness *(benevolentia)*, diligence *(diligentia* [= care]), and good sense *(prudentia* [= discretion]) both in managing my affairs *(in agendis nostris rebus)* and in forming plans and suggesting them *(in consiliis ineundis mihique dandis)* in your letters go to my heart wonderfully.

However, if you do anything with Silius, even on the very day of my arrival at Sicca's place [a literary companion of Cicero], please let me know, especially which piece of ground he wants to withdraw. You say, "the far end." Take care *(vide)* that it is not the very bit which, as you know, set me thinking about the thing at all.[245]

Discussions concerning various aspects of the negotiations for the shrine continue as a major subject of their correspondence. Note how heavily Cicero relies on Atticus to raise the necessary money:

[11] As to the money [to buy the gardens of a new prospective vendor, Scapula — the previous deals having fallen through], I see you are making every effort, or rather you have done so already. If you manage it, I shall owe the gardens to you . . .[246]

[12] If Faberius [*cf.* passage 8] comes, see that the right amount of the debt is put to my credit, if anything is. Eros [*cf.* passage 6] will tell you about it.[247]

[13] For my part I am so satisfied with the debtors you mention, that the only thing which disquiets me is that you seem to have doubts. For I don't take it at all kindly of you to refer the matter to me. If I managed my own business *(negotium meum gererem)*, I should never manage anything without your advice *(nisi consilio tuo)*. However I know you did it more from your usual carefulness *(diligentia)* than because you had any doubts about the debtors. The fact is you don't approve of Caelius [an agent of Caesar who apparently owes Faberius a large sum of money], and you don't like to increase their number.[248] I agree with you on both points. So we must make the best of them

---

245 Ibid., 12.34.2–3. Silius now wished to reserve part of his estate, and Cicero feared that it might be the same part as that upon which he was proposing to erect the shrine; Bailey, ibid.

246 Ibid., 13.1.2.

247 Ibid., 13.2a.1.

248 Apparently Faberius had offered to make over a number of debts due to him in payment of his debt to Cicero, with an alternative of a large debt from Caelius or smaller ones from several other debtors. Atticus is dissatisfied with either alternative; editor's note in the Loeb Classical Library edition, *ad loc.*

as they are. Sometime you would at long last have had to stand surety[249] — even in this sale [which Cicero by now knew did not meet Atticus' approval]. So now I shall pay in full myself . . .[250]

The above-cited passages may be supplemented by the general survey of Atticus' activities on behalf of Cicero contained in the following paragraph written by Gaston Boissier:

> Atticus became his man of business, we know his talent for this profession. He leased Cicero's property very dear, saved as much as he could out of the income and paid the most pressing debts. When he discovered new ones, he dared to scold his friend, who hastened to reply very humbly that he would be more careful for the future. Atticus, who did not much believe this, set to work to make up the deficit. He went to see the wealthy Balbus or other great bankers of Rome with whom he had business relations. If the calamities of the times made it difficult to get credit, he did not hesitate to dip into his own purse . . .[251]

As a matter of fact, the various verbs found in these passages which are used to cover the manifold tasks Atticus was called upon to perform are enough to indicate his usefulness as Cicero's agent: to take care of or to take charge of (*curare* and *gubernare*), to manage (*administrare*), to prepare or procure by buying (*parare*), to settle accounts (*conficere*), to apply pressure in the collection of debts (*exprimere*), to conduct financial transactions and business affairs (*agere, negotium gerere*), to see to it that something is carried out or that some precaution is taken (*videre*). This list is even more impressive when one is reminded that the verbs have been culled from only thirteen out of the hundreds of letters written by Cicero to Atticus. It is remarkable that from this small number of letters, the picture of Atticus' role in Cicero's life as, among other things, his business agent emerges with crystal clarity. Informally and non-contractually, Atticus was a kind of combined *negotiorum gestor*, *procurator omnium rerum* and *mandatarius*. Indeed, recalling the services and benefactions (*officia et beneficia*) catalogued in the

---

249 If Cicero did not get his money from Faberius and still bought the gardens, he would have had to ask for credit. In that case, he apparently expected Atticus to stand surety; Bailey, ibid.

250 *Ad Att.* 13.3.1.

251 Boissier, 141.

previous section, we already find in the relatively few letters heretofore excerpted numerous instances that neatly fit into the six categories which we enumerated and explained: the writing of letters containing words of encouragement and news information, granting of loans and acting as surety, using one's influence — e.g., with wealthy bankers — on behalf of one's friend, and, of course, the particular service of acting as one's agent in financial transactions involving property.

Especially instructive is the usage of such expressions as "we will investigate together *(coram videbimus)*" and "forming plans and suggesting them *(in consiliis ineundis mihique dandis)*." Such expressions serve as good examples of the value of a close and devoted friend serving as one's agent which is superior to that of a contractual, formal one. An agent who was also a trusted friend of his principal was in a better position, for instance, of dissuading the latter from following a course of action which would undoubtedly be to his *dis*advantage. Thus, Atticus, convinced that Cicero's desire to purchase gardens as a shrine for Tullia was a project which was beyond Cicero's means and would lead to Cicero's financial undoing, disapproved of the whole business and did not hesitate to make his feelings known to his friend.[252] Moreover, by occasional inaction, temporizing and the presentation of alternative suggestions, Atticus finally succeeded in prevailing upon Cicero. Cicero's enthusiasm was gradually dampened, and the hoped-for project was eventually given up.[253] A formal agent could not have had the same measure of influence on the thinking and the decisions of his principal.

In order to round out our description of non-contractual agency among friends in transactions involving property, we append here a brief catalogue of isolated acts which will serve to illustrate the thousands of similar acts which it would be pointless to enumerate.

Atticus very often bought books for Cicero.[254]

Similarly, Pliny the Younger called upon his scholar friend, Vibius Severus, whose good taste he knew and trusted, to buy some work of art for a friend of his:

252 *Ad Att.* 12.25.2; 12.41.3; 12.43.1–2; 13.3.1.
253 Carcopino, *Cic.*, 171–172.
254 *Ad Att.* 1.7; 13.8.

[14] Herennius Severus, a person of distinguished learning, is greatly desirous to have the paintings [i.e., pictures] of two of your fellow townsmen, Cornelius Nepos and Titus Catus, to adorn his library; and has entreated me, if they are to be met with where you are (as probably they may) that I would procure copies of them for him. That care *(curam)* I recommend to you, rather than to any other, not only because I know your friendship for me readily inclines you to comply with my requests . . .[255]

Equally pertinent are the remarks of the jurist who declares:

[15] In general we are considered to possess [through] who[mso]ever may be in actual possession in our name, e.g., a *procurator*, a guest or a friend.[256]

This declaration, contrary to the rule of the Roman civil law which states, "Through a person *sui iuris* nothing can be acquired for us,"[257] was a natural outcome of the material and substantial type of *beneficium (rē)* that a host performs by providing hospitality and lodging for his friend. Thus, if one's friend, living on one's estate, had made a path through the neighbouring farm or estate in such a way as to have gained the right of way *(iter, ius eundi)* or any other servitude *(ius in re aliena)*, it was his host, the proprietor, who was construed to have attained this right *(usus videtur itinere vel actu vel via).*[258]

The converse to Gaius' statement was enunciated by Paul (D. 41.2.41), namely, "One who, by right of friendship, enters his friend's land is not considered to take possession *(non videtur possidere)*, because he did not enter with the intention of possessing *(animo ut possideat)* though physically he is on the land" — ordinarily he would not seem to have even detention.[259] This, too, follows naturally from

---

255 Pliny *Epistulae* 4.28. Similarly, 3.6, where the addressee is probably also a friend. See passages 3.6.6 and 5.1.12 as a corrective to the remarks of Sherwin-White, 185.

256 Gaius, D. 41.2.9: *Generaliter quisquis omnino nostro nomine sit in possessione, veluti procurator hospes amicus, nos possidere videmur*; see also G. 4.15.3.

257 G. 2.95; Inst. 2.9.5; Paul, D. 45.1.126.2; 4.27.1 pr.

258 Ulpian, D. 43.19.1.7 and 3.4.

259 Zulueta.

the relationship of a host to his guest, classified above as a benefaction of hospitality.[260]

Continuing our catalogue of examples of agency among friends,
non-contractual and informal in conception and execution, we turn
our attention to commercial transactions. In this area, too, Cicero's
correspondence provides us with a wealth of illustrative material
most useful and instructive for our purposes.

While Cicero was governing Cilicia as *pro-praetor*, he did not
neglect his business affairs nor those of his friends. On his way to
his proconsular post in Cilicia (in 51), he halted at Ephesus. There
he used his influence and recommended to Minucius Thermus, the
Propraetor of Asia, Atticus' chief representatives in that province
— Marcus Seius and the freedman Philogenes. Such a recommendation, coming from so distinguished a Roman, undoubtedly had the
desired effect of advancing Atticus' business interests in the Asian
province by opening some key doors to his agents and by affording
them access to people of import. This detail is of significance to us
in that it is one of many examples which serves to correct the image
of the friendship between Atticus and Cicero as being of unilateral
advantage to the latter. Nothing could be further from the truth.
Numerous passages indicate that Cicero performed many services
and benefactions for Atticus. Our tendency has been to emphasize
Atticus' services on behalf of Cicero because of our interest in
agency. In the area of business transactions, Atticus' commercial
talent and acumen were so far superior to those of Cicero that it
was only natural that the former be the one to help the latter and
not *vice versa*. In other areas, the relationship was no wise as one-
sided.

---

260 Under certain circumstances, one could be rendered liable for some specific types of delict committed by one's friends who were staying as guests
at one's home. For example, under the Edict *de his qui effuderint vel
deiecerint*, the host was liable for damage caused by that which his guests
threw out of the window of his home. This was also true of similar deeds
done to his or his wife's freedmen and clients; Ulpian, D. 9.3.5.1. For a
description of hosts and guests based upon non-juristic sources, see
Wiseman, 33–38.

The same letter contains the following statement:

> [16]　In addition I submitted to Philogenes [Atticus' freedman] an account of the sum I got from you by negotiating a bill of exchange.[261]

Elsewhere we find the following statement:

> [17]　I have in *cistophori* [local currency] in Asia nearly 2,200,000 sesterces. By a bill of exchange for that amount it will be easy for you to maintain my credit.[262]

The Latin term for which the phrase "bill of exchange" serves as translation is *permutatio*. *Permutatio* is a banking term and generally represented a transaction between two banking firms to make payments from Rome to Italy and the provinces, and *vice versa*. Not a formal contract, it was akin in function to the modern check.[263] In the first passage, Atticus lent Cicero money, and Cicero was arranging for repayment through Atticus' freedman. In the second passage, Cicero, at Epirus in 48, asked Atticus to cover the money he owed by arranging a *permutatio* on the basis of the money he had in Asia.[264] But whether Atticus was Cicero's creditor or agent,[265] it is instructive to learn that friends used this banking instrument informally among themselves for their own needs and purposes — "informally," for there was no thought of any formal contract or legal relationship.

The multiplicity of commercial tasks that Cicero assigned to Atticus is most impressive. A random sampling from the first ten letters of Book V of Cicero's *Letters to Atticus* shows the following assignments: to act in behalf of and as representative of Cicero in the sale of an estate and to furnish the purchaser with proof of the validity of

---

261　*Ad Att.* 5.13.2: *Ego praeterea rationem Philogeni permutationis eius, quam tecum feci, edidi.*

262　Ibid., 11.1.2; *Ego in cistophoro in Asia habeo ad sestertium bis et viciens. Huius pecuniae permutatione fidem nostram facile tuebere.*

263　See Kiessling, 700.

264　All sorts of combinations were employed in arranging for the transfer of funds; *permutatio* was but one of them. See Frank, Ec. Surv., I, 352.

265　When at Brundisium in 47, Cicero wrote to Atticus to pay a 30,000 sesterce debt and, inasmuch as this payment exhausted his assets, to advance a loan to him. Thus, Atticus acted as agent and creditor simultaneously; *Ad Att.*, 11.11.2.

title;[266] to give Cicero's creditor formal assurance of his willingness, readiness and ability to pay the debt;[267] to arrange a payment;[268] to investigate an account, to examine a bill;[269] to settle a debt;[270] to pay the interest that has accrued on past debts.[271]

Occasionally, one letter would contain numerous tasks for which Cicero enlisted Atticus, mainly although not exclusively, as his agent. We cite two such letters *exempli gratia*:

(1) To act as Cicero's business *alter ego*. ("I received your letter on the 4th of February, and on the same day I accepted the inheritance formally according to the will. Of my many and miserable anxieties one is taken away, if, as you say, this inheritance is sufficient to maintain my credit and reputation, though I know you would have defended it even without the inheritance with all your resources.")

(2) To pay the second installment of Tullia's dowry due to Dolabella. ("I adjure you for heaven's sake to manage the whole business and protect the poor girl, a victim of my culpable carelessness, with my funds, if there are any, and out of your own, so far as you can without inconvenience.")

(3) To protect Cicero's house at Rome from confiscation or forced sale by the Caesarians

(4) To supply Cicero with cash and clothes.

(5) To send letters in Cicero's name. ("Please send letters in my name to such people as you think proper — you know my friends. If they wonder about the seal and handwriting [inasmuch as letters usually bear the supposed writer's seal, unless, written in his own hand and not in the hand of a secretary, his handwriting was distinctively recognized], please say I have avoided using them owing to the sentries.")[272]

---

266 *Ad Att.* 5.1.2. The phrase used is to give *satisdatio*, which usually meant to act as personal security — security on a loan and therefore would have nothing to do with agency. In context, however, it seems to refer to *satisdatio secundum mancipium* which had the effect of certifying title; see Tyrrell-Purser.

267 Ibid., 5.1.2. The creditor was Caesar, and the formal assurance — known as *apertio* — was made to Oppius, Caesar's agent to whom Cicero owed 80,000 sesterces; see Tyrrell-Purser. The same request of Cicero to Atticus to render this service was later referred to as *expositio (exponere)* ibid. 5.4.3.

268 Ibid., 5.4.3; *perficere*, literally, to execute or bring to completion.

269 Ibid., 5.4.3; *rationem cognoscere*.

270 Ibid., 5.4.3; *efficere*, literally, to carry out a transaction.

271 Ibid., 5.5.2; 5.9.2.

272 Ibid., 11.2. the first letter.

(6) To reassure Cicero's neighbour, M. Aelius, concerning a matter of an easement between them, to use discretion and tact.

(7) To collect the money owed to Cicero by his (Cicero's) scribe and freedman, Tullius.

(8) To supervise the sale of some of Tullius' property in order to pay money Cicero owed on the purchase of a block of flats.[273]

Then again, a friend or relative would be assigned to act as a general manager and/or agent with an explicit or implied general authorization to do whatever was necessary in the course of executing the assignment. The vagueness of the wording of these general commissions is sufficient evidence — as if the relationship of friendship were not enough — of their non-contractual nature. Pliny the Younger, for example, inspected the property of Fabatus, his wife's grandfather, and supervised the repair work that it needed.[274]

How far general agency could go, we learn from the following brief excerpt taken from another letter of Cicero to Atticus:

> [18] As to my co-heirs in Fufidius' property, there was no reason for you to write to me: for their demand is quite just, and anything you did I should think right.[275]

We see how a habitual *mandatarius* or a *procurator omnium rerum* could create an implied agency akin to that of a *negotiorum gestor* in as informal, natural, everyday fashion. Atticus was formally none of these, yet in fact he was acting like all of them. Note the assurance that ratification for the acts performed by Atticus on behalf of Cicero would most certainly always be forthcoming and therefore could always be relied upon.[276]

Indeed, when Cato was absent from Rome, Atticus undertook

---

273 Ibid., 15.26; see Carcopino, Cic., 45.

274 *Epistulae* 6.30.2. This type of general management undertaken by a friend or relative was in sharp contrast to the services rendered by a professional manager. The latter received a fixed wage and maintained a relationship with his employer that was of a more or less standardized nature recognized by law. Compare Pliny's role as a manager of the estate of his wife's grandfather with that of a professional manager whom Pliny had hired to supervise the farm he had presented to an old *nutrex*; see Sherwin-White, 358 and 390.

275 *Ad Att.* 11.13.

276 See also *Ad fam.* 7.28.1–2.

the management of his affairs in order to ingratiate himself with the distinguished Roman. Cato was very pleased, as a matter of fact.[277] It is clear that under such circumstances no contract (of *mandatum* or of *procuratio*) existed nor any agency in the formal sense (of *negotiorum gestio*) implied. Given the mentality of the men involved, their sense of dignity and their attitude toward duty, it is virtually impossible to envisage any recourse to litigation.

d. *From Friendship to Contract — A Concluding Note*

Reference has already been made at the beginning of this chapter to the significant thesis that "trade and contract are built upon the forms of gifts which, although theoretically voluntary, are in reality made or rendered to fulfil some obligation." With the risk of going beyond the limited scope of our study, it behooves us to discuss, at least briefly, the wisdom and truth of this thesis in the light of our study of friendship and agency in Roman life and law.

The integral relationship which existed between friendship and all that it connoted and between the contract of mandate, as well as the latter's indebtedness to the former for its origin, conception, and ground rules of operation, was enunciated as established doctrine in Roman legal sources.

> A mandate, unless gratuitous, is null and void; for it originates in goodwill and friendship: a reward therefore is inconsistent with mere good will, since by the introduction of money the business becomes more akin to a letting and hiring.[278]

A careful study of the use of *mandatum* and its relative verb in Plautus — either *mandatum* or *mandare* occurs in his plays about fifty times — reveals (1) that is was non-technical and non-legal in connotation, (2) that it had a wide scope and was used in greatly varying circumstances, and (3) that almost certainly its gratuitous-

---

277 Boissier, 135.

278 Paul, D. 17.1.1.4; *Mandatum nisi gratuitum nullum est: nam originem ex officio atque amicitia trahit, contrarium ergo est officio merces: interveniente enim pecunia res ad locationem et conductionem potius respicit.* See Dumont, 307–322; and the reservations of Watson, Mand., 15–16. *Cf.* further the remark of Kaser, Rev. C., 263–264.

ness was recognized as a principle from the beginning.[279] These features of *mandatum-mandare* are corroborated by Cicero's use of these terms in his correspondence with his friends.[280]

Equally striking is the fact that, in addition to right of action available to a party injured by violation of the rules of mandate, there lay the sanction of *infamia* for a breach. This stems directly from the conception of fidelity *(fides)* as the basis of the friendship relationship which, in turn, was the basis of the contract of mandate.[281] The praetorian Edict deprives one who violated the rules of mandate of the right to act as an advocate or as a representative of a party at a trial.[282] Explaining the reasoning upon which this edictal sanction was based, Ulpian stated as follows:

> The language of the Edict puts a mark [of *infamia* disqualifying one from acting as advocate or representative in court] not only on the party who undertook the mandate, but on anyone who fails to keep faith *(fides)* where the other relied on his doing so.[283]

Thus, *infamia*, the standard sanction for serious breaches of friendship, always was connected with the duty to render benefactions and services personally *(operā)* — even when such duty was converted to and formulated in terms of contract.[284]

As the classical period of Roman law progressed, however, friendship as a source of non-contractual agency in business gradually became more limited. Business enterprises had become larger, more numerous and more time-consuming. Then again, as a result of increases in the free population and the inclusion of foreigners and freedmen into the ranks of the citizenry, the stigma traditionally associated with commercial activity was seriously weakened; services generally regarded as agency were therefore increasingly per-

279 Watson, Mand., 11–16; *cf.* Costa, Dir., 389–397.
280 Eg., *Ad Att.* 1.5.7; 4.7.3; 5.9.2. *Ad fam.* 7.2.1.
281 See, for example, Cicero *Pro Roscio Amerino* 39.112: *Neque mandat quisquam fere nisi amico.*
282 The Latin term for this right is *postulare*. See Lenel, E.P., 76–78. Lenel also points out that this edictal deprivation is the praetorian forerunner of the Justinian *infamia*.
283 Ulpian, D. 3.2.6.5; *Verbis edicti notatur non solum qui mandatum suscepit, sed et is, qui fidem, quam adversarius secutus est, non praestat.*
284 See Michel, 589ff.

formed by such persons. Moreover, friendship came to include groups of people of lesser and lesser intimacy and closeness. Thus, the role of friendship as a source of agency became correspondingly more restricted, and, concomitantly, contractual relationships became the preponderant source of commercial representation.[285] Nevertheless, the mandate, even after it had become a formal contract, always retained the unmistakable signs of its origin in friendship. In addition to its formal gratuitousness as its basis and *infamia* as its sanction, the conceptual evolution of the contract of mandate out of friendship emerges most convincingly from the following words of Paul:

> Just as it is an act of free bounty and good feeling, rather than of compulsion, to make a loan to anyone, so too it is for the person who confers the benefit to lay down terms and limits with reference to it. But when this has once been done, when, that is, the party has made the loan, then such an act as that of laying down limits and going back on the terms and depriving the other, at the wrong time, of the use of the thing lent, is forbidden not only by good feeling (*officium*), but also by the obligation created by the handing over on the one hand and the receiving on the other. Each party does something for the other, and consequently rights of action are allowed on both sides, so as to leave no doubt that what was at first a matter of favour and mere bounty takes the form of an interchange of performances and of civil rights of action on both sides. We see something of the same kind in the case of a man who has taken some steps in the way of looking after the affairs of an absent man; such a one cannot divest himself of all concern for things which are liable to be lost, without being obliged to answer for it, as, if he had left the business alone in the first instance, perhaps someone else would have taken it up; taking up a *mandatum* is a matter of free choice, but to carry it through is a necessity.
>
> It is on this principle that if you lend me tablets for my debtor to use to give me an undertaking, you have no right to ask for them back before the proper time, as, if you had refused to lend them, I should either have bought others or else procured witnesses. It is the same thing if you lend timber to shore up a set of flats, and then carry

285 The contract of mandate governed the relationship of express agency between principal and *procurator*. Implied agency was embodied in the rules of *negotiorum gestio* which governed the relationship between principal and unauthorized agent. In the latter half of the classical period there also emerged the broker *(proxeneta)* as an agent in financial transactions.

> them away again, or perhaps even lend me some which you know
> to be rotten; when something is done as a favour, a man ought to be
> the better for it, not to be taken in.[286]

This passage contains two remarkable insights, of great significance
for our study. Gratuitous contracts in general and *mandatum* in
particular occupied a unique place in the entire realm of legal institutions, for they operated upon the basis of law, with legal sanctions,
and simultaneously upon the basis of social usage, with social sanctions, i.e., those of public opinion. Secondly the gratuitous service
underwent a significant conceptual transformation. Born out of good
will *(voluntas)* and granted freely, it, once granted, became subject
to legal coercion and partook of the nature of legal necessity and
compulsion *(necessitas)*.[287]

2. *Relatives* sui iuris

Except for the areas of inheritance and guardianship, relatives outside the immediate family — that is, beyond one's wife and children — played no special legal role. In other words, in the (classical)
law of property, obligations and procedure, agnates,[288] cognates[289]
and *a fortiori* clansmen[290] were of no particular significance. Thus,
in the specific areas of transactions involving property (i.e., acquisition or alienation of ownership and possession) as well as in general
commercial transactions, the legal rule, "Through a person *sui iuris*
nothing can be acquired for us," made no distinction between these

---

286 D. 13.6.17.3.
287 Michel, 594–595.
288 Agnates were those persons who are under the power of the same
Ancestor, or would have been if he were alive. The tie among agnates
was created by their descendants *in the male line* from a common
ancestor.
289 Cognates were blood relations related through females as well as through
males. It was therefore a more inclusive term than agnates. It also included agnates who were given in adoption, emancipated or otherwise
lost their agnatic kinship.
290 Kinsmen who belonged to the same clan *(gens)*.

relatives and total strangers — just as it made no distinction between friends and guests and total strangers.

On the other hand, despite the lack of any such distinction in the civil law, Roman mores and social norms created practically the same catalogue of duties and services *(officia et beneficia)* that relatives were obligated to render each other as were friends and neighbours. Or, as already pointed out, the very existence of these duties and the seriousness with which Romans regarded them made it unnecessary for the civil law to address itself to this area of Roman life.

It would be pointless to repeat the entire catalogue of *officia* and *beneficia* contained in the previous chapter to show how they were rendered mutually among relatives. If anything, the mutual interchange of these services and benefactions was even more intense. As Publius Nigidius, "a man of prodigious learning," is reputed to have explained, "A brother is so called because he is, as it were, 'almost another self'."[291] Nevertheless, a few examples of extra-legal and non-contractual agency among relatives are in order.

> (1) Why, then did you write to me about the exchange? As though I was not being supported as it is by your resources. And it is just there that I see and feel, alas, what a crime I have committed, seeing that you are forced to satisfy your creditors by drawing upon your own and your son's very lifeblood, while I have squandered to no purpose the money I had received from the treasury *on your account.* Anyhow the amount you mentioned in your letter has been paid to M. Antonius, and the same amount to Caepio [creditors of Quintus].[292]

The opening sentence indicates that Quintus had offered to negotiate some transaction of exchange, when he arrived at Rome, on behalf of Cicero, and the money would be paid to Cicero at Thessalonica whither Cicero had fled to escape the dangerous counter-attacks of the supporters of the slain Catilinarians.[293]

In order to understand the rest of this most instructive passage it must be recalled that while Quintus had been *pro-praetor* of Asia

---

291 Aulus Gellius, *Noctes Atticae* 13.10.4. The etymology was based upon the phonic similarity between *frater*, brother, and *fere alter*, almost another.
292 Cicero *Ad Quintum fratrem* 1.3.7.
293 See Tyrrell-Purser; and Carcopino, *Cic.*, 196f.

(60–58), he had the right to draw from the public Treasury the sums allocated by decree of the Senate for the expenses of running the province, the expenditure essential to the dignity and prestige of his post. To simplify the transfer of remittances, Quintus had given his brother the authority to draw the money for him and to use it as he thought best. Cicero arranged that these monies due from the treasury to Quintus in Asia should be paid in Roman currency *(denarii)* and not in Asiatic coins *(cistophori).* When Cicero obtained the money, he proceeded to use it for himself — as Cicero confesses so pathetically in the above passage; in all probability he spent a good part of it in bribes in an attempt to save himself from the necessity to flee into exile. Quintus probably forgave his exiled brother in consideration of his distress. In any event, the thought most remote from either brother's mind was that of recourse to litigation in court.[294] In the last sentence, Cicero informs his brother that, before having left Rome, he had paid the latter's debts owed to the creditors named — probably out of the very monies he had received *suo nomine*, on Quintus' account.[295]

(2)   In 56, while Quintus was in Sardinia, Cicero rented a house for him so that, upon his return, Quintus could have a place to live inasmuch as the home he had bought was not ready for occupancy. In addition, Cicero rented out Quintus' house in the Carinae quarter[296] to tenants:

> A house has been taken for you that belonged to Licinius, near Piso's pool, but in a few month's time, say after July 1,[297] you will move into your own. Your house in the Carinae has been taken on lease by some genteel tenants, the Lamiae.[298]

(3)   Cicero's care and supervision over Quintus' real estate, the

---

294 Litigation among brothers had to be avoided at all costs. Elsewhere Cicero wrote, "Do not allow brothers to engage in litigation and have their heads banged together in discreditable litigation" (*Ad fam.* 9.25.3).

295 *Ad Att.* 2.6 and 2.16, at end; Tyrrell-Purser, ibid.; and Carcopino, ibid., 65–66.

296 Cicero himself had inherited this house from his father and later gave it to his younger brother; Carcopino, ibid., 43.

297 The usual time for the expiration of the terms of occupancy of rented houses in Rome; Tyrrell-Purser.

298 *Ad Quintum fratrem* 2.3.7.

building and repair of his houses, his negotiations with and orders to the latter's contractors, and his constant stream of information concerning these matters to his brother[299] remind one vividly of the similar services performed by Atticus on behalf of Cicero himself with regard to the *Tusculanum* and garden-shrine projects.

(4) Cicero, the great connoisseur of books, bought and sold books on behalf of his brother in order to replenish Quintus' Greek library, to arrange a profitable exchange of books, and to buy for him Latin ones.[300]

A final example that comes to mind is that of the emancipated son. After the Punic wars, family ties were loosened. As one scholar has put it:

> The relaxation of the religious ties which held the family together and the increase in luxurious habits would have tended to increase the number of sons who would seek and obtain emancipation. The emancipated son, however — now *sui iuris* — might well continue for a time at any rate in an employment on his father's behalf.[301]

Although the *potestas* relationship no longer obtained, formal contractual bonds did not take its place.

Similar services would be performed on behalf of kinsmen more distantly related, albeit usually with lesser frequency and with somewhat less devotion — nevertheless in the same spirit of *fides* and in the same non-contractual framework.[302]

299 Ibid., 2.4.2; 2.5.4–5; 3.1.2; 3.6.24; 3.9.7.
300 Ibid., 3.4.5; also 3.6.6.
301 Powell, 43.
302 E.g., one's son-in-law (*Ad fam.* 2.16.5) and the grandfather of one's wife (Pliny *Epistulae* 6.30).

CONCLUDING SUMMARY

Chapter One deals with the extent to which agents could be utilized in transactions involving property. Civil law rules *(ius civile)* excluded acquisition of ownership and possession through independent persons *(sui iuris)*. The only agents who could be employed to accomplish these acts were subordinates in one's power *(potestas)*, i.e., slaves and children. Even one's wife was excluded, since in classical times the ancient *manus*-marriage, whereby a wife entered the power of her husband, was rarely practiced; it had given way to the "free" marriage, i.e., that type of marriage where a woman was "free' of her husband's power.

The ability to acquire ownership through those in one's power, however, did not imply that these subordinates were agents in the jurisprudential sense. Rather, slaves and children in power were conceived as chattel of the head of family — actual, in the case of slaves, and vestigial, in the case of sons. Their acts of acquisition were construed as nothing more than the physical accession of additional property. Moreover, slaves and sons were precluded from true agency by the civil law rule, "Our slaves [and sons in power] can better our condition, but cannot make it worse." Hence, their capacity to perform acts of alienation was severely limited, namely to those acts which the head of family had given his express consent.

The second chapter is devoted to a thoroughgoing discussion of the institution of the *peculium*, the name given to funds and items of property granted to slaves and sons by their respective masters and fathers. This *peculium* functioned as the patrimony of the subordinate slave or son. The subordinate could, and was expected to, undertake business enterprises on the basis of his *peculium* fund. But legal title thereof was retained by the master, and all business transactions based upon it were technically in the name of the master. By setting up this fund, the head of the family was in effect declaring that he was authorizing the business transactions that would be conducted by his subordinate and therefore was accepting liability for any breach of contract by the subordinate. Obstacles presented by the *ius civile* were overcome by the praetorian recognition of the *peculium* arrangement and by the praetorian provision for the actions necessary to make the arrangement commercially and legally effective. At the same time, by separating the *peculium* fund from the rest of his estate, the head of the family was also declaring that he would not accept liability beyond the limits of the *peculium* unless he appropriated the profits of his subordinate's transactions for himself. Hence, his liability, by praetorian law, was a limited one.

After a description of the role of the *peculium* in the economic life of Rome, the mode of its administration and its juridical nature, there follows an extended exposition of the nature of the liability of the subordinate administering it as well as of the head of family in whom legal title to it is vested. This exposition develops the position clearly that the *peculium* arrangement was far removed from any theoretic concept of true agency as understood by lawyers. Nevertheless, the arrangement is found to have served on the practical, economic level in a manner similar to that associated with agency. Any transaction conducted by a subordinate in power on the basis of the *peculium* granted to him by the head of the family created indirect credits and debits for the latter via the profits and losses sustained by the fund whose legal title was vested in him. It also created for the head of family rights and liabilities that arose out of that transaction, the liabilities limited to the extent of the *peculium*. The creation of the credits, debits, rights and liabilities stemmed from the act whereby the head of family had granted his subordinate the *peculium* in the first place, an act which was essentially the appointment of a business agent.

Moreover, where the head of the family accepted for himself (not for the *peculium*) any of the payments or other benefits that arose out of the transaction, the enrichment was no longer indirect. In such cases, the direct enrichment of the principal predicated an agency formed by implied ratification; the liability of the principal for the transactions of his subordinate agent, then, was no longer limited to the extent of the *peculium*. The liability was for the whole transaction, as it is usually the case for normal principal-agent arrangements today. Therefore, whenever the profits derived from business enterprises which were being conducted on the basis of a *peculium* were applied, wholly or partially, to the accounts of the head of the family more or less regularly, there was created *de facto* a normal agency relationship between subordinate and master. As indicated, however, the agency thus formed was not based upon any theoretical concept of agency; the principal's liability was, rather, grounded in a theory akin to enrichment, i.e., the idea that one who finances a transaction and reaps the profits thereof ought to assume the risks and liabilities that it involves.

The third chapter of this book concerns itself with the various types of *authorized* non-contractual agents who could carry out commercial transactions *outside* of the institution of the *peculium*. This chapter represented the triumph of praetorian law in adapting the Roman legal system to revolutionary economic necessities and to new social realities. The chapter contains an exposition of the exercitorian and institorian arrangements as the key to commercial transactions conducted by generally authorized agents. After the Punic and Macedonian wars, Roman commerce expanded in every way. Business transactions were undertaken in much greater numbers, much larger sums of money were involved in each transaction, and commercial dealings were increasingly taking place between businessmen far apart from and unknown to each other. In maritime commerce, shipowners began to employ shippers and, alternatively, shippers employed shipmasters to act as their agents. These employers were known as *exercitores*, hence the term, "exercitorian arrangement." On land, capitalists were wont to employ shopkeeper agents to run their businesses. These shopkeepers were called *institores*, hence the term, "institorian arrangement." It thus became more and more necessary to assure traders that the obligations which their customers had assumed, whether in their own name or — as was increasingly becoming the usual practice — in the name of their principal-employer, would be satisfactorily discharged. Here, too, it was the law of the praetor which overcame what from the modern lawyer's point of view would be viewed as the exaggerated ancient civil law idea of privity of contract by rendering the employers liable for the transactions entered into by their agents.

The fourth chapter is a study in depth of the principal-agent relationship which, although not regulated by formal contract, was not governed by *potestas* either.

Agency in commercial transactions that were entered into under the general authorization of the principal, the central subject of the previous chapter, was the major feature of the exercitorian and institorian arrangements, the former at sea and the latter on land. In these arrangements, those who acted as agents were not only slaves working on behalf of their owners or sons functioning on behalf of their fathers, but also freedmen striving on behalf of their patrons, and wives acting on behalf of their husbands. In the case of slaves and sons who acted as agents of their masters and fathers, the principal-agent relationship was defined by the agent's status as a subordinate in the power of his principal. In the case of freedmen, however, the principal-agent relationship cannot be defined so simply. Being *sui iuris*, they were, like wives, free of the status of *potestas*. On the other hand, their services as agents of their patrons could very well be governed by the terms of contract which governed the agency of freemen who were shippers, ship captains and shopkeepers, namely *locatio conductio, mandatum* and *negotiorum gestio*. Nevertheless, many freedmen acted as the agents of their patrons in a fashion that cannot be explained in terms of contract. Although subjected at manumission to an oath of service which gave rise to contractual obligations, there was often a supplementary moral tie that bound the freedman to his patron. The many years of servitude, as well as the present duties subsumed under *obsequium, officium* and *operae*, engendered in numerous former slaves habits of obedience and service that were totally devoid of contractual considerations. Thus, freedmen often served their former masters as agents in the exercitorian and institorian arrangements and outside these arrangements in a manner above and beyond the requirements of contract. Wives in the classical period were generally without *manus*; yet they, too, were a constant, albeit modest, source of non-contractual agency.

The exercitorian and institorian arrangements, then, provided for the employment of agents who were well within the family structure, *i.e.*, slaves and sons in power and wives; agents who were on the periphery of the *familia* circle, i.e., freedmen who maintained quasi-familial ties with their former masters; and agents who were totally divorced from the *familia* of the principal, i.e., freedmen who had achieved total independence from their patrons and freemen. Thus, the employment of the exercitorian and institorian agents who were totally outside the familial structure indicates the replacement of *potestas* by contract.

Although the "when" of this transition is shrouded in mystery, the "how" of it is not. It is to be found in the patron-freedman relationship. It was this relationship which preserved the acts, dealings and arrangements which obtained between citizens and their former slaves. The slave-shopkeeper and the slave-shipmaster upon manumission would often remain in the same position of general agent for principal as had been true before manumission. Since manumission took place frequently and in large numbers, the Roman business world was often faced with the *de facto* situation of a manumitted slave, now a freedman, acting as an agent in a maritime or commercial establishment with ties to his principal which, originally based on *potestas*, were now replaced by an implied contract. The contract between them was taken as "implied" because it was entered into unwittingly by both principal and agent; it was the jurist who inferred that the general terms of this "contract" were defined by the tacit agreement of the parties involved to continue the same arrangement that had existed prior to the manumission. Once this contract which arose *de facto* was recognized and categorized — and the agent was construed as a hired employee, as a mandatary, or as an unauthorized manager — the relations between principal and agent had been redefined while the services of the agent on behalf of the principal with regard to third parties continued uninterrupted and unabated. Once the transition from *potestas* to implied contract and then to defined contract had been accomplished, the results could be applied directly to govern the relationship of two persons *sui iuris* who wished to establish between themselves an exercitorian and institorian agency arrangement *ab initio*.

The bridge, then, between generally authorized agency based upon *potestas* and that based upon contract was the manumitted slave who became the freedman of his former master. Recalling the famous theory of Sir Henry Maine that "the movement of progressive societies has hitherto been a movement from *Status* to *Contract*," the non-contractual services of the freedman on behalf of his patron may be regarded as the transitional midpoint in this movement.

All of this is placed within the economic and social realities of the times by constant reference to non-legal data culled from the non-juristic literature and inscriptions.

The second half of Chapter Four completes the picture of non-contractual agency in classical Rome by describing the role of friends and relatives. Friendship among the Romans was qualitatively different from that which obtains among us today. It entailed the performance of a number of serious and very real duties and services *(officia et beneficia)* which, although formally gratuitous, engendered or were the result of the duty to reciprocate by rendering similar duties and services. Among these services were acts of agency and representation that friends and relatives performed for each other. Non-contractual in character, they nevertheless were felt by the Roman to be obligatory in a very real way. Thus, friends and relatives must be included as an ever-present source of non-contractual agency.

GLOSSARY *

LATIN

Actio, an action of a plaintiff bringing suit

Actio de in rem verso, an action available to the creditors of a *peculium* against the father or master who had enjoyed a profit from the transaction concluded with the son or slave who had been managing it

Actio de peculio, an action available to the creditors of a *peculium* directly against the father or master who had set it up

Actio ex conducto, actio conducti, an action based upon a contract of lease and hire

Actio exercitoria, an action available directly against the owner or manager of a ship based upon the dealings of his shipper or captain

Actio institoria, an action available directly against the owner of a shop based upon the dealings of the shopkeeper he had set up in business

Actio mandati, see: *mandatum*

Actio negotiorum gestorum, see: *negotiorum gestio*

Actio quod iussu, an action available directly against a father (or

---

* *cf.* Berger, Enc., *passim.*

206

master) based upon the authorization he had given his son (or slave) to conclude a transaction

Actio utilis, an action introduced through the activity of praetors and jurists by the modification of an existing formula to cover a legal situation or transaction for which the original formula did not suffice

Actiones adiecticiae qualitatis, actions against a principal bearing the quality of being added to the primary actions available directly against the agent himself

Actor, manager of a business; see: *vilicus*

Alieni iuris, someone who is legally dependent upon the power of another

Amicus, a friend

Cognomen, a surname following the first name *(praenomen)* and the name of the tribe of a person *(nomen gentilicium)*

Condictio, an action *in personam* based upon unjust enrichment

Condictio furtiva, an action available against a thief

Dominium, the owner's power over his possessions

Dominus negotii, a party to a transaction, a prinicpal

Ex ante gestis, for the earlier transactions

Ex peculiari causa, through the enlargement of the *peculium*

Exercitor, a shipper

Extranea persona, an outside person, one not belonging to a certain family

Familia, family, household

Filiafamilias, daughter

Filiusfamilias, son

Gestio, an act of management or of performance; see: *negotiorum gestio*

In factum, adapted to the questions of fact (rather than questions of law) of the particular case

In solidum, in full

Institor, shopkeeper

Intellectu iuris, according to the understanding of the law

Ius civile, the classical Roman law (derived from statutes, plebiscites, decrees of the senate, imperial enactments, juristic authorities)

Ius honorarium, Roman law derived from the Praetor (the judicial magistrate)

Ius patronatus, the right of a patron to formal duties from his client

Ius Quiritium, the *ius civile* of earlier times

Libertus, a freedman

Locatio conductio, a contract of lease and hire

Magister navis, shipmaster

Mandatum, a contract by which a person assumed the duty to conclude a legal transaction or to perform a service gratuitously in the interest of the mandator or of a third person

Manus, husband's power over his wife

Negotiorum gestio, the management of another's affair without the authorization by the person interested

Obsequium, a respectful behaviour incumbent upon a freedman towards his patron.

Officium, a moral duty incumbent upon a freedman towards his patron

Paterfamilias, head of household

Patria potestas, the power of the head over the members of his household

Patrimonium, the whole property of a person

Peculium, a sum of money, a commercial or industrial business, or a small separate property granted by a father to his son or by a master to his slave, for the son's (or the slave's) use, free disposal and fructification through commercial and other transactions

Potestas, the father's power over his children and the master's power over his slaves

Praepositio, setting someone up in business

Pro solido, see: *In solidum*

Procurator, agent

Procurator omnium bonorum, general agent

Res ipsa loquitur, the matter speaks for itself

Signaculum, a seal or signet

Sui iuris, someone independent of another's power

Traditio, formal delivery

Universitas, a union of persons or a complex of things treated as a unit (a whole)

Vilicus, a farm-bailiff, administrator of a country estate; see: *actor*

Voluntas, will, desire, intention

Glossary

bonitary ownership, the ownership over something given by the praetor to a person without regard to the dictates of the formal *ius civile*

extraordinary procedure, the latest form of civil proceedings, in contrast to the earlier formulary procedure

paetorian law, see: *ius honorarium*

Quiritarian, in accordance with the *ius Quiritium*

usufruct, the right to use another's property and to take produce therefrom, without impairing its substance

BIBLIOGRAPHY

PRIMARY LITERATURE

Juristic

Codex Gregorianus et Hermogenianus. Ed. by Paul Krueger. Berlin: Weidmann, 1890.

Codex Theodosianus cum Constitutionibus Sirmondianis et Leges Novellae ad Theodosianum pertinentes. Ed. by Theodor Mommsen and P.M. Meyer. 3 vols. Berlin: Weidmann, 1905.

Corpus Iuris Civilis. Vol. I: *Institutiones.* Ed. by Paul Krueger. *Digesta.* Ed. by Theodor Mommsen and Paul Krueger. 15th stereotype edition. Vol. II: *Codex Iustinianus.* Ed. by Paul Krueger. 10th stereotype edition. Berlin: Weidmann, 1928–1929. *Digesta Iustiniani Augusti.* Ed. by Theodor Mommsen and Paul Krueger. 2nd. ed. "lucis ope expressa." 2 vols. Berlin: Weidmann, 1962–1963.

The Digest of Justinian. Transl. by Charles Henry Monro. 2 vols. containing titles I–XV. Cambridge: Cambridge University Press, 1909.

Fontes Iuris Romani Anteiustiniani. Vol. II: *Auctores.* Ed. by J. Baviera, C. Ferrini, J. Furlani. 2nd ed. Florence: Barbèra, 1940.

Johnson, Allan Chester; Coleman-Norton, Paul Robinson; Bourne, Frank Card; edd. *Ancient Roman Statutes: A Translation with Introduction, Commentary, Glossary, and Index.* Austin: University of Texas Press, 1961.

Non-juristic

Aristotle *Nicomachean Ethics*

Aulus Gellius *Noctes atticae*

Caesar *Bellum civile*

[⟨Cicero⟩ *Ars Rhetorica ad Herennium*] *Incerti auctoris De ratione dicendi ad C. Herennium lib. IV.* Edited by Frederick Marx. Rev. by Winfried Trillitzsch. Leipzig: B.G. Teubner, 1964.

Bibliography

Cicero *De officiis*
    De oratione
    De republica
    De senectute, de amicitia, de divinatione. Loeb Classical Library.
    Transl. by William Armstead Falconer. London: William Heinemann,
    1923.
    Epistulae ad Atticum
    Epistulae ad familiares
    Epistulae ad Quintum fratrem
    In Verrem II
    Pro Caecina
    Pro Plancio
    Pro Publio Quinctio
    Pro Roscio Amerino
    Pro Tullio
    Tusculanarum disputationum
Cornelius Nepos *De latinis historicis*
Corpus Inscriptionum Latinarum, consilio et auctoritate Academiae Litterarum
    Borussicae editum. Berlin: W. de Gruyter, 1863–1955.
Dessau, Hermann, ed. *Inscriptiones Latinae selectae.* 2nd ed. 3 vols. in 5.
    Berlin: Weidmann, 1955.
Dio Cassius *Roman History.* Transl. by Earnest Cary. Loeb Classical Library.
    9 vols. London: William Heinemann, 1914–1927.
Martial *Epigrammata*
Plautus *Comoediae*
Pliny the Younger *Epistulae*
Plutarch *Lives*: "Cato Major".
Quintilian *Institutio oratoria*
Rhetorica ad Herennium. See: Cicero *Ars Rhetorica*
Seneca *De beneficiis*
Terence *Comoediae*

SECONDARY WORKS

Albertario	Albertario, E. *Studio di diritto romano.* 6 vols. Milan: A. Giuffrè, 1933–1935.
Angelini, Osserv.	Angelini, P. "Osservazioni in tema di creazione dell' 'actio ad exemplum institoriae'." *Bullettino dell' istituto di diritto romano,* LXXI (1968), 230–248.
Angelini, Proc.	Angelini, P. Il 'procurator'. Milan: A. Giuffrè, 1971.
Ankum	Ankum, J.A. " 'Utilitas causa receptum': On the pragmatical methods of the Roman Lawyers." *Symbolae Juridi-*

cae et Historicae Martino David Dedicatae. I, 1–31.
Leyden: E.J. Brill, 1968.

Arangio-Ruiz   Arangio–Ruiz, V. Il mandato in diritto romano. Naples:
E. Jovene, 1949.

Arms   Arms, J.H.D'. Commerce and Social Standing in Ancient
Rome. Cambridge, Mass.: Harvard University Press,
1981.

Bailey, Cic.   Bailey, D.R.S. Cicero. London: Duckworth, 1971.

Bailey, Ep.   Bailey, D.R.S. Cicero: Epistulae ad familiares. 2 vols.
Cambridge: Cambridge University Press, 1977.

Bailey, Letters   Bailey, D.R.S. Cicero's Letters to Atticus. 7 vols. Cambridge: Cambridge University Press, 1965–1970.

Balogh   Balogh, E. "Adaptation of Law to Economic Conditions
According to Roman Law." Atti del congresso inter-
nazionale di diritto romano e di storia del diritto. Verona,
II, 261–355. Milan: A. Giuffrè, 1948.

Balsdon, Cic.   Balsdon, J.P.V.D. "Cicero, the Man." Cicero. T.A.
Dorey, ed. 171–214. London: Routledge and Kegan Paul,
1964.

Balsdon, Life   Balsdon, J.P.V.D. Life and Leisure in Ancient Rome.
London: The Bodley Head, 1969.

Balsdon, Rom.   Balsdon, J.P.V.D. Roman Women: Their History and
Habits. London: The Bodley Head, 1962.

Barrow   Barrow, R.H. Slavery in the Roman Empire. London:
Methuen & Co., 1928.

Behrands   Behrands, O. "Die Prokuratur des klassischen römischen
Zivilrechts." Z.S.S., LXXXVIII (1971), 215–298.

Benöhr, Besitz   Benöhr, H.-P. Der Besitzerwerb durch Gewaltabhängige
im klassischen römischen Recht. Berlin: Drucker und
Humblot, 1972.

Benöhr, Irrtum   Benöhr, H.-P. "Irrtum und guter Glaube der Hilfs-
person beim Besitzerwerb." Studien im römischen Recht.
Max Kaser zum 65. Geburtstag gewidmet . . . Edd. Dieter
Medicus and Hans Hermann Seiler. Berlin: Duncker
und Humblot, 1973. 9–32.

Berger, Enc.   Berger, A. Encyclopedic Dictionary of Roman Law
[= Transactions of the American Philosophical Society,
New Series. Vol. XLIII, Part 2]. Philadelphia: The
American Philosophical Society, 1953.

Berger, Nota   Berger, A. "Nota minima sul servus vicarius." IURA,
VIII (1957), 122–125.

Berger, Pap.   Berger, A. "Papirius Fronto." R.E., XVIII: 3. P. 1059.

Beseler, Beit.   Beseler, G. Beiträge zur Kritik der römischen Rechts-
quellen. 5 vols. Tübingen: Verlag von J.C.B. Mohr (Paul
Ziebeck), 1910–1931.

Bibliography

Beseler, Misc.   Beseler, G. "Miscellanea critica." *Z.S.S.*, XLIII (1922), 415–438.

Beseler, Rom.   Beseler, G. "Romanistische Studien." *Z.S.S.*, XLVII (1927), 53–74.

Besnier   Besnier, R. "L'état économique de Rome de 264 à 133 av.J.C." *Revue historique de droit français et étranger*, LIV (1976), 5–33.

Betti, Ist.   Betti, E. *Istituzioni di diritto romano.* 2nd ed. Padua; Cedam, 1942.

Biondi   Biondi, B. *Prospettive romanistiche.* Publicazioni delle Università cattolica del Sacro cuore. Ser. 2: Scienze giuridiche, vol. XXXVII. Milan: Società editrice "Vita e pensiero," 1933. [= *Scritti Giuridici*, I, 221–322. Milan: A. Giuffrè, 1965.]

Biscardi   Biscardi, A. "La capacita processuale dello schiavo." *Labeo*, XXI (1975).

Boissier   Boissier, G. *Cicero and His Friends: a Description of Roman Society in the Time of Caesar.* Transl. with an index and table of contents by Adnah David Jones. London: Ward and Lock, n.d.

Bonetti   Bonetti, P. "Per la storia del diritto del lavoro nel mondo romano (Appunti su *officina* e *taberna* nelle fonti)". *Bullettino della Scuola di perfezionamento e di specializzazione in diritto del lavoro e della sicurezza sociale: Università degli studi di Trieste*, V:13 (1959), 14–16.

Bonfante   Bonfante, P. *Corso di diritto romano* — Vol. I. *Diritto di famiglia*, Vol. III. *Diritti reali.* 2nd ed. Milan: A. Giuffrè, 1963, 1972.

Bretone, Ad.   Bretone, M. "'Adquisitio per procuratorem'?" *Labeo*, I (1955), 280–292.

Bretone, Serv.   Bretone, M. *Servus Communis.* Publicazioni della Facoltà giuridica dell' Università di Napoli, XXX. Naples: Eugenio Jovene, 1958.

Brewster   Brewster, E.H. *Roman Craftsmen and Tradesmen of the Early Empire.* Menasha, Wisc.: George Banta Publishing Co., 1917.

Brunt, Am.   Brunt, P.A., "'Amicitia' in the Late Roman Republic," *Proceedings of the Cambridge Philosophical Society*, N.S. II (1965), 1–20.

Brunt, Soc.   Brunt, P.A. *Social Conflicts in the Roman Republic.* London: Chatto & Windus, 1971.

Buckland, Inst.   Buckland, W.W. *The Main Institutions of Roman Private Law.* Cambridge: Cambridge University Press, 1931.

Buckland, Per.   Buckland, W.W. "Per liberam personam nihil adquiri posse" (transl. G. Cornil). *Academie royal des sciences, des lettres et des beaux arts de Belgique. Bulletin de la*

classe des lettres et des sciences morales et politiques. 5°
serie XXV (1939), 188–210.

Buckland, Slavery   Buckland, W.W. *The Roman Law of Slavery.* Cambridge: Cambridge University Press, 1908.

Buckland, Text.   Buckland, W.W. *A Textbook of Roman Law from Augustus to Justinian.* 3rd ed. Revised by Peter Stein. Cambridge: Cambridge University Press, 1963.

Burdese   Burdese, A. " 'Actio ad exemplum institoriae' e categorie sociali," *Studi in memoria di Guido Donatutti,* I. Milan: Cisalpino-Goliardica, 1973. 191–210.

Carcopino, Cic.   Carcopino, P. *Cicero, The Secrets of His Correspondence.* Transl. by E.O. Lorimer. New Haven: Yale University Press, 1951.

Carcopino, Life   Carcopino, J. *Daily Life in Ancient Rome.* Edited with bibliography and notes by Henry T. Rowell. Translated from the French by E.O. Lorimer. New Haven: Yale University Press, 1940.

[Carcopino, Sec.]   [Carcopino, J. *Secrets.*] *Cf.* Reviews by J.P.V.D. Balson, *Classical Review,* N.S. II (1952), 178–181 and *Journal of Roman Studies,* XL (1950), 134–135.

Carrington   Carrington, R.C. "Studies in the Campanian 'Villae Rusticae'." *Journal of Roman Studies.* XXI (1931), 110–130.

Cary   Cary, M. "Tesserae gladiatoriae sive nummulariae." *Journal of Roman Studies,* XIII (1923), 110–113.

Casson, Anc.   Casson, L. *The Ancient Mariners: Seafarers and Sea Fighters of the Mediterranean in Ancient Times.* Fourth Printing. New York: Macmillan, 1967.

Casson, Ships   Casson, L. *Ships and Seamanship in the Ancient World.* Princeton: Princeton University Press, 1971.

Corbett   Corbett, P.E. *The Roman Law of Marriage.* Oxford: Clarendon Pres, 1930.

Cosentini, Studi   Cosentini, C. *Studi sui liberti: Contributo allo studio della condizione giuridica dei liberti cittadini.* 2 vols. Catania: Facoltà giuridica, 1948–1950.

Costa, Az.   Costa, E. *Le azioni exercitoria e institoria.* Parma: L. Battei, 1891.

Costa, Dir.   Costa, E. *Il diritto privato romano nelle comedie di Plauto.* Turin: Fratelli Bocca, n.d.

Dahlheim   Dahlheim, W. *Struktur und Entwicklung des römischen Völkerrechts.* Munich: C.H. Beck, 1968.

Daube, Act.   Daube, D. "Actions between *pater familias* and *filius familias* with *peculium castrense.*" *Studi in memoria de Emilio Albertario.,* I, 433–474. Milan: A. Giuffrè, 1950.

Daube, Praet.   Daube, D. "The Peregrine Praetor." *Journal of Roman Studies,* XLI (1951), 66–70.

Daube, Text — Daube, D. "Text and Interpretation in Roman and Jewish Law." *The Jewish Journal of Sociology*, III (1961), 3–28.

Daube, R.L. — Daube, D., and Nelson, L.W. *Roman Law: Linguistic, Social and Philosophical Aspects*. Edinburgh: Edinburgh University Press, 1969.

Dernberg — Dernberg, H. *System des römischen Rechts*. Revised by Pavel Sokolowski. 2 vols. Berlin: H.W. Müller, 1912.

Didier — Didier, P. "Les obligations naturelles chez les derniers Sabiniens." *Révue internationale des droits de l'antiquité*, 3° série, XIX (1972), 239–273.

Dill — Dill, S. *Roman Society from Nero to Marcus Aurelius*. 2nd ed. London: Macmillan and Co., 1911.

Diósdi — Diósdi, G. *Ownership in Ancient and Preclassical Roman Law*. Budapest: Akadémiai Kiadó, 1970.

Donatuti — Donatuti, G. Review of *Ricerche sull' "obligatio naturalis"* by Giovanni E. Longo. *Bullettino dell' istituto di diritto romano*, LXV (1962), 310–317.

Douglas — Douglas, A.E. "Cicero the Philosopher." *Cicero*. T.A. Dorey, ed. Pp. 135–170. London: Routledge and Kegan Paul, 1964.

Duff, A.M. — Duff, A.M. *Freedmen in the Early Roman Empire*. Oxford: Clarendon Press, 1928.

Duff, J.W. — Duff, J.W. "Social Life in Rome and Italy: Slaves and Freedmen; Economic Factors." *Cambridge Ancient History*. XI, 755–762. Cambridge: Cambridge University Press, 1936.

Dugas — Dugas, L. *L'amitié antique d'après les moeurs populaires et les théories des philosophes*. Paris: Alcan, 1894.

Düll, Stell. — Düll, R. "Stellvertretung im Bereich von Stipulationen?" *Studi in onore di Vincenzo Arangio-Ruiz*, I, 309–316. Naples: E. Jovene, n.d.

Ehrlich — Ehrlich, E. *Fundamental Principles of the Sociology of Law*. Transl. by Walter L. Moll. Introd. by Roscoe Pound. Cambridge, Mass.: Harvard University Press, 1936.

Eisele — Eisele, F. "Zur Diagnostik der Interpolationen in den Digesten und im Codex." *Z.S.S.*, VII (1886), 15–31.

Erman — Erman, H. *Servus vicarius*. 321–527. Faculté de droit de l'Université de Lausanne, 1896.

Ernout — Ernout, A. and Meillet, A. *Dictionnaire étymologique de la langue latine*. 4th ed. Paris: Librairie C. Klincksieck, 1959.

Fabricius — Fabricius, P. *Der gewaltfreie Institor im klassischen römischen Recht*. Würzburg: H. Sturtz A.G., 1926.

Finley   Finley, M.J. *The Ancient Economy*. Berkeley: University of California Press, 1977.

Francisci   Francisci, P. de. "Sull' acquisto del possesso per mezzo dello schiavo." *Rendiconte dell' Istituto Lombardo di Scienze e Lettere*, serie 2ª, XL (1907), 1002ff.

Frank, Aspects   Frank, T. *Aspects of Social Behavior in Ancient Rome*. Cambridge, Mass.: Harvard University Press, 1932.

Frank, Ec. Hist. Frank, T. *An Economic History of Rome*, 2nd ed., rev. London: J. Cape, 1927.

Frank, Ec. Survey Frank, T. *An Economic Survey of Ancient Rome*, In collaboration with T.R.S. Broughton and others. 5 vols. Baltimore: John Hopkins Press, 1933–40.

Frank, Italy   Frank, T. "Italy." *Cambridge Ancient History*. VIII, 326–356. 2nd ed. Cambridge: Cambridge University Press, 1954.

Frank, Rom.   Frank, T. *Roman Imperialism*. New York: Macmillan Co., 1914.

Friedländer   Friedländer, L. *Roman Life and Manners under the Early Empire*. Authorized transl. of the 7th enl. and rev. ed. of the *Sittengeschichte Roms*. New York: Barnes and Noble,1965.

Friedmann   Friedmann, W. *Legal Theory*. 5th ed. London: Stevens, 1967.

Gallo   Gallo, F. " 'Potestas' e 'dominium' nell' esperienza giuridica romana." *Labeo*, XVI (1970), 17–58.

Gay   Gay, J.L. "L'in rem versum a l'époque classique." *Varia, Etudes de droit romain*, II (1956), 155–296.

Girard, Man.   Girard, P.F. *Manuel élémentaire de droit romain*. 8th ed. Revised by Felix Senn. Paris: Rousseau et Cie., 1929.

Gordon   Gordon, W.M. "Acquisition of Ownership by *traditio* and Acquisition of Possession." *Revue internationale des droits de l'antiquité*, 3ᵉ serie, XII (1965), 279–300.

Guarino   Guarino, A. "Actiones adiecticiae qualitatis." *N.N.D.I.*, I¹, 270–272.

Guillemin   Guillemin, A.M. ed. and transl. *Pline le Jeune: Lettres.* 4 vols. Paris: Societé d'édition "Les Belles Lettres," 1927–1947.

Gummerus   Gummerus, H. "Industrie und Handel." *R.E.*, IX, 1381–1535.

Hands   Hands, A.R. *Charities and Social Aid in Greece and Rome*. London: Thames and Hudson, 1968.

Heitland   Heitland, W.E. *Agricola: A Study of Agriculture and Rustic Life in the Greco-Roman World from the Point of View of Labour*. Cambridge: Cambridge University Press, 1921.

Bibliography

Herskovits   Herskovits, M.J. *Economic Anthropology: A Study in Comparative Economics.* 2nd ed., rev., enl., rewritten. New York, Knopf, 1952.

Herzog   Herzog, R. "Aus der Geschichte des Bankwesens im Altertum — Tesserae nummulariae." *Abhandlungen der Giessener Hochschulgesellschaft,* I. Giessen: Topelmann, 1919.

Hoebel   Hoebel, E.A. *The Law of Primitive Man: A Study in Comparative Dynamics.* Cambridge, Mass.: Harvard University Press, 1954.

Hogbin   Hogbin, H.I. *Law and Order in Polynesia: a Study of Primitive Legal Institutions.* Introd. by Bronislaw Malinowski. Reprint: Hamden, Conn.: Shoe String Press, 1961.

Hunter   Hunter, W.A. *A Systematic and Historical Exposition of Roman Law in the Order of a Code.* Translation of the Institutes of Gaius and the Institutes of Justinian by Ashton Cross. 4th ed. London: Sweet, 1903.

Huschke   Huschke, E.P. *Iurisprudentiae anteiustinianae quae supersunt.* 4th ed. Leipzig: B.G. Teubner, 1879.

Huvelin   Huvelin, P. *Études d'histoire du droit commercial romain.* Published posthumously by Henri Levy-Bruhl. Paris: Librairié du Recueil Sirey, 1929.

Imbert   Imbert, J. "De la sociologie au droit: la 'Fides' romaine." *Droits de l'antiquité et sociologie juridique: Mélanges Henri Lévy-Bruhl.* Publications de l'institut de droit romain de l'université de Paris, XVII. 407–415. Paris: Sirey, 1959.

Ihering   Ihering, R. von. *Geist des römischen Rechts auf den verschiedenen Stufen seiner Entwicklung.* 3 vols. 6th ed.

Jolowicz, Dig.   Jolowicz, H.F. *Digest XLVII.2: De furtis.* Cambridge: Cambridge University Press, 1940.

Jolowicz, Hist. Introd.   Jolowicz, H.F. *Historical Introduction to the Study of Roman Law.* 2nd ed. reprinted. Cambridge: Cambridge University Press, 1954.

Kaden   Kaden, E.H. Review of *Die Geschäftsführung im klassischen römischen Recht* by Mario Morelli. *Z.S.S.,* LVI (1936), 342–345.

Karlowa   Karlowa, O. *Der römische Zivilprozess zur Zeit der Legisactionen.* Berlin: Weidmann, 1872.

Kaser   Kaser, M. *Das römische Privatrecht.* 2 vols. Munich: C.H. Beck's Verlagsbuchhandlung, 1955–1959. Vol. 1, 2nd ed., 1971. [All citations are from the later edition.]

Kaser, Con.   Kaser, M. "The Concept of Roman Ownership." *Rapports généraux au VI⁰ Congrès international de droit comparé.*

	Edited by Jean Limpens. 37–51. Brussels: Établissements Emile Bruyhard, 1964.
Kaser, Eig.	Kaser, M. *Eigentum und Besitz im älteren römischen Recht.* 2nd ed. Köln-Graz: Böhlau Verlag, 1956.
Kaser, Inh.	Kaser, M. "Der Inhalt der *patria potestas.*" *Z.S.S.*, LVIII (1938), 62–87.
Kaser, Rev. C.	Kaser, M. *Review of Contract of Mandate in Roman Law* by A. Watson. *Tijdschrift voor Rechtsgeschiedenis,* XXX (1962), 262–272.
Kaser, Rev. P.	Kaser, M. *Review of Pécule et capacité patrimoniale* by Gabriel Micolier. *Z.S.S.*, LIV (1934), 392–402.
Kaser, Rev. S.	Kaser, M. Review of *Scritti di diritto romano. I* by Siro Solazzi. *Z.S.S.*, LXXIII (1956), 418–423.
Kaser, Wes.	Kaser, M. "Zum Wesen der römischen Stellvertretung." *Romanitas*, 9 (1970), 333–355.
Kelly	Kelly, J.M. *Roman Litigation.* Oxford: Clarendon Press, 1966.
Kiessling	Kiessling, E. "Giroverkehr." *R.E.*, Suppl. 4, 696–709.
Klingmüller	Klingmüller, E. "Institor." *R.E.*, IX$_2$, 1564–1565.
Koschaker	Koschaker, P. "Die Eheformen bei den Indogermanen." *Deutsche Landesreferate zum II. Internationalen Kongress für Rechtsvergleichung im Haag. 1937.* Berlin: Verlag Walter de Gruyter und Co., 1937.
Kunkel	Kunkel, W. "Das Konsilium im Hausgericht." *Z.S.S.*, LXXXIII (1966), 219–251.
Lambert	Lambert, J. *Les operae liberti: Contribution à l'histoire des droits de patronat.* Paris, 1934.
Lavaggi	Lavaggi, G. "Nuovi studi sui liberti." *Studi in onore di Pietro Francisci*, II, 73–111. Milan: A. Giuffrè, 1956.
Lemonnier	Lemonnier, H. *Étude historique sur la condition privée des affranchis aux trois premiers siècles de l'Empire romaine.* Paris: Librairie Hachette, 1887.
Lenel, E.P.	Lenel, O. *Das Edictum Perpetuum.* 3rd ed., reprinted. Leipzig: B. Tauchnitz, 1956.
Lenel, Pal.	Lenel, O. *Palingenesia iuris civilis.* Supplement by Lorenz E. Sierl. 2 vols. Graz: Akademische Druck und Verlagsanstalt, 1960.
Lenel, Zur	Lenel, O. "Zur sog. *actio de in rem verso utilis.*" *Archiv für zivilistische Praxis*, LXXVIII (1892), 354–362.
Lepien	Lepien, U. " 'Utilitatis causa'; Zweckmässigkeitsentscheidungen im römischen Recht." *Studia et Documenta Historiae et Iuris*, XXXV (1969), 51–72.
Levy, Konk.	Levy, E. *Die Konkurrenz der Aktionen und Personen im klassischen römischen Recht.* 2 vols. Berlin: Vahlen, 1918–1922.

Levy, Pauli — Levy, E. *Pauli sententiae: A Palingenesia of the Opening Titles as a Specimen of Research in West Roman Vulgar Law.* Ithaca, N.Y.: Cornell University Press, 1945.

Levy-Strauss — Levy-Strauss, C. *Les structures élémentaires de la parenté.* 2nd ed. Paris: Mouton, 1967.

Loane — Loane, H.J. *Industry and Commerce of the City of Rome (50 B.C.–200 A.D.).* Baltimore: John Hopkins Press, 1938.

Longo, Act. — Longo, G. "Actio Exercitoria, Actio Institoria, Actio Quasi Institoria." *Studi in onore di Gaetano Scherillo,* II. Milan: Cisalpino-Goliardica, 1971.

Longo, Ap. — Longo, G. "Appunti critici in tema di peculio." *Studia et Documenta Historiae et Juris,* I (1935), 392–422.

Longo, Con. — Longo, G. "Il concetto classico e il concetto giustinianeo di administratio peculii." *Archivio giuridico,* XVI (1928), 184–203. [= Reprinted: Longo, Gianetto. *Ricerche romanistiche.* 367–385. Milan: A. Giuffrè, 1966.]

Longo, Lib. — Longo, G. "*Libera administratio peculii:* I limiti e lo spirito di una innovazione giustinianea." *Bullettino dell' istituto di diritto romano.* XXXVIII (1930), 29–46. [= Reprinted: Longo, Gianetto. *Ricerche romanistiche.* 387–404. Milan: A. Giuffrè, 1966.]

Longo, Ric. — Longo, G.E. *Ricerche sull' "obligatio naturalis."* Milan: A. Giuffrè, 1962.

MacCormack, Form. — MacCormack, G. "Formalism, Symbolism and Magic in Early Roman Law." *Tijdschrift voor Rechtsgeschiedenis,* XXXVII (1969), 439–468.

MacCormack, Role — MacCormack, G. "The Role of Animus in the Classical Law of Possession." *Z.S.S.,* LXXXVI (1969), 105–145.

Maine — Maine, H. *Ancient Law.* Introd. by J.H. Morgan. Reprint. London: J.M. Dent, 1954.

Mandry — Mandry, G. *Das gemeine Familiengüterrecht mit Ausschluss des ehelichen Güterrechts.* 2 vols. Tübingen: Verlag der H. Laupp'schen Buchhandlung, 1871–1876.

Martino, Anc. — Martino, F. de. "Ancora sull' actio exercitoria." *Labeo,* IV (1958), 274–300 [= Mnemeion Siro Solazzi. Naples: E. Jovene, 1964, 25–51.]

Martino, Ex. — Martino, F. de. "Exercitor," *N.N.D.I.,* VI, 1088–1092.

Martino, Stud. — Martino, F. de. "Studii sull' actio exercitoria." *Rivista del diritto della navigazione,* VII (1941), 7–31.

Maschi — Maschi, C.A. *Il diritto romano. I. La prospettiva storica della giurisprudenza classica (diritto privato e processuale).* 2nd ed. Milan: A. Giuffrè, 1966.

Mauss, Gift — Mauss, M. *The Gift: Forms and Functions of Exchange in Archaic Societies.* Transl. by Ian Cunnison. Introd.

by E.E. Evans-Pritchard. Glencoe, Illinois: Free Press, 1954.

Mauss, Soc.
Mauss, M. *Sociologie et anthropologie*. Introd. by Claude Levy-Strauss. 3rd ed. Paris: Presses universitaires de France, 1966.

McDermott
McDermott, W.C. "M. Cicero and M. Tiro." *Historia*, 21 (1972), 259–286.

Meylan
Meylan, P. "Per procuratorem possessio nobis adquiri potest." *Festschrift Hans Lewald*. 105–114. Basel: Helbing Lichtenhahn, 1953.

Michel
Michel, J.H. *Gratuité en droit romain*. Brussels: The Free University–Institut de Sociologie, 1962.

Micolier
Micolier, G. *Pécule et capacité patrimoniale. Étude sur le pécule, dit profectice, depuis l'édit "de peculio" jusqu'à la fin de l'époque classique*. Lyon: Bosc Frères, M. et L. Riou, 1932.

Mitteis
Mitteis, L. *Die Lehre von der Stellvertretung nach römischem Recht mit Berücksichtigung des österreichischen Rechts*. Vienna: Hölder, 1885.

Mitteis, Op.
Mitteis, L. "*Operae officiales* und *operae fabriles*." *Z.S.S.*, XXI (1900), 143–158.

Mitteis, R.P.
Mitteis, L. *Römisches Privatrecht bis auf die Zeit Diokletians*. Only vol. 1 published. Leipzig: Duncker und Humblot, 1908.

Mitteis, Trap.
Mitteis, L. "Trapezitika." *Z.S.S.*, XIX (1898), 198–260.

Mommsen, Staats.
Mommsen, T. *Römisches Staatsrecht*. 3 vols. in 5. 3rd ed., reprinted. Basel: Schwabe, 1952.

Moritz
Moritz, L.A. *Grain-Mills and Flour in Classical Antiquity*. Oxford: Clarendon Press, 1958.

Münzer
Münzer, F. "Ofilius." *R.E.*, XVII² 2039–2041.

Münzer–Kübler
Münzer, F. and Kübler, B. "'Servius Sulpicius Rufus,'" *R.E.*, IV A¹, no. 95. 851–860.

Nicosia, A.
Nicosia, G. "Acquisto del possesso 'per procuratorem' e 'reversio in potestam domini' delle 'res furtivae'." *IURA*, XI (1960), 189–201.

Nicosia, L.
Nicosia, G. *L'acquisto del possesso medianti i "potestati subjecti."* Publicazione della Facoltà di Giurisprudenza: Università di Catania, 38. Milan: A. Giuffrè, 1960.

Niederländer
Niederländer, H. *Die Bereicherungshaftung im klassischen römischen Recht; der Ursprung der Haftungsbefreiung durch Wegfall der Bereicherung*. Böhlau, 1953.

Norden
Norden, F. *Apulejus von Madaura und das römische Privatrecht*. Leipzig: B.G. Teubner, 1912.

Oertel
Oertel, F. "The Economic Unification of the Mediterranean Region: Industry, Trade and Commerce." *Cam-*

	bridge Ancient History, X, 382–424. Cambridge: Cambridge University Press, 1934.
Park	Park, M.E. *The Plebs in Cicero's Day. A Study of their Provenance and of their Employment.* Cambridge, Mass.: Cosmos Press, 1921.
Pearce	Pearce, T.E.V. "The Role of the Wife as *Custos* in Ancient Rome." *Eranos*, LXXII (1974), 16–33.
Pernice	Pernice, A. *Marcus Antistius Labeo. Das römische Privatrecht im ersten Jahrhundert der Kaiserzeit*, 3 vols. 2nd ed. Halle: Waisenhaus, 1873–1905.
Perozzi	Perozzi, S. *Istituzioni di diritto romano.* 2 vols. 2nd ed. Rome: Atheneum, 1928.
Pescani	Pescani, P. *Le "Operae libertorum": Saggio storico-romanistico.* Quaderni del Bullettino della Scuola di perfezionamento e di specializzazione in diritto de lavoro e della sicurezza sociale, 23. Trieste: Università degli studi, 1967.
Poste	Poste, S. *Gai Institutiones.* 4th ed. Revised and enlarged by E.A. Whittuck. Historical introduction by A.H.J. Greenidge. Oxford: Clarendon Press, 1904.
Pound	Pound, R. "A Survey of Social Interests." *Harvard Law Review*, LVII (1943), 1–39.
Powell	Powell, R. "Contractual Agency in Roman Law and English Law." *Buttersworth South African Law Review* (1956). 41–56.
Prachner	Prachner, G. *Die Sklaven und Freigelassenen in arretinischen Sigillatagewerbe.* Wiesbaden: Franz Steiner Verlag GMBH, 1980.
Prichard	Prichard, A. "Terminology in Mancipatio." *Law Quarterly Review*, LXXVI (1960), 412–428.
Pringsheim, G.A.	Pringsheim, F. *Gesammelte Abhandlungen.* 2 vols. Heidelberg: Carl Winter, 1961.
Pringsheim, Un.	Pringsheim, F. "The Unique Character of Classical Roman Law." *The Journal of Roman Studies*, XXXIV (1944), 60–64.
Pugliese	Pugliese, G. "In tema di 'actio exercitoria'." *Studi in onore di Francesco Messineo*, IV, 287–326. Milan: A. Giuffrè, 1959. [= *Labeo*, III (1957), 308–343.]
Quadrato	Quadrato, R. "D. 3.3.1 pr. e la definizione di 'procurator'." *Labeo*, XX (1974), 210–224.
Rabel	Rabel, E. "Ein Ruhmesblatt Papinians: Die sogenannte actio quasi institoria." *Festschrift für Ernst Zitelman.* 1–26. Munich: Duncker und Humblot, 1913. [= *Gesammelte Aufsätze*, IV, 269–293. Tübingen: J.C.B. Mohr, 1971.]

Riccobono, Rec.   Riccobono, S. "The Reception of the Forms of Agency in Roman Law." *New York University Law Quarterly Review*, IX (1932), 271–279.

Riccobono, Term.   Riccobono, S. "Zur Terminologie der Besitzverhältnisse." *Z.S.S.*, XXXI (1910), 321–371.

Robertis   Robertis, F.M. de. *I rapporti di lavoro nel diritto romano*. Milan: A. Giuffrè, 1946.

Robinson   Robinson, M.B. *The Digest or Pandects of Justinian. Book 46, titles 1 and 2*. Notes by R.J. Pothier. Grahamstown, Cape Colony: African Book Company, 1910.

Roby   Roby, J.H. *Roman Private Law in the Times of Cicero and of the Antonines*. 2 vols. Cambridge: Cambridge University Press, 1902.

Rostovtzeff   Rostovtzeff, M.I. *Social and Economic History of the Roman Empire*. 2 vols. 2nd ed. Oxford: Clarendon Press, 1957.

Rotondi   Rotondi, G. *Leges publicae populi romani. Elenco cronologico con una introduzione sull' attività legislativa dei comizi romani*. Reprint. Hildesheim: G. Olms, 1966.

Sachers   Sachers, E. "Potestas patria." *R.E.*, XXII: 1. 1046–1175.

Salkowski   Salkowski, C. *Zur Lehre vom Sklavenerwerb*. Leipzig: Verlag von Bernhard Tauchnitz, 1891.

Savigny   Savigny, F.K. von. *System des heutigen römischen Rechts*. 8 vols. 3rd ed. Introduction and Index by O.L. Hauser. Leipzig: Veit, 1863.

Scherillo   Scherillo, G. "Sulla stipulazione del *servus* e del *filius familias*." *Studi in onore di Pietro Bonfante*, IV, 203–241. Milan: Fratella Treves, 1930.

Schiller   Schiller, A.A. "The Business Relations of Patron and Freedman in Classical Roman Law." *Legal Essays in Tribute to Orrin Kip McMurray*. Edited by Max Radin and A.M. Kidd. 623–639. Berkeley, Ca.: University of California Press, 1935. Republished: Schiller, A. Arthur. *An American Experience in Roman Law*. 24–40. Gottingen: Vandenhoek und Ruprecht, 1973.

Schneider   Schneider, K. "Vicarius als Sklave." *R.E.*, VIII A$_2$, 2044–2053.

Schulz   Schulz, F. *Classical Roman Law*. Oxford: Clarendon Press, 1951.

Schulz, Fr.   Schulz, F. "Fr. 63 D. 41.1 (Zur Lehre vom Schatzerwerb)." *Z.S.S.*, XXXV (1914), 94–112.

Schulz, Lehre   Schulz, F. "Die Lehre vom erzwungenen Rechtsgeschäft im antiken römischen Recht." *Z.S.S.*, XLIII (1922), 171–261.

Schulz, Princ.   Schulz, F. *Principles of Roman Law*. Transl. by Marguerite Wolff. Oxford: Clarendon Press, 1936.

Seavey   Seavey, W.A. and Hall, L. *Cases on the Law of Agency.* St. Paul, Minn.: West Publishing Co., 1956.

Sella   Sella, L. de. "Sull' acquisto del possesso 'domino ignoranti'." *Mnemeion Siro Solazzi.* Naples: E. Jovene, n.d. 432–462.

Serrao   Serrao, F. *Il procurator.* Milan: A. Giuffrè, 1947.

Sherwin-White   Sherwin-White, A.N. *The Letters of Pliny: a Historical and Social Commentary.* Oxford: Clarendon Press, 1966.

Sohm   Sohm, R. *Institutionen, Geschichte und System des römischen Privatrechts.* 17th ed. Edited by Ludwig Mitteis and Leopold Wenger. Munich: Verlag von Duncker und Humblot, 1924.

Solazzi, Rev.   Solazzi, S. Review of *Varia. Études de droit romain II. IURA,* VIII (1957), 539–545.

Solazzi, Scritti   Solazzi, S. *Scritti di diritto romano.* 6 vols. Naples: E. Jovene, 1955–1972.

Solin   Solin, H. *Beiträge zur Kenntnis der griechischen Personennamen in Rom.* Helsinki: Societas Scientiarum Fennica, 1971.

Staerman   Staerman, E.M. *Die Blütezeit der Sklavenwirtschaft in der römischen Republik.* Transl. by M. Bräuer-Pospelova. Wiesbaden:. F. Steiner, 1969.

Taubenschlag   Taubenschlag, R. *The Law of Greco-Roman Egypt in the Light of the Papyri.* 2nd ed. Warsaw: Panstwowe Wydawnictwo Naukowe, 1955.

Tomulescu   Tomulescu, C. St. "Problémes de droit romain, I. L'affet extinctif de la *litis contestatio* a l'époque des legis actiones." *IURA,* XXIV (1973), 62–77.

Treggiari   Treggiari, S. *Roman Freedmen During the Late Republic.* Oxford, Clarendon Press, 1969.

Tuhr   Tuhr, A. von. *Actio de in rem verso, zugleich ein Beitrag zur Lehre von der Geschäftsführung.* Freiburg: J.C.B. Mohr (Paul Siebeck), 1895.

Tyrell–Purser   Tyrell, R.Y. and Purser, L.C. *The Correspondence of M. Tullius Cicero Arranged According to its Chronological Order; with a Revision of the Text, a Commentary and Introductory Essays.* 7 vols. Dublin: Hodges, Figgis and Co., 1890–1906.

Vážny   Vážny; J. "Naturalis obligatio." *Studi in onore di Bonfante,* IV. 129–180. Milan: Fratelli Treves Editori, 1930.

Veyne   Veyne, P. "Vie de Trimalcion." *Annales: économies-sociétés-civilisations,* 16 (1961), 213–247.

Vogel   Vogel, C.J. de, ed. *Greek Philosophy.* 3 vols. Leyden: E.J. Brill, 1950–1959.

Volterra	Volterra, E. "Sui *mores* della *familia* romana.'" *Accademia Nazionale dei Lincei. Atti. Roma. Rendiconti.* Series VIII, Vol. IV (1949), 516–534.
Walker	Walker, B. *Selected Titles from the Digest, Part I. Mandati vel contra. Digest, XVII.l.* Cambridge: Cambridge University Press, 1879.
Wallon	Wallon, H.A. *Histoire de l'esclavage dans l'antiquité.* 3 vols. 2nd ed. Paris: Librairie Hachette, 1879.
Watson, Ac. O.	Watson, A. "Acquisition of Ownership by 'Traditio' to an 'Extraneus'." *Studia et Documenta Historiae et Juris,* XXXII (1967), 189–209.
Watson, Ac. P.	Watson, A. "Acquisition of Possession and Usucapion *Per Servos et Filios.*" *Law Quarterly Review,* 78 (1962), 205–227.
Watson, Ac. P.E.P.	Watson, A. "Acquisition of Possession *Per Extraneam Personam.*" *Tijdschrift voor Rechtsgeschiedenis,* XXIX (1961), 22–42.
Watson, Mand.	Watson, A. *Contract of Mandate in Roman Law.* Oxford: Clarendon Press, 1961.
Watson, Ob.	Watson, A. *The Law of Obligations in the Later Roman Republic.* Oxford: Clarendon Press, 1965.
Watson, Per.	Watson, A. *The Law of Persons in the Later Roman Republic.* Oxford: Clarendon Press, 1967.
Watson, Prop.	Watson, A. *The Law of Property in the Later Roman Republic.* Oxford: Clarendon Press, 1968.
Wesenberg	Wesenberg, G. "Praetor." *R.E.,* XXII$_2$, 1581–1605.
Westermann, Sk.	Westermann, W.L. "Sklaverei." *R.E.,* Supplementband VI, 894–1068.
Westermann, Slave	Westermann, W.L. *The Slave Systems of Greek and Roman Antiquity.* Philadelphia: American Philosophical Society, 1955.
White	White, K.D. *Roman Farming.* London: Thames and Hudson, 1970.
Wieacker	Wieacker, F. Review of *Contractus* by Sven Erik Wunner. *Tijdschrift voor Rechtsgeschiedenis,* XXXV (1967), 129–145.
Wiesmüller	Wiesmüller, K. "Exercitor." *R.E.,* Supplementband XII, 365–372.
Windscheid	Windscheid, B. *Lehrbuch des Pandektenrechts.* 3 vols. 9th edition. Revised by Theodor Kipp. Frankfurt am Main: Literarische Anstalt Rutten und Loening, 1906. Reprinted, Aalen: Scientia Verlag, 1963.
Wiseman	Wiseman, T.P. *New Men in the Roman Senate 139 B.C.–A.D. 14.* London: Oxford University Press, 1971.
Wunner	Wunner, S.E. *Contractus: Sein Wortgebrauch und Wil-*

	lensgehalt im klassischen römischen Recht. Köln-Graz: Böhlau, 1964.
Wylie	Wylie, J.K. *Solidarity and Correality.* Edinburgh: Oliver, 1923.
Zeber	Zeber, I. *A Study of the Peculium of a Slave in Pre-Classical and Classical Roman Law.* Wroclaw: Wydawnictwo Universytetu Wroclawskiego, 1981.
Zulueta	Zulueta, F. de. *Digest 41.1 and 2.* Oxford: Clarendon Press, 1953.
Zulueta, Gaius	Zulueta, F. de. *The Institutes of Gaius.* 2 vols. Oxford: Clarendon Press, 1946.

INDICES

Index of Sources
(cited in the Text)

JURISTIC

Lenel, *Das Edictum Perpetuum*
258   105
282   76

Gaius, *Institutiones*
2.86   7
2.95   1 13 25
4.71   92

Justinian, *Institutiones*
3.17.12   11
4.6.10   48

Justinian, *Digesta*
2.13.4.3   158
3.2.6.5   194
4.9.7pr.   119
13.6.17.3   196
14.1.1pr.   91
14.1.1.5   101–103
14.1.2   115
14.1.5.1   62 112
14.3.11.2–4   107
14.3.14   114
14.3.19.1   157
15.1.1.1   79
15.1.3.11–12   61

15.1.4pr.
15.1.5.4   33
15.1.19.3   111
15.1.21.3   50
15.1.29.1   57
15.1.42   ¡55
15.1.44   65
15.3.1pr.   84
17.1.1.4   193
37.15.9   128
41.1.32   15
41.2.1.8   23
41.2.9   188
41.2.41   188
41.2.34.2   19
41.2.49.1   18 37
43.16.1.22   29
45.1.38.17   1 13 25
50.17.133   27
50.17.206   85

NON-JURISTIC

Cicero

De amicitia
8.26   166

Indices

Index of Roman Jurists

Index of Names

Index of Authors